IRISH WRITERS AND RELIGION

THE IRISH LITERARY STUDIES SERIES

ISSN 0140–895X

1. *Place, Personality & the Irish Writer*. Andrew Carpenter (editor)
2. *Yeats and Magic*. Mary Catherine Flannery
3. *A Study of the Novels of George Moore*. Richard Allen Cave
4. *J. M. Synge & the Western Mind*. Weldon Thornton
5. *Irish Poetry from Moore to Yeats*. Robert Welch
6. *Yeats, Sligo, & Ireland*. A. Norman Jeffares (editor)
7. *Sean O'Casey, Centenary Essays*. David Krause & Robert G. Lowery (editors)
8. *Denis Johnston: A Retrospective*. Joseph Ronsley (editor)
9. *Literature & the Changing Ireland*. Peter Connolly (editor)
10. *James Joyce: An International Perspective*. Suheil Badi Bushrui & Bernard Benstock (editors)
11. *Synge: the Medieval & the Grotesque*. Toni O'Brien Johnson
12. *Carleton's* Traits and Stories *& the 19th Century Anglo-Irish Tradition*. Barbara Hayley
13. *Lady Gregory, Fifty Years After*. Ann Saddlemyer & Colin Smythe (editors)
14. *Woman in Irish Legend, Life & Literature*. S. F. Gallagher (editor)
15. *'Since O'Casey' & other Essays on Irish Drama*. Robert Hogan
16. *George Moore in Perspective*. Janet Egelson Dunleavy (editor)
17. *W. B. Yeats, Dramatist of Vision*. A. S. Knowland
18. *The Irish Writer & the City*. Maurice Harmon (editor)
19. *O'Casey the Dramatist*. Heinz Kosok
20. *The Double Perspective of Yeats's Aesthetic*. Okifumi Komesu
21. *The Pioneers of Anglo-Irish Fiction, 1800–1850*. Barry Sloan
22. *Irish Writers & Society at Large*. Masaru Sekine (editor)
23. *Irish Writers & the Theatre*. Masaru Sekine (editor)
24. *A History of Verse Translation from the Irish 1789–1897*. Robert Welch
25. *Kate O'Brien, A Literary Portrait*. Lorna Reynolds
26. *Portraying the Self, Sean O'Casey and the Art of Autobiography*. Michael Kenneally
27. *W. B. Yeats & the Tribes of Danu. Three Views of Ireland's Fairies*. Peter Alderson Smith
28. *Theatre of Shadows: Samuel Beckett's Drama 1956–76 from* All that Fall to Footfalls. Rosemary Pountney
29. *Critical Approaches to Anglo-Irish Literature*. Michael Allen & Angela Wilcox (editors)
30. *'Make Sense Who May': Essays on Samuel Beckett's Later Works*. Robin J. Davis & Lance St. J. Butler (editors)
31. *Cultural Contexts and Literary Idioms in Contemporary Irish Literature*. Michael Kenneally (editor)
32. *Builders of My Soul: Greek and Roman Themes in Yeats*. Brian Arkins
33. *Perspectives of Irish Drama and Theatre*. Jacqueline Genet & Richard Allen Cave (editors)
34. *The Great Queens. Irish Goddesses from the Morrigan to Cathleen ni Houlihan*. Rosalind Clark
35. *Irish Literature and Culture*. Michael Kenneally (editor)
36. *Irish Writers and Politics*. Okifumi Komesu & Masaru Sekine (editors)
37. *Irish Writers and Religion*. Robert Welch (editor)
38. *Yeats and the Noh*. Masaru Sekine & Christopher Murray
39. *Samuel Ferguson: the Literary Achievement*. Peter Denman
40. *Reviews and Essays of Austin Clarke*. Gregory A. Schirmer (editor)
41. *The Internationalism of Irish Literature & Drama*. Joseph McMinn (editor)
42. *Ireland and France, A Bountiful Friendship: Literature, History and Ideas*. Barbara Hayley and Christopher Murray (editors)

IRISH WRITERS AND RELIGION

edited by Robert Welch

Irish Literary Studies: 37
IASAIL — Japan Series 4

1992
COLIN SMYTHE
Gerrards Cross, Buckinghamshire

First published in 1992 in Great Britain by
Colin Smythe Ltd., Gerrards Cross, Buckinghamshire

British Library Cataloguing in Publication Data

Irish writers and religion. – (Irish literary studies
ISSN 0140–895X; 37) (IASAIL-Japan series
ISSN 0267–6079; 4)
I. Welch, Robert, *1947*– II. Series
820.99415

ISBN 0–86140–236–7

Produced in Great Britain
Printed and bound by Billing & Sons Ltd., Worcester

IASAIL-JAPAN Series
ISSN 0267-6079

In Memory of Barbara Hayley

CONTENTS

INTRODUCTION

ROBERT WELCH

In a lecture given at the Shelbourne Hotel in Dublin on 23 November, 1962, the bilingual poet, Eoghan Ó Tuairisc, spoke of 'Religio Poetae', (The Religion of Poetry) as follows:

> This term, *religio*, derives from Latin, *Religare*, that is a bond or link between two things. But more than this is involved, because in the word *religio re* is the pre-particle of emphasis, so *religio* implies making a strong bond, a link not easily broken.
>
> What are the two things which are bonded in this *religio* ? The two worlds. The other world and this world. *Religio* links together the two aspects of reality, that is to say, god and man. The two aspects of history: tradition and race. The two aspects of the universe: matter and form[1]

Ó Tuairisc goes on to argue that matter, which was conceived of by nineteenth century materialist philosophy as a fixed determined and quantifiable thing, has been revealed by modern physics to be essentially mysterious. So the 'religious' attitude, in Ó Tuairisc's definition, allows us a way of considering the material world which is more complex, therefore more valuable, than that afforded by the commonsensical notion that measurement and weighing tell us all we need to know about the world we live in. The 'religious' attitude considers matter as being animated by form; and suggests that this animation is essentially mysterious, an unknown quantity, though common to all experience.

It is interesting to observe that Ó Tuairisc does not write the word 'god' with the usual capital ('dia' in the original Irish), because it is part of his strategy to insist on the normality of the 'religious' instinct, its everyday quality. But what is there to the eyes every day becomes filmed over with the dust of familiarity, so we need ritual, poetry and art to awaken us to the 'charge' that holds things together in form in the most common everyday things. 'The world is charged with the grandeur of God', wrote Hopkins; but the Welsh poet, David Jones, and Patrick Kavanagh, in their different ways wrote of this charge inhabiting the merest utensils, the most apparently lacklustre situations.

W. B. Yeats was drawn to Irish folklore because it represented to him an alternative to the mechanical world view of nineteenth century positivist philosophy and utilitarian values. Though no scientific folklorist, Yeats, with Lady Gregory, was an extremely assiduous collector of folklore, which he worked hard upon and studied. He was right in thinking that folklore preserved the theme of interpenetration of this world with the other world from the oldest Irish and Celtic traditions. The sídh, the fairies, are the other world people of Ireland, and their presence can be felt in the tales of the Mythological Cycle (*Cath Maighe Tuiredh*, for example) and in the anecdote he took down from 'a witch doctor' on the borders of Clare. The informant is explaining how the fairies take good dancers away from this world into their own:

> There was a boy was a splendid dancer. Well, one night he was going to a house where there was a dance. And when he was about half way to it, he came to another house where there was music and dancing going on. So he turned in, and there was a room all done up with curtains and with screens, and a room inside where the people were sitting, and it was only those that were dancing sets that came to the outside room. So he danced two or three sets and then he saw that it was a house they had built up where there was no house before for him to come into. So he went out, but there was a big flagstone at the door, and he stumbled on it and fell down. And in a fortnight after he was dead.[2]

Yeats was convinced that Ireland was unlike other European countries because down to the seventeenth century pagan, Druidic belief persisted in 'peasant and noble alike'; and he further held that this belief was sustained amongst the Western peasants down to his own time. Whether or not Ireland is unlike other European countries in this regard is probably impossible to say; but certainly some forms of pre-Christian belief have survived down to the twentieth century and even to the present day.

Towards the end of his life, in that difficult and controversial essay, 'A General Introduction to my Work', Yeats recalled his belief in a Druidic 'backdrop' to Irish tradition, united it with his concept of Christ, and went further to argue for its relevance in the decades to come, when the last remnants of materialism will have been shaken off:

> I am convinced that in two or three generations it will become generally known that the mechanical theory has no reality, that the natural and supernatural are knit together, that to escape a dangerous fanaticism we must study a new science; at that moment Europeans may find something attractive in a Christ posed against a background not of Judaism but of Druidism, not shut off in dead history, but flowing, concrete, phenomenal.[3]

These last phrases hauntingly anticipate the Christ of writers as various as Patrick Kavanagh, Francis Stuart, Brian Coffey, Denis Devlin, Seán Ó Ríordáin, Caitlín Maude, Paul Durcan. 'Flowing, concrete, phenomenal': if Christ is now alive he must be so amidst the phenomena; and the writer, in trying to recall our attention to him will refer not to institutions but to actualities. The other will be located in the here and now:

> A year ago I feel in love with the functional ward
> Of a chest hospital. . .[4]

Or, in 'Red Square — the Hours', under an epigraph from Karl Marx that reads, in part, 'Religion is the sigh of the oppressed creature, the heart of a heartless world, just as it is the spirit of spiritless conditions', Paul Durcan writes:

> At some stage God must have been alive
> In St. Peter's Square
> But she is certainly not alive there now —
> Poor murdered woman.
>
> God lives in Red Square.
> It is the first thing that strikes you
> On a February morning . . .[5]

The angle of vision is 'wrenched round' (to adopt from Francis Stuart a phrase descriptive of the technique required to accommodate new perspectives) to look at the actual in a new way. Exactly the same spirit informs the metaphysical interconnections between phenomena explored in Stuart's later fiction, or in the classic poems of Christian angst of Seán Ó Ríordáin. Ó Ríordáin's aesthetic, too complex to explore in brief here, but fully outlined in his magisterial introduction to *Eirebaill Spideoige* (1952), argues for a poetic that locates the form of individual things; which form, he says, is the prayer each thing continuously transmits. It is that thing's otherness.[6] Poetry, art, is the means of reaching towards such forms, and the encounter with them is registered always, he says, with 'a thrust of joy' — 'geit áthais'. Ó Ríordáin's poem 'Siollabadh' ('Syllables' or, more correctly, 'Syllablizing') transmits such a charge as the otherness inherent in the actual invades the consciousness, the poem and the reader's mind. It is set in a T.B. ward:

> A nurse in a hospital
> On a brief afternoon;
> Arteries in dormitories
> Effortlessly pulsing;

And she stood at each beside
Waiting and counting,
Writing down the metric
Of the syllables in her fingers;
And she syllabled rhythmically
Out of the room,
Leaving a symphony
Of arteries counting;
And the Angelus
Syllabled in murmurs,
And 'Amen' all concluded
In a whisper in the sick room;
But the chanting continued
In the monastery of the flesh,
Acolytes like arteries
Murmuring the nones.[7]

This heightened response and active creative outrush is a kind of probe ('aisling', in the sense of 'a going out of the head') into what Yeats called 'the labyrinth of another's being';[8] his or her otherness. Such a probe goes out and in its departure from the fixed, inert conditions inspires, inspirits (i.e. breathes life into) another world; not an *alternative* world, but *another* world. Such is Yeats's 'Byzantium'; such is Bran's Land of the Women; such is the place Conn Cédchathach sees in *Baile in Scáil* ('The Phantom's Frenzy'), where he is given a drink from a vat of red beer by a girl called 'Flaitheas Éireann', the sovereignty of Ireland. Red is the colour of the underworld, and of blood. Hence Yeats's Red Hanrahan, who, in the story of that title sees the same girl, but cannot speak to her, because he is afraid.[9]

Stress has been laid upon the persistence of the pagan belief in the interaction of this world and the otherworld, because such a concept is particularly appropriate for a time in which the nature of matter, of what is often, loosely, called 'reality', has been brought into question. Perhaps Yeats was right: that a 'Druidic' backdrop, emphasising the fluid nature of phenomena, is the one against which the contemporary phantasmagorias are being played out.

But it should also be remembered that Irish tradition was always extremely accommodating. The pagan belief systems rapidly assimilated the Christian one; and the early Irish church evolved a reconciliation with paganism that preserved much even of the caste distinctions and social classifications that belonged to pre-Christian times. So that when, in the thirteenth century, the poet Giolla Brighde Mac Con Midhe implores the Trinity for a child, because his marriage is barren, he uses the old bardic convention whereby a poem is dedicated to a noble lord, and the poet expects a gift in return:

> Holy Trinity, which gave light
> to the blind, have pity on me;
> though it's more difficult to push grass
> through rock, don't leave me childless.
>
> O Father, pity the man who can't see it,
> you put flowers through the stalk top,
> blossom through the branch tip; Creator
> how may it be harder to bring me issue?[10]

The religious instinct is a permanent feature of Irish writing; as indeed may be the case with all writing that seeks to respond to the creative impulse. In the Irish tradition, it may be said, the continuous awareness of the otherworld sharpens the sense of the here and now. This interplay, from Manannán's poem in *The Voyage of Bran* to Heaney's 'Clearings' in *The Haw Lantern*, leads us, in the end, to an open consideration of the thing itself, there, before us, baffling in its actuality, a precarious balance of matter and form. It is perhaps fitting to conclude this introduction with the pure and strangely consolatory interrogation of 'out there' by Samuel Beckett:

> something there
> where
> out there
> out where
> outside
> what
> the head what else
> something there somewhere outside
> the head.[11]

PAGANISM AND SOCIETY IN EARLY IRELAND

In Memory of Heinrich Wagner

SÉAMUS MACMATHÚNA

'It came to pass in that year that on the same night as the Holy Patrick was celebrating Easter, there was an idolatrous ceremony which the gentiles were accustomed to celebrate with manifold incantations and magical contrivances and with other idolatrous superstitions, when the kings, satraps, chieftains, princes and great ones of the people had assembled, and when the druids, singers, prophets, and the inventors and practitioners of every art and of every gift had been summoned to Loígaire, as once to king Nabcodonossor, at Tara, their Babylon.'[1]

By the time that Muirchú wrote these words in his seventh century life of Saint Patrick, the druid had been ousted from his position of power in society by the cleric and the Church had defeated organised paganism. The Church's triumph is celebrated in a number of religious works of the eighth and ninth centuries. In *Fiacc's Hymn*, which was composed c.800 A.D., a summary account is given of Patrick's life. As a result of his mission, the old pagan sites of Emain Macha and Tara are desolate, while Armagh and Downpatrick flourish; the true Godhead has replaced the pagan idols and life has triumphed over iniquitous heathendom.[2] The same sentiments are expressed in the *Félire Óengusso*, 'the Calendar of Oengus', which was written at about the same time. The great heroes of the past are recalled, only to be rejected in favour of Patrick, Brigit, Ciarán and other saints of the Christian church. 'The situation could not be clearer', says David Greene; 'it is to substitute a set of Christian heroes for the pagan ones, to form an Irish literature which will be exclusively Christian in subject.'[3]

Fiacc's Hymn is prefaced by a short prose passage which relates that, during the reign of Loígaire at Tara, Patrick visited the chief-poet of Ireland, Dubthach maccu Lugair, in order to seek a candidate for the bishopric of Leinster. According to other sources, Dubthach was an early convert to Christianity, and the story which they tell of his acceptance of Saint Patrick seems to be a myth which was propounded in order to explain the accommodation which was reached between the Church and the native learned classes of *filid* 'poets' and *brithemain* 'lawyers'.[4] In contrast to the druids and seers, who rejected Patrick and who are enemies of the Church, the poets and lawyers accepted him and have clerical approval.

The accommodation which was reached between the intelligentsia of the native oral tradition and the clerical *literati* was one of unusual sensitivity and mutual sympathetic understanding. Indeed, it has been suggested recently that, long before the surviving texts of the Old Irish period were written, these two streams had merged to form 'a single mandarin caste'.[5] As far as written literature is concerned, this suggestion seems to be well-founded: Old Irish literature is the product of monastic scriptoria and it was written by Christian authors and scribes. While it is proper, therefore, to reaffirm the influence of Christian Latin ecclesiastical culture, it must also be emphasised that it is not a univocal literature, and that, in general, it represents a compromise between the Christian and native traditions. The Christian authors and scribes are clearly in tune with the traditions of secular society; they are creatures of their own environment,[6] reflecting in their writings the realities and tensions of contemporary society. Moreover, it is certain that an oral culture of prestige continued to flourish alongside the written literature of the monasteries.[7]

Church documentation indicates that, in the sixth century, Christians were believers in the midst of pagan practices. *Fiacc's Hymn* makes the important observation that before Patrick's mission these customs included the worship of the *síde*:

> *For túaith Hérenn bái temel; túatha adortais síde:*
> *ní creitset in fírdeacht inna Trindóte fíre*

(On the folk of Ireland there was darkness; the people used to worship the *síde*: they did not believe the true Godhead of the true Trinity).[8]

These lines support the view that *síd*—religion was the essential form of grassroots paganism. The *síde*, or the *áes síde* 'the people of the *síd*', were the gods and spirits of Ireland. A man of the *síd* is called a *fer síde*, a woman of the *síd*, a ben *síde* — the banshee of folk belief who keens the dead. *Síd*, (which is cognate with Latin *sedes* 'seat'), is the word for the dwelling place of these supernatural beings.[9] They live in different places — in heights and in mounds, in caverns, on islands in the sea, and under lakes. They are also called the Túatha Dé Danann, 'the tribes of the goddess

Danu', and they have their own place in the pseudo-historical traditions of early Ireland.

According to these traditions, having spent a period of time in the northern islands of the world learning the arts of druidry and magic, they invaded Ireland in dark clouds, doing battle in the first instance with the Fir Bolg, and later with the Fomoire. Eventually, they were themselves defeated by the Sons of Míl (the Gaels) at the Battle of Tailtiu, and the country was divided into two halves — an upper half and a lower one. The Túatha Dé Danann were assigned to the half below the earth's surface, and the Dagda, their chief-god, distributed the fairy mounds among their leaders. The Dagda is a *día talman* 'a god of the earth', and the *síde* in general are referred to in the *Book of Armagh* as 'gods in the earth' (*side aut deorum terrenorum*).[10]

It is appropriate that they should be known as earth gods, for they are spirits of growth and fertility — gods of agriculture. This conclusion emerges from a study of early literary sources and of modern folk belief. After their defeat at the Battle of Tailtiu, they destroyed the wheat and milk of their conquerors, the Sons of Míl. They were still in possession of the secrets of agriculture, however, and it was not until a treaty was concluded with the Dagda that the Sons of Míl were able to harvest their corn and milk their cows. The *síde* had then to be propitiated with sacrifices of various kinds in order to ensure continued health and welfare. Modern fairy belief, for example, entailed the custom of pouring libations of milk for the fairies and of making offerings of food to them. The Dindshenchas of Mag Slécht gives the following account of ritual sacrifice in pagan times:

> It was there that the king idol of Ireland was, namely the Crom Cróich, and round him twelve idols made of stone; but he was of gold. Until Patrick's arrival, he was the god of every people who colonized Ireland. To him they used to offer the firstlings of every issue and the chief scions of every class. It is to him that the king of Ireland, Tigernmas, son of Follach, went at Samain (Hallowe'en), together with the men and women of Ireland, in order to adore him. And they all prostrated themselves before him . . . and three-quarters of the men of Ireland perished at these prostrations; whence Mag Slécht 'Plain of Prostrations'.[11]

The metrical version of this prose text also says that 'worship was paid to stones till the coming of noble Patrick to Armagh'. Stones were venerated and were believed to contain supernatural powers. The *Lia Fáil* is the classic example of this: it was the magic stone which was brought to Ireland by the Túatha Dé Danann. As the inauguration stone of Tara, it screamed when the rightful king sat on it. Supernatural spirits were also contained in other things. Weapons, for example, had unseen powers. In *Táin Bó Cúailnge*, Cú Chulainn's earthly father, Sualtaim, perished by his own sword because he had spoken before the druid.[12]

Since pagan Irish religion was animistic in nature, it is not surprising to find that there were strong cults of sacred animals, and of rivers, lakes and wells. These latter were deemed to be either gods or goddesses, or to contain a sacred presence. The Boyne river (*Boand* in Irish), for example, is derivable from *bou-vindá*, which means 'cow-white (goddess)'. Boand plays an important role in mythological tales. She is the mate of Nechtan, (or Nuadu Necht), who is identical with the fisher god Nodens of early Britain. Nechtan may also be compared with the Roman water-god Neptunus. As Mircea Eliade has pointed out, cults of rivers, lakes and wells are based ultimately on the sacredness of water. Water gives life and strength; it aids fertility, it purifies, it cures illness, and it continually renews itself.[13] Little wonder that it was considered to be the manifestation of the sacred. Here is an example from the *Vita Tripartita*, 'the Tripartite Life (of Saint Patrick)':

> Patrick went to the well of Findmag. Slán is its name. They told Patrick that the heathen honoured the well as if it were a god . . . the magi, i.e., the wizards and druids used to reverence the well Slán and offer gifts to it as if it were a god.[14]

Another well — that of Segais — was the source of all wisdom and occult knowledge. It was located in the otherworld, and 'around it were hazel-trees, the fruit of which dropped into the well and caused bubbles of mystic inspiration' (*na bolcca immais*) to form on streams which issued from the well. The nuts of the trees passed into the river Boyne, and those who drank the *imbas* from them became accomplished poets.[15] Cults of holy wells were so strong that they were carried over into Christian times, with many of the ancient pagan rites associated with them intact.[16]

In circumstances in which the forces of life have to be propitiated and kept under control, the magician and soothsayer play a central role, for it is they who are capable of communicating with the gods and spirits by means of spell, rite, charm and incantation. In early Ireland, magico-religious beliefs and practices permeated every aspect of individual, social and political life.

Organised paganism had its caste of established holy men — the druids of pre-Christian Ireland. Originally they had a high status, comparable to that of their counterparts in Gaul and Britain. Julius

Caesar remarks that the whole Gaulish people were much given to religious matters (*natio est omnis Gallorum admodum dedita religionibus*),[17] a comment which echoes that of Livius who says that they were not a *negligens gens* in this regard.[18] According to Caesar, the druids were the sacerdotal class who officiated at sacrifices, made prophecies, enforced legal decisions and conducted the system of education. References to the druids in Irish sagas and saints' lives suggest that the same was true of pagan Ireland. 'The druid (Old Irish *druí*) was priest, prophet, astrologer, and teacher of the sons of nobles. According to the sixth century *First Synod of Saint Patrick* oaths were sworn in his presence.'[19] With the advance of Christianity, however, he lost a number of his functions, and by the time the law-texts were written, he is more akin to a sorcerer or witch-doctor than to a priest of an organised religious institution. Nevertheless, he was sufficiently prominent to be included in the list of *dóernemid* (dependent privileged class) in *Uraicecht Becc*, a law-text dealing with rank in early Irish society.[20]

Rank was crucial in society. In a classic statement on the distinguishing characteristics of early and modern Irish society, D. A. Binchy defined the early period as 'tribal, rural, hierarchical, and familiar (using this word in its oldest sense to mean a society in which the family, not the individual, is the unit) — a complete contrast to the unitary, urbanized, egalitarian and individualist society of our time'.[21] While this definition is not beyond controversy — there are problems with the interpretation of the term 'tribal' and the assumed egalitarian nature of modern society may be more a wish than a reality — the statement nonetheless highlights in fairly accurate and succinct wording the central differences between the two types of society.

The *túath* (pl. *túatha*), petty kingdom, was the basic political and territorial unit: it designates both the people and the territory ruled by a king (*rí*). According to F. J. Byrne, there were about 150 *túatha* in the country at any given time between the fifth and the twelfth centuries.[22] It is stated in one law-text that no *túath* was properly constituted unless it had an ecclesiastical scholar, a cleric, a poet and a king.[23] Society was tribal in that the king of the *túath* (*rí túaithe*) was the 'true' king, and that people, with the exception of the learned classes, had no legal standing outside their own *túath*; it was not tribal in the sense that this infers distinct religious and cultural differences between *túatha*. As regards the hierarchical or stratified nature of society, it was divided into three classes corresponding roughly to king, lords and commons — in Irish, *rí*, *flatha* and *bó-airig*. This tripartite division is found in other Indo-European societies. It corresponds to Caesar's division of Gaulish society into *druides, equites* and *plebs*, and to the Indian classification into *brahmans* (priests), *ksatriyas* (warriors) and *vaishyas* (farmers). Classical accounts of Gaulish society, most of which are based on that of the Stoic ethnographer Posidonius of Apamea, make a further tripartite division of the learned classes into *vates* (seers/poets), *bardoi* (bards) and *druides* (druids). *Vates* corresponds etymologically to Ir. *fáith* (pl. *fátha*), *bardoi* to Ir. *bard* (pl. *baird*), and *druides* to Ir. *druí* (pl. *druíd*). By the time the Old Irish laws were written, the *fili* (pl. *filid*) 'poet, seer', is the dominant member of the learned classes, having taken over many of the functions of the others.

The law-texts of the seventh and eighth centuries which deal with rank in society distinguish between those people who are *nemed* 'privileged' and those who are not *nemed*, and between those who are *sóer* 'free' and those who are *dóer* 'unfree'. The basic meaning of the word *nemed* is 'sacred, holy', and it is cognate with the Gaulish word *nemeton* which is used of sacred places. As Fergus Kelly says, this suggests 'that the privileges of rank were originally sustained by religious feeling as well as respect for wealth and power'.[24] The main categories of *nemed* were kings, lords, clerics, and poets (*filid*).

One of the main functions of the *filid* was to praise and to satirise. They also had the power of prophecy, and they were originally the guardians of the traditions (*senchas*) of the *túath*. They derived their status from the pagan practices of *imbas forosna* 'encompassing knowledge which illuminates', *teinm láeda* 'breaking of marrow(?)' and *díchetal di chennaib* 'chanting from heads'. According to the account of the ninth century bishop-king Cormac mac Cuilennáin, St. Patrick banned the first two of these customs because of their pagan associations.[25]

The *filid* worked for the *status quo*, for the maintenance of their own status and that of the king. They protected the king against sorcery and they were tightly bound to him in a form of mutual obligation and support. The Irish word for king, *rí*, is cognate with Sanscrit *rāj*, Latin *rēx*, Gaulish *rīx*. The king was a sacred personage, capable of tracing his descent to an ancestral deity. Many of the founders of early Irish dynasties — such as Conn, Lug and Nuada — are euhemerised divinities. The right of the king to rule — to stretch, extend, protect (cf. Old Irish *rigid*, the verb with which the root noun *'rēg-s* king' is associated) depended on *fír flaithemon* 'prince's justice (or truth)'.[26] *Fír flaithemon* encompasses the concepts of cosmic and ethical truth and justice. The cosmic order, and consequently the well-being of his kingdom, depended on the king's justice. He was the representative of the gods on earth, a *día talmaide* 'an earthly god'. The opposite of *fír flaithemon* is *gáu* (gó) *flaithemon* 'prince's injustice (or falsehood)'; it causes severe hardship and disadvantage for the king and his *túath*; it leads to the overthrow of the king, and often to his death.

Few themes are as pervasive in Irish literature and mythology as that pertaining to kingship and to the relationship of the king with the forces of the otherworld. It is in those texts containing the theme that we approach an understanding of the religiously sacred nature of Irish political institutions. One of the most important works on the subject is the *Audacht Morainn*, 'the Testament of Morann', a wisdom-text dating from the late seventh century.[27] According to this text, the king's justice brings about fertility of man, woman, beast, land, and river. The weather is good and the king's reign prosperous; his injustice, on the other hand, produces the opposite effects.

This theme, along with the allied one of the *hieras gamos*, the symbolic mating of the king with the Earth goddess, echoes down the centuries — from the ideal kingship of Cormac mac Airt, during whose reign Ireland is reputed to have become a land of promise, to the Jacobite poetry of the seventeenth and eighteenth centuries which view Ireland as a wasteland in consequence of her rightful spouse being overseas. The ceremony which marks the inauguration of the king is a religious fertility rite: he 'sleeps with' or 'marries' (Ir. *feis, ban-feis*) the Earth goddess. The most celebrated of these rites in early Ireland were associated with the royal sites of Tara, Cnuachu and Emain Macha.

Many texts of the early Irish period demonstrate that the cosmos was viewed as an interlocking system of relationships in which animate and inanimate matter were merged together in mutual sympathy and support. This delicately balanced universe was held together by the proper functioning of its respective parts, and the king, who more than anyone else embodied the hidden forces of nature on account of his kinship with the gods, was the one who was accepted by the community to ensure that things were kept 'in proper order'. He did this through the exercise of his *fír flaithemon*, by adhering strictly to its principles. Irish kingship is similar in this respect to kingship in many primitive societies, and Heinrich Wagner has demonstrated that *fír flaithemon* bears remarkable resemblances to Vedic *Rta*, 'cosmic and ethical truth', and to Egyptian *Ma-a-t*, the goddess of cosmic and ethical truth.[28]

Kings and heroes were hedged about with taboos: these are

prohibitions of a religious nature, called *geisi* (sg. *geis*), which forbid the performance of certain acts. The basis of taboo is to insulate the sacred personage against the malign forces of the otherworld and to ensure that he maintains harmony between the two worlds. The druids and seers, who acted as intermediaries between the natural and supernatural realms, were capable of divining what was favourable and unfavourable for the king to do. If he broke his taboos, whether wittingly or unwittingly, it led to disaster and probable doom.

The breaking of taboos is the subject of the tragic story of *Togail Bruidne Da Derga* 'The Destruction of Da Derga's Hostel'. The tragedy is set against the background of a Golden Age of peace and plenty in the mythical past when the young hero-king, Conaire Mór mac Etarscélae, ruled at Tara. Faced with the dilemma of choice between the love of his foster-brothers who had begun thieving in the land and his duty as a king of cosmic and ethical truth, Conaire fails to act swiftly and justly with the effect that he violates one of his taboos. This starts a chain of events over which he has no control and which leads to the breaking of his other taboos and to his death in Da Derga's hostel.

The saga of Conaire Mór presents us with an example of the myth of the semi-divine hero — his conception, birth, life and death. In treating of the relationship between man and the gods, myth embodies the essence of religion and reflects the ideology of a given culture. The central theme of early Irish literature and mythology is precisely this intercourse and link between the world of men and the world of the gods: it is a theme which occupied not only the aristocrats of learning throughout the ages of Gaelic civilisation, but also, until recent times, the ordinary people themselves.

The otherworld of Irish belief and poetic imagination is a place of wonders (*Tír Ingnad*), a pleasant or great plain (*Mag Mell / Mag Már*), a land of the Ever-living (*Tír inna mBéo*); it is also a land of beautiful women and young maidens (*Tír inna mBan*). In its benevolent aspect, it is a land of peace and harmony. The words of peace (*síth*) and the otherworld (*síd*) are homonymous in Old Irish, something which did not go amiss on the early *litteratéurs*.[29] The peace of the natural world under the rule of the true prince is a reflection of that found in the otherworld, which is its source. The supernatural world defies rational definitions of time and space: it may be reached at almost any time and in any place, and many of the finest Early Irish compositions treat of journeys to and sojourns in it.

Nowhere in Early Irish literature is the theme of the otherworld expressed so poetically, or with such creative and intellectual sensitivity, as in *Immram Brain*, 'The Voyage of Bran'. This work consists of two poems, each containing twenty-eight quatrains, together with short introductory, linking and final prose passages. The success of the composition lies in the author's superb lyricism, and in his artistic blending and harmonising of ecclesiastical and native elements to produce a work with a clear Christian message. In the following stanzas, Manannán mac Lir, the god of the sea and the happy otherworld, addresses Bran, who has started on his voyage across the sea to see if he might reach the Land of Women (*Tír inna mBan*):

> Bran thinks it is a wondrous beauty
> in his coracle over the clear sea;
> as for me, in my chariot from afar,
> it is a flowery plain around which he drives
>
> What is clear sea,
> for the prowed ship in which Bran is,
> is a pleasant plain with abundance of flowers
> for me in a two-wheeled chariot
>
> Bran sees
> many waves breaking over the clear sea;
> I myself see in Mag Mon
> red-topped flowers without flaw
>
> Sea-horses glisten in summer
> as far as Bran has stretched the glances of his eye;
> flowers pour forth a stream of honey
> in the land of Manannán mac Lir[30]

Here we have reciprocity and juxtaposition of opposites as the poet unfolds the theme of the relativity of matter. The force permeating both these stanzas and the entire composition is that of the *coincidentia oppositorum*: all the islands which are described mirror one another, yet they are also finely differentiated. The woman at the beginning of the tale is a *ben síde*, but she is also Eve; Bran is Adam; Manannán is God; Mongán is Jesus. This interlocking, linking and resembling could be carried on to infinity. But some measure of order is necessary in order to establish firm ground. Firmness, certainty and finitude are sought in the infinite, in Him who made all these islands, the earth and the sea, the sea-horses and the flowers, the pleasant plain and paradise. It is He — the Christian God — who has the key to the similarities and differences. And so the circle can be closed: the sea and the plain, the fish and the calves, the woman and Eve, Bran and Adam, Manannán and God, this world and the otherworld.

Having sifted the evidence relating to pagan Irish religion, one arrives at the conclusion that the Celts brought their gods with them when they came to Ireland. By the time of our written sources, these gods are 'faded deities' in mortalised form. Moreover, they were probably superimposed upon a vibrant animistic religion. One of the most important sources of information on the gods, and on Early Irish mythology in general, is the tale of *Cath Maige Tuired* 'The (Second) Battle of Mag Tuired'. It preserves an independent literary account of the battle between the Túatha Dé Danann and the Fomoire. It is a long and quite complex tale which has been interpreted in various ways by different scholars. Tomás Ó Cathasaigh sees three main parts in it: the first deals with the kingship of Ireland, the second with the battle, and the third with the fertility of the land. The Túatha Dé Danann get the kingship, they prove their superiority in battle, and they finally succeed in wresting from the Fomoire the secrets concerning the fertility of the land.[31]

Ó Cathasaigh's analysis of the tale in terms of exemplary myth, with a direct bearing upon contemporary society, has the added merit of incorporating the powerful theory of Georges Dumézil, who views it as a reflex of an old Indo-European myth in which the gods of the first and second functions unite against the third. Dumézil has argued convincingly that there was in Indo-European ideology a functional tripartite classification of the natural and supernatural worlds: Ireland and India, for example, manifested this classification in their stratification of classes and castes. The first function is concerned with magico-religious aspects of life (represented by *druids* and *brahmans*) and with law and government (*kings*), the second with physical force (*flatha and ksatriyas*), and the third with fertility (*bó-airig* and *vaishjas*). This division of functions is also found in the Indian pantheon of gods: Varuna and Mitra represent the respective aspects of the first function, Indra that of the second function, and the Ashvins, the third. While such a hierarchy of functions is not clear in the case of Irish deities, Dumézil nevertheless argues that, notwithstanding the complexities involved, the Túatha Dé Danann may be taken to represent the first and second functions while the Fomoire embody the third; thus Bres, the leader of the Fomoire, who has the secrets of fertility which the Túatha Dé Danann lack, supplies the latter with the necessary information: he tells them when and how to plough, to sow and to reap.[32]

In our appraisal of such tales as *Cath Maige Tuired*, and indeed of Irish mythology in general, we must not lose sight of the fact that the 'religious' content relates in the first instance in many cases to the value system of society. Thus another scholar, who has recently edited *Cath Maige Tuired*, points out that the victory of the Túatha Dé Danann is 'a symbolic recognition of the fact that the strength of a society depends upon balanced relations between king and subject, upon the bonds of both maternal and paternal kinship, and upon co-operative relations among affinal groups';[33] Pádraig Ó Riain is undoubtedly correct in stressing that 'the implication surely is that the connexions with Greek, Scandinavian or more remote Indo-European themes, the role as a "myth of Samain" or the expression of an alliance between representatives of the two higher functions of the Indo-European range of divinities against the third (Dumézil's interpretation, sections of which are expertly accommodated by Ó Cathasaigh to his view of the tale's social function), reflect less the narrative's underlying meaning than the conservatism of the society it portrays'.[34]

The hero of *Cath Maige Tuired* is Lugh, who, according to other sources, belonged to the *áes síde* and dwelt at Brugh na Bóinne (Newgrange), from whence he came to beget Cú Chulainn, the great hero of the Ulster cycle: he is therefore Cú Chulainn's divine father. Many Irish families and dynasties claimed descent from Lug, and Eoin MacNeill takes this to have been the claim of all the Irish at one time.[35] Pádraig Ó Riain draws attention to the Dál Modula, an historical east Limerick family, who traced their descent back to Daul — probably a cover-name for Lug — 'through a sequence of no less than five synonyms of Lug, beginning with Find and continuing with Lugaid Lámluath, Lug Lethderg, Luchta and Láimthech in that order'.[36] Moreover, the same scholar's researches into Irish hagiography show that it was to some degree a mirror-image of its pagan precursor and that the pagan deity Lug has been recycled as a Christian saint in many instances. Examples include Lugaid of the Dál Modula, Molua of the Uí Fidgeinte (founder of the monastery of Killaloe), Molacca of the Fir Maige Féne and Bishop Lugach of the Luigne 'Lug's people'.[37]

That the cult of Lug was widespread in the Celtic world is clear from Gaulish inscriptions, and from placenames, such as Lyon, Laon and Leyden (from *Lugudunum*, 'Lug's Fort'), or Luguvalium (from *Luguvalos*, 'strong like (or in) Lug'), the Romano-British name of Carlisle in Northern England. The Festival Of Lughnasa (from *Lug-nasad*, 'Lug's feast') occurred on 1 August and traditionally lasted a month, fifteen days before and fifteen days after

1 August. Two of the greatest Irish assemblies were held at this time — the Oenach Tailten and Oenach Carmain, both of which were associated with important goddesses. *Lughnasa* was an agrarian festival, one of the four great festivals of the Irish and Celtic year, the others being *Imbolg* which was celebrated on 1 February, *Beltaine* on 1 May, and *Samain* on 1 November. *Samain* was the most important of these from a religious point of view, for it was at this time that there was unhindered access between this world and the otherworld. As Máire MacNeill has demonstrated in her great work on the subject, *Lughnasa* was celebrated throughout all parts of Ireland and was intimately connected with hill-tops.[38] We may note also here that Crom Cróich — the pagan idol whom we mentioned earlier — is associated with the festival in folk tradition under the name of Crom Dubh. He is also connected with it in the earlier *dindshenchas* sources.

In *Cath Maige Tuired*, Lug is the *Samaildánach*, the master of all arts and crafts, who ousts the old king of Tara, *Nuada Argatlám* 'Nuada of the Silver Hand', and defeats his own maternal grandfather, Balar of the baleful eye. He is also 'the divine prototype of human kingship', the exemplary model to be followed by the kings of this world. All this tends to confirm the view that he is identical with Mercury, whom Caesar says the Gauls regarded as the inventor of all arts, and who was the one to whom they paid the greatest worship.

It appears that the divine order was modelled, to some extent not yet fully clear, upon tribal hierarchy and organisation. Thus, it has been argued by some scholars that each tribe had a distinct god just as it had a distinct king — a multifunctional deity who was the ancestor of his people. Like the king, he was responsible for the well-being of the *túath* and its people.[39] A common oath in the Ulster cycle of stories is the invocation of the god of the tribe — *tongu do día toinges mo thúath* (or *toingte Ulaid*), 'I swear to the god by whom my tribe (or 'the Ulaid') swears'; and many Gaulish names of deities appear only once and have purely local reference. T. F. O'Rahilly, on the other hand, held that there was only one polyvalent deity who appears under different names and guises. While it is true that different gods frequently perform similar functions, certain gods have quite distinct and specific functions.[40] Examples of the latter are Goibniu, the smith god; Dian Cécht, the leech; and Donn, 'the brown one', the lord of the dead to whose home (*Tech Duinn*) all of the Irish will come after death.

In a country in which fertility played such a prominent role, earth or mother goddesses were particularly important: they were chiefly concerned with fertility of land and beast, with sexuality, and, in defence of their territory, with war. Thus we have Anu, the goddess of plenty, whose maternal function is indicated by the name of the Paps mountains in Co. Kerry with which she is closely associated; Medb 'the intoxicated one' (or 'the one who intoxicates'), to whom so many kings were mated; and the Morrígan, the raven war-goddess who appears in triple form, and who also has a sexual function. The female deity in triadic form is a common Celtic phenomenon: in Ireland there is the Morrígan/Badb/Nemain complex, the three Machas, and the three Brigits.

According to Cormac mac Cuillenáin, Brigit was the goddess whom the *filid* adored. An expert in poetry and traditional lore, she was the daughter of the Dagda 'the good god' — the Great Father (Eochaidh Ollathair), and the god of knowledge and druidry (Rúad Rófhessa, 'The Mighty One of Great Knowledge'). The importance of Brigit is underlined by the fact that, according to Cormac, the general name for a goddess was Brigit. Her functions were taken over by the Christian St. Brigit whose feast-day fell on 1 February, the date of the old pagan spring festival of *Imbolg*. In her Christian guise, Brigit is connected with fertility, healing and craftsmanship.

For a variety of reasons, many of the gods and goddesses referred to in this essay failed to make a lasting impression on folk memory. Some probably never made the transition from heroic society to peasant culture. Paganism, however, did not come to an end with the demise of the druid. At grassroots level, the peasant continued to cherish the ruder prototypes of the gods whom the druids and poets had glorified: belief in the *síde* survived. And certain gods and heroes continued to hold a fascination for the imagination. Fertility goddesses, in particular, held a special place in folk belief. Among these was the Caillech Bérri, or 'The Hag of Beare'. She has a cosmogonic function: she moves islands, drops cairns from her aprons, builds mountains, and has a close association with megalithic monuments, particularly with that of Knowth in Co. Meath. Her names include Dige, Digde and Duinech, and as Buí (or Boí), she is said to be wife of Lug and thus the goddess of sovereignty and fertility. The divine ancestress of many people, she is a woman of tremendous longevity who has lived through seven cycles of youth: 'she passed into seven periods of youth, so that every husband used to pass from her to death of old age, so that her grandchildren and great-grandchildren were peoples and races.'[41]

In our discussion of *Immram Brain* above, attention was drawn to the sensitivity with which the author treated the theme of the relationship between pagan and Christian beliefs. At approximately the same time as the author of this work was engaged at his composition, another writer took up a similar theme and produced what seems to many to be the greatest of all Irish poems — 'The Lament of the Old Woman of Beare'. In this poem the Caillech Bérri contrasts her earlier years of youth, love and companionship on the rich plain of Feven with her present solitary state of withering old age on the bleak island of Beare. The image which is sustained throughout the poem is the ebb and flow of life, an image capable of encompassing many rich veins of interpretations. Perhaps the final ebb of the hag is to be equated with the end of the pagan past, but, if it is, this author knew, as did the author of *Immram Brain*, that tradition in Ireland withers and ebbs neither slowly nor serenely:

> The ebbing that has come to me
> is not the ebbing of the sea.
> What knows the sea of grief or pain?
> Happy tide will flood again
> I am the hag of Buí and Beare —
> the richest cloth I used to wear,
> Now with meanness and with thrift
> I even lack a change of shrift . . .
> Those whom we loved, the plains
> we ride today bear their names;
> gaily they feasted with laughter
> nor boasted thereafter . . .
> These arms you see,
> these bony scrawny things,
> had once more loving craft
> embracing kings . . .
> When Maytime comes
> the girls out there are glad,
> and I, old hag, old bones,
> alone am sad . . .
> But for Feven's plain
> I envy nothing old;
> I have a shroud of aged skin,
> Feven's crop of gold . . .
> Great wave of flood
> and wave of ebb and lack!
> What flooding tide brings in
> the ebbing tide brings back . . .
> Blessed the islands of the great sea
> with happy ebb and happy flood.
> For me, for me alone, no hope:
> the ebbing is for good.[42]

LITERATURE AND RELIGION IN EIGHTEENTH CENTURY IRELAND

A Critical Survey

JOSEPH McMINN

Literature in eighteenth-century Ireland, whether in Gaelic or English, is the fruit of insecurity. The Aisling of the Munster poets, inspired by a dream of national recovery, or the pamphlets of Protestant reformers on the economy, full of anger and despair at Ireland's chaotic management, though the expression of mutually antagonistic cultures, share the same sense of frustrated possibility. The century began with revolution and conquest, a settlement which guaranteed power to a Protestant minority through the political dispossession of the Catholic majority. Writing and literature for the rest of the century is usually an argument with the terms and consequences of that settlement.

Literary culture in these circumstances is a deeply precarious activity, almost threatened with extinction. Protestant, English-speaking Ireland, which constitutes roughly a quarter of the population,[1] looks to London for both political security and cultural assurance: Catholic, Gaelic-speaking Ireland, in its traumatic condition of loss, has no such focus for support. Ireland in this period has two, legally-separate, linguistically-distinct cultures, denominated, above all else, by religious affiliation. Ireland is governed in the Protestant interest, while Catholicism, under the Penal Laws, is defined as an interest incompatible with loyalty to the State. Constitutional principles and parliamentary legislation make religion the badge of political and cultural acceptability. For eighteenth-century writers, religion is not a chosen subject or a casual allegiance: for the minority it legitimises colonial rule, while for the majority it explains exclusion from the State.[20]

It is difficult to generalise about 'literature' in eighteenth-century Ireland, since the terms which may be usefully applied to one culture fail to suggest the quite different nature of imaginative composition and expression in the other. The social, legal, even technological conditions under which authors in both cultures produced their work were worlds apart. Protestant writers, from William Molyneux and Jonathan Swift onwards, were able to address a literate, educated class which, if it did not actually wield power, certainly identified with the interests of government. Protestant Ireland had its own parliament, although executive power lay with London.[3] In their attempts to influence public opinion, Protestant writers took for granted the rapid circulation of copies through the printing press. The exchange of ideas was part of normal, civilised public-debate and an enjoyable custom. If we insist on the term 'literature' when discussing imaginative or fictive writing in Catholic Ireland, we are faced with a radically different set of assumptions and practices. The great majority was illiterate, though not unfamiliar with artistic culture. Verses from Gaelic poets barely reached the printing-press by the end of the century, since the custom was to preserve and circulate the work in manuscript.[4] With the collapse of the traditional nobility's patronage, Gaelic poets often seemed unsure exactly who they were addressing, if anyone.

Writing in English is quite a new affair. Once it gets under way, it is largely the constitutional status of Ireland and the economy which preoccupy Protestant writers. This is the literature of the public pamphlet, designed for appeal and instruction, not diversion or entertainment. Gaelic verse of the period, though proud of its ancient pedigree and noble traditions, seems in a state of shock. Its enterprise is to express, often with a dignified anger, the loss of security. For each culture, writing is a form of desperation. Despite occasional rhetoric about the 'Irish nation', the country has a quite schizoid character. If we are to appreciate the mixed literary culture of eighteenth-century Ireland, then we will have to take each part separately, in its own terms, and then see what overall picture emerges.

Most Anglo-Irish writers in this period come from middle-class, clerical back-grounds.[5] Some of the most outstanding, like Swift and Berkeley, rise to high positions in the Church of Ireland. Many of them, including Sheridan and Goldsmith, once they finish studies at Trinity College Dublin, look to England for a serious career as writer or churchman. This is why J. C. Beckett refers to these writers as the representatives of a 'cross-channel' culture,[6] in the sense that educated men like them could not associate Ireland with literary culture. Only England could offer the living practice of public writing with a clearly-defined audience, shared values grounded in custom, no continuing political crisis, and, most importantly, a feeling of literary tradition behind the writers. In Ireland, there was always the problem of economic survival, a hostile majority, depressed trade, and the strain of trying to preserve an English identity in barbarous conditions — it was, unfortunately, a place to leave.

Swift, more than any other Protestant writer, addressed himself consistently to the Irish question. Significantly, his ambition for an English career is the key to his commitment to Protestant Ireland. Thwarted in his desire to secure an English bishopric, and then being appointed the Dean of St. Patrick's Cathedral in Dublin, Swift becomes the most articulate and coherent spokesman for the Anglican part of Protestant Ireland. A clergyman for nearly fifty years, we should not underestimate the part which religion played in his defence of an Ireland loyal but not subservient to the Crown.[7] Given the generally uneven and unpredictable character of writing during this period, religious orthodoxy was one of the very few ideological certainties available to the public-spirited writer, especially when he was a priest in the State Church. With such a close identification between the authority of the Church of Ireland and the State, religious values would necessarily and quite naturally inform matters of political controversy. Also, religion could offer to figures like Swift the only visible form of tradition, in a country which offered no other forms of security.

Swift's *Drapier's Letters* (1724) are a good example of this inseparability of religious and political values or, more precisely, the way religious orthodoxy is summoned to reinforce a political argument. By 1724, a considerable body of public opinion in Ireland had expressed its disquiet over a patent granted to an English speculator, William Wood, to mint small coinage for Ireland. Swift joined in with this opposition and produced a series of seven polemical pamphlets under the fictional guise of a humble, Dublin drapier. By appealing to a range of classes and interests, Swift tried to broaden public concern and knowledge with regard to the constitutional legality of a move approved by London, but directly opposed by official opinion in Ireland, including the Irish Houses of Parliament.[8] Using a mock-naif persona like the Drapier had several, related purposes: as a trader in a commodity of importance to the economy of Ireland, he could speak from direct knowledge and experience; as a man of sufficient but unsophisticated learning, he could give the impression of honest common-sense; using a mask, he could protect himself from direct legal recognition; and, most important, as a Christian and a patriot, he could appeal to the religious and political idealism of the Protestant middle-class.

Throughout the *Letters*, the Drapier explains his unprecedented involvement with political questions usually above his head. He does this using the explicitly alarmist terms of Christian duty in the public interest. The first pamphlet, *A Letter to the Shopkeepers*, opens solemnly:

What I intend now to say to you, is, next to your duty to God, and the care of your Salvation, of the greatest Concern to yourselves, and your Children; your Bread and Clothing, and every common Necessary of Life entirely depend upon it. Therefore I do most earnestly exhort you as Men, as *Christians*, as *Parents*, and as *Lovers of your Country*, to read this paper with the utmost Attention, or get it read to you by others.[9]

This careful ranking of duties is central to the instructive nature of the pamphlets. It is retained at the rhetorical climax of the fourth letter, *To the Whole People of Ireland*:

The Remedy is wholly in your own Hands; and therefore I have digressed a little, in order to refresh and continue that *Spirit* so seasonably raised amongst you; and to let you see, that by the laws of GOD, of NATURE, of NATIONS, and of your own Country, you ARE and OUGHT to be as FREE a People as your Brethren in *England*.[10]

The Drapier, on Swift's behalf, is trying to show his audience that this seemingly local, irritating affair of Wood unfortunately raises the constitutional status of Ireland in relation to England. Swift never accepted Ireland's 'dependent' status, as defined in the 1720 Declaratory Act, and argued that Protestant loyalty was always to the Crown and Constitution, not to legislators and politicians of the day.[11] This convenient distinction between a sacred ideal and a changeable reality explains Swift's enduring distrust of English politicians and his confident interpretation of the Constitution as a contract between equal partners based on mutual consent. The Drapier's religious emphasis on the sacredness of this freedom may be taken literally, and not just as a rhetorical device to achieve dramatic authority. For the Drapier, Irish 'dependency' is a smear, probably invented by clever-speaking lawyers confident that most people are easily intimidated by big words:

. . . a *depending kingdom* is a *modern term of art*, unknown, as I have heard, to all *ancient* Civilians and *Writers upon Government*: and *Ireland* is on the contrary called in some statutes an *Imperial crown*, as held only from God: which is as high a Style as any Kingdom is capable of receiving.[12]

The Drapier's contempt for this 'modern term of art' is part of a consistent reliance on the traditional nature of Ireland's claim to legislative independence under the Crown. Speculators like Wood in economics, Churchmen in theology, or lawyers on the Constitution, have a perverse love and need of abstraction to justify their authority. For Swift and his Drapier, the truth of the matter was obvious, susceptible to ordinary reason, and best illustrated by a plain way of talking. Forever suspicious of complex reasoning as a form of deception, the Drapier encourages his audience to 'take the whole matter nakedly as it lies before us, without the refinements of some people, with which we have nothing to do'. The Drapier's style is a perfect demonstration of Swift's religious orthodoxy.

Although the persona of the Drapier had several tactical advantages, especially authorial concealment, the Dean could not resist openly applauding the patriotic stance of his fictional self. Late in the campaign against Wood, he wrote *A Letter to the Lord Chancellor Middleton*, and signed his initials to the letter.[13] Here the identification between the political and the religious, the fictional and the real, is made quite explicit:

> If this Fact be truely stated; I must confess I look upon it as my Duty, so far as God hath enabled me, and as long as I keep within the Bounds of Truth, of Duty, and of Decency, to warn my Fellow Subjects . . . never to admit this pernicious coin. . . For if one single Thief forces the Door, it is in vain to talk of keeping out the whole Crew behind.[14]

More than any of the other letters, this one seeks to explain and justify the public intervention of writers committed to Ireland's defence in the face of arbitrary government. For Swift, this was not simply a choice, but a duty inspired by conscience. When this same writer was a clergyman, that intervention and the cause which it espoused would naturally draw on the moral and religious authority of the Established Church. Pamphlets on Ireland were now part of Swift's pastoral politics. In the letter to Middleton, Swift remarks, 'I did very lately, as I thought it my duty, preach to the people under my inspection upon the subject of Mr Wood's coin', and concludes that the very idea of preaching politics from the pulpit would be considered seditious by the Law.

The actual text of this sermon, entitled *Doing Good*,[15] tries to explain the need for practical patriotism in a situation where the nation's well-being is under attack from self-interested individualism. In a patient elaboration of the many varieties of love, from self-love, love of our neighbours, to love of our country, Swift argues that patriotism is the supreme, because all-inclusive, love:

> This love of the public, or of the commonwealth, or love of our country, was in antient times properly known by the name of *Virtue*, and because it was the greatest of all virtues, and was supposed to contain all virtues in it.[16]

Offences against the public interest, it is argued, cannot be considered or judged merely in secular terms, but 'are very great and aggravated sins in the sight of God'. Faced with corrupt English politicians who ignore the constitutional rights of loyal Protestants, or as Swift earlier called them, 'the true English people of Ireland', individualism and self-interest must give way to a higher, collective interest for the sake of survival. In his sermons and pamphlets, Swift always assumes Ireland's moral superiority over English political venality.

At the same time, he is equally aware of the danger within – Irish apathy and ignorance. For Swift as writer and clergyman, the ultimate political authority is, simply, God himself:

> All government is from God, who is the God of order, and therefore whoever attempts to breed confusion or disturbance among a people, doth his utmost to take the government of the world out of God's hands, and to put it into the hands of the Devil, who is the author of confusion. By which it is plain, that no crime, how heinous soever, committed against particular persons, can equal the guilt of him who doth injury to the public.[17]

This near-feudal or mediaeval identification of Church and State, based on the ideal of absolute, uncompromising uniformity and allegiance, is explicable partly by reference to the sectarian character of Ireland at the time. Surrounded by Presbyterians, who numbered almost half the Protestant minority, and by Catholics, who outnumbered all Protestants by three to one,[18] the reality of division and dissent seriously questioned the principle of such authority. The precariousness of the Established Church forced Swift to define his political patriotism in such extreme terms. In matters political and religious, Swift's conservatism looked back to archaic models based on authority beyond inquiry.

But Irish Protestantism owed its existence to a very different, even contradictory, principle – the right to oppose authority. The 'Glorious Revolution' of 1690 was consistently interpreted as the result of lawful dissent in the interests of government by consent. Protestants were born to protest. Yet only two decades after such an achievement, Irish protest was usually branded as sedition. Swift is pulled in two directions simultaneously: a loyal Protestant, he has a duty to speak out; a conservative churchman, he knows that such defiance only contributes to a situation which authority must not tolerate.

The strain of being caught between these tensions, considered in terms of his personality as well as his ideology, resulted in a major shift towards an ironic perspective on the effectiveness of reasonable appeal. Circumstances became so ludicrous that, as Swift says, 'whoever happens to think out of Fashion, in what relates to the Welfare of this Kingdom, dare not so much as complain of the *Toothache*' . . .[19] That same sense of genuine despair conditions the ironic bitterness of *A Modest Proposal*:

> . . . as to my self; having been wearied out for many Years with offering vain, idle, visionary Thoughts; and at length utterly despairing of Success, I fortunately fell upon this Proposal. . .[20]

A Modest Proposal is best viewed as self-criticism, as an exasperated parody of faith. Its ferocity could only have derived from a conviction that Ireland was more appropriately governed by the rules of an abbatoir than by the laws of Christianity. In the year before this valedictory pamphlet, Swift had rehearsed his rejection of a blind and unresponsive public through the awesome manner of a revengeful and pitiless God:

> *Wisdom crieth in the Streets; because I have called and ye refused; I have stretched out my Hand, and no Man regarded. But ye have set at nought all my Counsel, and would none of my Reproof. I also will laugh at your Calamity, and mock when your Fear cometh*[21]

There is a sense here of the man of religion having been contaminated by an unworthy and thankless involvement in public affairs, and this results in an even greater assertion of priestly authority. After a decade of pamphleteering on behalf of his moral and political constituency, Swift turned away in disgust from public writing, and for the last decade of his life withdrew to the more secure and predictable area of Church interests.

In the last decade of his life, Swift wrote eight pamphlets on religious matters. They were concerned with two major controversies, the material conditions of the lower clergy in the Church of Ireland, and the renewed threat to legalise Toleration for Presbyterians. Both issues had an important and familiar factor in common — the authority of the Established Church.[22] In *Concerning That Universal Hatred Which Prevails Against The Church* (1736), Swift attacks the figure of Henry VIII, that 'Monster and Tyrant', for having dispossessed the clergy of most of 'their legal possessions', and for having begun a policy of contemptuous mistreatment of the Church which survived up to the present. The fact that Henry exposed the tyranny of the Pope is of less consequence to Swift than the King's robbery of Church property. The fact that it was the Church of Rome is irrelevant, for it 'was then, the national, and established faith'. This interpretation of the English Reformation shows clearly Swift's preference for a mediaeval arrangement whereby the Church is protected by the State, and also makes clear his consistent emphasis on the need for a strong material base for religious authority. A poor Church cannot command respect. To contemplate Toleration for Presbyterianism would be to diminish even further the prospect of a unified Church with exclusive authority based on legal and material security. It is quite characteristic of Swift's contradictory image that on the issue of clerical rights he should seem radical and populist, and on the question of Toleration seem reactionary and elitist. In matters religious as well as political, Swift is dogmatic, materialistic and uncompromising, utterly opposed to theoretical or speculative debate. This kind of fundamentalism was not easy to protect in the volatile and complex situation of Protestant Ireland. The dissenting rhetoric of Swift's pamphlets is inspired by the radical roots of Protestantism: but his version of Catholicism suggests a kind of order more pleasing to his outlook.

Bishop Berkeley's brief commentary on Irish affairs provides an instructive comparison with Swift's sustained entanglement. After the usual pattern of education at Kilkenny College and Trinity, Berkeley took Holy Orders and eventually became Dean of Derry and Bishop of Cloyne. Like so many of his contemporaries, he was a strong, conservative advocate of reforms, though these were either proposals for the American Colonies or, as with the eccentric *Siris* (1744), a recipe for a universal panacea. Mostly absent from his clerical administration, his main work on Ireland is *The Querist*, a series of three pamphlets published in Dublin between 1735 and 1737, which are written in the form, not of an argument, but of a relentless questionnaire.[23] The need for a national Bank for Ireland is the unifying concern of *The Querist*, but the pamphlets also reveal Berkeley's attitudes on several related issues. His thoughts on Ireland show a strong, but unacknowledged, debt to Swift, and a very different political perspective.[24]

Both men deplored the waste of Ireland's natural and human resources, and argued that greater economic self-reliance, coupled with a ban on all foreign, imported luxuries would be an effective means of achieving the kind of normal prosperity enjoyed by most European nations. These ideas were first proposed by Swift in *A Proposal for the Universal Use of Irish Manufacture* (1720), and charged with sedition.[25] At the end of that pamphlet, Swift had ridiculed the idea of a national Bank as a lunatic superstition, mainly because it would encourage credit, an invisible form of money. Berkeley argues that a Bank, controlled in the public interest, would enrich Ireland by regulating its wealth. Speculation would be a proper part of economic growth. The materialist in Swift could never put his faith in such a chimera, but for Berkeley it was the sign of a modern form of prosperity. If London, Amsterdam and Hamburg were thriving cities, then why not Dublin? Berkeley had to concede that Ireland's dependent relation with England whereby Ireland, uniquely in the context of European nations, had no national Mint, ensured its continuing backwardness.

The clerical background of both writers enforced a distinctively puritan attitude towards all forms of luxury, especially when it is identified with women and the gentry. Berkeley questions:

> Whether it would not be better for this island, if all our fine folk of both sexes were shipped off, to remain in foreign countries, rather than that they should spend their estates at home in foreign luxury, and spread the contagion thereof through their native land?[26]

Like Swift, Berkeley views the condition of Ireland as a series of material obstacles to be banished or overcome in order to arrive at a self-sufficient economy which works for the public interest. Because of their Irish situation, both clergymen support free-trade with critical and determined reservations, the principal one being that the private interest should never be allowed to obstruct the national welfare of the State. For Swift, this had already been vindicated in the case of Wood's half-pence; for Berkeley, the fight was against private bankers who wished to set up in Ireland, thereby contributing to the country's disastrous exploitation by adventurers. Berkeley agreed that Ireland could not afford the luxury of self-interested individualism.

On the evidence of *The Querist*, Berkeley supports limited and conditional Toleration for Catholics if it means greater security for the State. He proposes a college for loyal Catholics who could study alongside Trinity and thereby 'prevent the prejudices of a foreign education', as well as keep their money in Ireland. Catholicism, taken purely as a religion, is not to be feared or disallowed, since it will remain outside politics:

> Whether the case be not very different in regard to a man who only eats fish on Fridays, says his prayers in Latin, or believes transubstantiation, and one who professeth in temporals a subjection to foreign powers, who holdeth himself absolved from all obedience to his natural prince and the laws of his country?[27]

Like many Anglican clergymen, including Swift, there is also a certain note of envy for the homogenous, uniform nature of the Catholic ecclesiastical organisation which has 'a clergy suited to all ranks of men . . . from cardinals down to mendicants'. This observation is always a sad reminder of divisions within Irish Protestantism.

The outstanding difference between the two Churchmen lies in their attitudes towards England. Though a loyalist, Swift never has a good word to say about England. Berkeley, however, seems sycophantic by Swift's critical standards. In the English edition of *The Querist*, Berkeley made a point of criticising Swift for his ungenerous attitude towards the mother-country.[28] In a series of questions, he shows a faith and trust which Swift had long abandoned:

> Whether London is not to be considered the metropolis of Ireland?
> Whether it is not our interest to be useful to them rather than rival them: and whether in that case we may not be sure of their good offices?
> Whether we can propose to thrive so long as we entertain a wrong-headed distrust of England?
> Whether the Protestant colony in this kingdom can ever forget what they owe to England?[29]

Two years before this was published, Swift had remarked on Englishmen, including Bishops, who enjoyed so many of the top Irish posts:

> They had no common Ligament to bind them with us;
> they suffered not with our Sufferings, and if it were
> possible for us to have any Cause of Rejoycing,
> they could not rejoyce with us.[30]

Both writers recognised that England was very much part of the Irish problem, since executive authority lay with London not Dublin. On this question, Berkeley sounds much more reasonable, but Swift sounds much more convincing. Swift has a commitment which is never felt in reading Berkeley. Even the form of *The Querist*, its dizzying interrogation, its formulaic rhetoric, shows the outlook of a disengaged dilletante of opinions.

While Protestant Ireland in this period shows a very uneven, sometimes non-existent pattern of literary activity, Catholic Ireland reveals the survival of a poetic tradition. English-speaking Ireland is concerned with politics, the economy and the constitution; its characteristic literary form is the pamphlet. Gaelic-speaking Ireland expresses itself, almost exclusively, through inherited poetical forms; its characteristic tone is elegaic. The former is looking for a new beginning, and has yet to find a voice and imagination suited to the contemplation of its ambiguous situation. Its best minds are concerned with survival or exile. The latter has a long tradition of poetic craft, which is now employed to lament its own collapse.

Gaelic poetry in this period is usually identified with the sophisticated verse of a few surviving Munster poets, especially Aogán Ó Rathaille (c. 1675–1729) and Eoghan Rua Ó Suilleabháin (1748–1784). A poet like Ó Rathaille voices both a personal and a racial sense of loss in the face of foreign conquest. In the midst of confusion and retreat, there is an extraordinary assertiveness about the verse:

> Do thonnchrith m'inchinn, d'imigh mo phríomhdhóchas,
> poll im ionathar, biora nimhe trím dhrólainn,
> ár bhfonn, ár bhfothain, ár monga 's ár mínchóngair
> i ngeall le pinginn ag foirinn ó chrích Dhóbhair
>
> Do bhodhar an tSionainn, an Life, s' an Laoi cheolmhar,
> abhainn an Bhiorra Dhuibh, Bruice 'gus Bríd, Bóinne,
> com Loch Deirg 'na ruide 'gus Toinn Tóime
> ó lom an cuireata cluiche ar an rí coróinneach.
>
> Wave-shaken is my brain, my chief hope gone.
> There's a hole in my gut, there are foul spikes through my bowels.
> our land, our shelter, our woods and our level ways
> are pawned for a penny by a crew from the land of Dover.
>
> The Sionainn, the Life, the musical Laoi, are muffled
> and the Biorra Dubh river, the Bruice, the Bríd, the Bóinn,
> Reddened are Loch Dearg's narrows and the Wave of Tóim
> since the Knave has skinned the crowned King in the game.[31]
>
> ('Cabhair Ní Ghairfead', 'No Help I'll Call')

This is a political verse, using all of Nature as its metaphorical weapon. Its simple anger prevents this kind of lyricism from ever becoming an innocent form of pastoral. Given the background of the Penal Laws which reduced figures like Ó'Rathaille from professional poet to pauper, it is interesting to note that Catholicism, as a form of cultural identity, hardly enters his verse. Yet religious imagery provides him, and many others, with the form of the period's best known poetry — the Aisling. This visionary form is an unusual combination of the political, the religious and the erotic. It employs religious allegory, in the form of a miraculous apparition of female beauty, and directs the longing towards the political hope of the Pretender's restoration. Political ambition is translated into a mystical form:

Aisling ghéar do dhearcas féin
ar leaba 's mé go lagbhríoch,
an ainnir shéimh darbh ainm Éire
ag teacht im ghaor ar marcaíocht,
a súile glas, a cúl tiubh casta,
a com ba gheal 's a mailí,
dá mhaíomh go raibh ag tíocht 'na gar
a díogras, Mac an Cheannaí.

A bitter vision I beheld
in bed as I lay weary:
a maiden mild whose name was Éire
coming toward me riding,
with eyes of green hair curled and thick,
fair her waist and brows,
declaring he was on his way
— her loved one *Mac an Cheannaí*.[32]
('Mac an Cheannaí', 'The Redeemer's Son')

These hopes were contrasted with the fears of many in Protestant Ireland that such an invasion might occur. But after the final defeat of the Stuarts at Culloden in 1745, (the year of Swift's death), such verse 'grew out of touch with reality'.[33] Even in the work of Eoghan Rua Ó Suilleabháin at the end of the century, in poems like 'Ceo Draíochta' ('Magic Mist'), it begins to sound like a formal exercise for the sake of times past.

But the Aisling verse of the Munster poets, while deservedly renowned for its dramatic and technical virtuosity, does not tell the entire story of Gaelic poetry in this period. It was the verse of an elite, comprehensible and available to very few. Its studied formality often has a ceremonial character, a ritualised form of anger and grief. For a quite different kind of expression we should consider popular and occasional verse.

The two great occasional poems of Gaelic Ireland in the eighteenth century are *Caoineadh Airt Uí Laoghaire* (Lament for Art O'Laoghaire) by Eilín Dhubh ní Chonaill and *Cúirt an Mheáin Oíche* (The Midnight Court) by Brian Merriman. Both deal with Justice. One is a personal lament for the murder of a beloved husband, whose death is placed in the context of the Penal Laws which oppress Catholics; the other is a comic parody of the Aisling in which women's rights are restored in order to retrieve hope for the Irish nation.

The popularity of Eilín Dhubh's lament lies in the symbolic attraction of its martyred subject. Art O'Laoghaire, at home on leave from service in the army of the Austro-Hungarian empire, murdered in a quarrel over a law forbidding Catholics to own a horse over a certain value, represents the most emotive issues of the century for Catholic Ireland. His aristocratic and military image seems like the realisation of the old dream of restoration. His murder reinforces a whole people's sense of injustice. The wife's lament ends with a determined expression of revenge:

> Tá fhios ag Íosa Críost
> ná beidh caidhp ar bhaitheas mo chinn
> ná léine chnis lem thaoibh
> ná bróg ar thrácht mo bhoinn
> ná trioscán ar fuaid mo thí
> ná srian leis an láir ndoinn
> ná caithfidh mé le dlí
> 's go raghad anonn thar toinn
> ag comhrá leis an rí,
> 's mura gcuirfidh ionam aon tsuim
> go dtiocfad ar ais arís
> go bodach na fola duibhe
> a bhain díom féin mo mhaoin.
>
> Jesus Christ well knows
> there's no cap upon my skull
> nor shift next to my body
> nor shoe upon my foot-sole
> nor furniture in my house
> nor reins on the brown mare
> but I'll spend it on the law;
> that I'll go across the ocean
> to argue with the King,
> and if he won't pay attention
> that I'll come back again
> to the black-blooded savage
> that took my treasure.[34]

Despite the frenzied determination to seek justice from the monarch himself, in the absence of any local justice, the balance favours personal retribution. Apart from its powerful and controlled expression of formal grief, *Caoineadh Airt Uí Laoghaire* is an important document of eighteenth-century Ireland, in the way it contains and dramatises the sensibility of a people outside the law and without power.

The comic irony of Merriman's *Cúirt an Mheáin Oíche* converts dream into nightmare, a burlesque development of the Aisling. The hapless wanderer finds the entire social and sexual order turned upside down, a situation in which the women of Ireland have assumed responsibility for the government of the country. This is necessary because the men of Ireland have proved their sexual and political incompetence. Although much of the poem's comic drama, based on a mock-legal proceeding, concerns itself with the traditional war between the sexes, it includes a significant commentary on the state of Ireland at the time:

> Is dóch nach iongantas laigeacht na gréine
> is fós gach tubaist dár imigh ar Éire,
> mar mheath gach ceart gan reacht gan dlí againn,
> ár mba a bhí bleacht gan lacht gan laoigh acu
> is dá dtagadh níos mó de mhórscrios tíortha –
>
> No wonder, I say, that the sun shines weak,
> no wonder the horrors that happen in Ireland
> – no law nor order, Justice blighted,
> our milch cows giving no milk or calves,
> and the rest of the ruin that's over the land – [35]

Irish manhood is charged with responsibility for joyless sex, frustration of love within marriage, and the infertile state of the nation. One of the most extraordinary and subversive proposals for improvement is that the Catholic clergy should be allowed to marry, since they have the best-fed men in Ireland. This appeal is part of the poem's satirical intent, whereby the Catholic Church is shown to feed, like animals, off the misery of its flock. Like Swift, Merriman has a strong sense of the grotesque contrast between the forms of order and the imagery of suffering. The spiritual leaders of Catholic Ireland, with their 'bull-like voices' and 'huge hindquarters' must now assume responsibility for the corrupt injustices which afflict Ireland. Yet the poem is not an appeal for anarchy or libertinism. On the contrary, it is a comic exposure of moral and imaginative failure, and seeks to restore some kind of natural order in which the body and the spirit may thrive. As an ironic fantasy, it is quite unique in Gaelic poetry. Only Swift's *A Modest Proposal*, which contemplates very similar distortions of Nature, bears any imaginative correspondence.

For the student of this period, however, *Cúirt an Mheáin Oíche* is a freak. Its range and ambition include an interesting documentary element, but there are no successors. Its style is often compared with, even attributed to, Swift or Rabelais, but there is little substantial evidence for this.[36] The literary sources of the poem, like the life of its author, lie within an unrecorded culture beyond official recognition.

The anonymous folk-poetry of Gaelic Ireland is a substantial body of work, often showing an awareness of inherited and traditional modes of expression. One famous example from this period is 'Róisín Dubh' ('Little Black Rose'), a short, simple form of Aisling in which the political intent is couched in a blend of religious and sexual imagery:

> Dá mbeadh seisreach agam threabhfainn in aghaidh na gcnoc
> is dhéanfainn soiscéal i lár an aifrinn de mo Róisín Dubh;
> bhéarfainn póg don chailín óg a bhéarfadh a hóighe dom
> is dhéanfainn cleas ar chúl an leasa le mo Róisín Dubh.
>
> Beidh an Éirne 'na tuilte tréana is réabfar cnoic,
> beidh an fharraige 'na tonnta dearga is an spéir 'na fuil
> beidh gach gleann sléibhe ar fud Éireann is móinte ar crith
> lá éigin sul a n-éagfaidh mo Róisín Dubh.
>
> If I had six horses I would plough against the hill
> I'd make Roisin Dubh my Gospel in the middle of Mass
> I'd kiss the young girl who would grant me her maidenhead
> and do deeds behind the *lios* with my Róisín Dubh!
>
> The Erne will be strong in flood, the hills be torn,
> the ocean be all red waves, the sky all blood,
> every mountain valley and bog in Ireland will shake
> one day, before she shall perish, my Róisín Dubh.[37]

Political devotion is expressed through frank, blunt sexual imagery. Religion simply provides a conventional mode of declaring faith, which here is political. Alongside this enduring feature of Gaelic verse, we must also take account of the survival of simple, unsophisticated devotional verse. Kinsella and Ó Tuama point out that 'Many hundreds of rhythmical prayers — devotional, doctrinal, occasional — exist in the Irish folk tradition',[38] and Ó Cuív singles out the survival of a considerable body of Catholic religious poetry and devotional prose.[39] In Catholic Ireland, there is a clear separation of literary activity between a small group of individual poets of learning and sophistication, but without any rooted social audience, and a popular, anonymous folk-verse, closely tied to tradition, including loyalty to the Catholic Church. This separation within the same linguistic community is preserved by the absence of an agreed written form of Gaelic, and the existence of regional dialects.[40] These features are not part of literary activity in Protestant Ireland. The gap between spoken and written Gaelic, the virtual absence of an agreed, printed form of the language, the precarious and private transmission of work in manuscript form, even the encouragement of the English language by the Catholic Church after the establishment of Maynooth College in 1795 — all these factors suggest the splintered character of literature in Catholic Ireland.

It was this literary culture, very different from the one she was brought up in, which inspired Charlotte Brooke to undertake a modest Celtic Revival by publishing her *Reliques of Irish Poetry* in 1789, a collection of contemporary and ancient Gaelic verses. This romantic publication, an Irish answer to Bishop Percy's *Reliques of Ancient Poetry* (1765),[41] is the first determined and sympathetic attempt to bridge what up till then had been two mutually incomprehensible literary cultures. Born into a clerical family in Co. Cavan, daughter of Henry Brooke, who had written *The Tryal of the Roman Catholics* (1761)[42] to argue for the easing of the Penal Laws, she collected and translated her specimens of Gaelic verse to show that Ireland's literary culture was of ancient pedigree and, therefore, worthy of civilised interest:

> The productions of our Irish Bards exhibit a glow of cultivated genius — a spirit of elevated heroism, — sentiments of pure honour, — instances of disinterested patriotism, — and manners of a degree of refinement, totally astonishing, at a period when the rest of Europe was nearly sunk in barbarism.[43]

Such effusive and exaggerated claims for the worthiness of what civilized contemporaries wrongly prejudiced as barbarous were part of the predictable manner of the enthusiastic antiquarian. Brooke introduces her specimens, complete with facing originals in Gaelic orthography, with a kind of ecumenical zeal:

> As yet, we are too little known to our noble neighbour of Britain; were we better acquainted, we should be better friends. The British muse is not yet informed that she has an elder sister in this isle; let us then introduce them to each other! Together let them walk abroad from their bowers, sweet ambassadresses of cordial union between two countries that seem forced by nature to be joined by every bond of interest and of amity. Let them entreat of Britain to cultivate a nearer acquaintance with her neighbouring isle. Let them conciliate for us her esteem, and her affection will follow of course.[44]

While this kind of defensive idealism is quite common in early Anglo-Irish literature,[45] including that of Maria Edgeworth (a close friend of Brooke), it defies the imagination to understand how a perusal of Gaelic verse could ever achieve such a union of minds. Published in Dublin, with an impressive list of wealthy and influential Irish subscribers, the *Reliques* seem to be an attempt by a liberal section of Protestant Ireland, not to educate England, but to understand itself. Although many Anglo-Irish texts of this period address themselves to the sympathies of an English audience, hoping to prove the decency and maturity of the native Irish, it may equally be the case that such Protestant 'go-betweens' as Brooke and Edgeworth are trying to convert themselves. After a century of virtual apartheid, in which Catholic Ireland has not rebelled, the native culture is safe for cultural scrutiny. Literary initiatives from the minority are the first signs of a sense of shared nationality, uncomplicated by political differences or religious persuasion. Such an aspiration which would have been incomprehensible to Swift.

Edmund Burke, looking back over the eighteenth-century, singled out the Penal Laws as the principal source of Ireland's dishevelled condition. Writing in 1792, when Parliament was discussing measures to alleviate the condition of Catholics,[46] he argued that the security of the Church of Ireland and of the Constitution was not incompatible with civil liberties for the majority. On the contrary, it seemed that this penal system would bring about those very circumstances it was supposed to hold at bay, namely, 'the great danger of our time, that of setting up number against property'. For Burke, the security of the State demanded that Catholics should be allowed to identify with that State. To this end, he proposed a system of 'Virtual Representation', through which propertied Catholics could enjoy the franchise. In this way, the vast majority in Ireland could play a vicarious but effective role in the country's affairs. Burke's letter can be read as an answer to the stubborness of Swift, exposing its practical blindness. For Burke, toleration was not part of Christian charity, but 'a part of moral and political prudence'. His description of the Irish Penal system is worth recall:

> For I must do it justice: it was a complete system, full of coherence and consistency; well-digested and well composed in all its parts. It was a machine of wise and elaborate contrivance, and as well fitted for the oppression, impoverishment and degradation of a people, and the debasement in them of human nature itself, as ever proceeded from the perverted ingenuity of man.[47]

The barely-controlled sarcasm of this judgement shows Burke's offended sense of reason in the face of misapplied intelligence. He may be exaggerating his view of the reality of eighteenth-century Ireland,[48] but the fact that he feels obliged to remind the Irish legislature of the distortions of its rule shows that the country was still in a schizophrenic state, a place composed of 'not only separate nations, but separate species'. The distracted state of literature under such conditions should come as no surprise.

RELIGION AND SOCIETY IN NINETEENTH CENTURY IRISH FICTION

BARBARA HAYLEY

Classification by religious affiliation is a sharp binary one in nineteenth-century Anglo-Irish fiction. It categorises in a more rigid way than class, rank, money, moral worth, works or deeds, and it does so by dividing into two irreconcilable opposing forces. If one is not Catholic one is Protestant. From that proposition depend all one's habits, foibles, virtues or vices, and social attitudes. In fiction, characters are seen as good or bad depending on whether their religious denomination is that of their author.

The assumption is that to all Protestants, Catholics are either deluded (the parish) or deluding (the priests). Other qualities probably follow: Catholics are superstitious, naive, wasteful, incompetent, because their priests are misleading, guileful and crafty. Catholics give, their priests receive; so Catholics are profligate, their priests greedy, gross and venial. Protestants (to the Protestant author), on the other hand, are hardworking, self-sufficient, intelligent, responsible. This assumption is made not only by the authors but by the characters, and presumably by the readers.

Underlying all this is a further assumption about class. If you are a Protestant, you are rich, upper class, ascendancy; if by any mischance you happen to be a peasant, you are a better class peasant than the common-or-farmyard Catholic kind. (But also something of a freak, a hitch in the system.) The ground rules of this game put Protestants on the winning side, and they automatically put the Catholic 'Poor Paddy' where the English novel would put the nondenominational peasant.

Mrs C. F. Alexander (1818–95), an Irishwoman, wrote an otherwise lovely hymn for the *Church of Ireland Hymnal* in 1848, 'All things bright and beautiful', which precisely places Protestant within the big house, Catholic without:

> The rich man in his castle,
> The poor man at his gate,
> God made them, high and lowly,
> And ordered their estate.[1]

The majority of nineteenth century Irish novelists were Protestant; however liberal they were they wrote from within the castle or at least from within the Pale. Of all the writers mentioned in this essay only Gerald Griffin and the Banim brothers were Catholic; William Carleton had become a convert to Protestantism by the time he started to write. So the overall balance of fiction seems uneven, as indeed is the balance between rich and poor in English novels of the mid-nineteenth century, where the 'interest' lies in the upper or middle classes, and the poor tend to be local colour rather than heroes and heroines.

George Brittaine's *Irish Priests and English Landlords* (1830) is the paradigm of the novel which sets forth the opposition of poor-deluded-Catholic and rich-civilised-Protestant. In a tug-of-war about children attending a 'proselytising school' denounced by the Catholic Bishop, an exchange takes place between the Protestant Rector Mr Leighton and the English returned landlord, Mr Eyrebury, which reveals the Protestant view of Catholicism. The Rector thinks that it is 'the source of all the evils, under which this unhappy country suffers'.

He asks 'Does Popery ever restrain vice?' and answers himself that the coaxing of a sentimental Catholic pastoral or a thundering scolding from the altar are equally disregarded:

> 'Yet the authority of the priesthood over their flock is unbounded — witness the blind submission with which they are obeyed in every instance, when they are in earnest, even when their commands are in direct opposition to the good feelings or wishes of the people. They can array the tenant against the landlord, though ruin stare him in the face — they can force them to rear their children in ignorance, when they are most anxious for education — they can persuade them to burn, or drown, or bury the Bible — in fact, they can keep them from all good; but if asked, why they do not exert their influence to repress the outrages against order and humanity, which are of daily occurrence, they must either confess, they have not the power, or that they will not exert it: and in either case, such a system wants the essence of true religion, and must be productive of manifold evils'.[2]

Mr Eyrebury tries to moderate the Rector's opinion that Catholicism destroys the social order, and to suggest that the English lower classes are as badly educated as the Irish peasantry, but the Rector wishes to pit himself and his Bible against the priests with their whips in the struggle to educate the peasantry.

The title of this novel also pinpoints the Englishness of the Protestant landlord class. The absentee landlord was a cliché of Irish fiction, but Edward Eyrebury, having thought of the law and the

Church as professions, finally falls into an Irish estate 'of ten thousand a year clear', through a remote connection who left him his heir 'for no other reason, as he specified, but that of not knowing a nearer relation'.[3] Protestants are in fact perceived if not as English, as English-orientated. Eyrebury comes to Ireland 'with the laudable intention of promoting the welfare of the people among whom he had determined to fix his residence', but the 'real English cottages' into which he transforms half a dozen dilapidated cabins, his schoolhouse, his folly, even the Popish Chapel which he endows, please nobody. 'The Roman Catholics complained of every thing because their children were not clothed'.[4] Dr McRoyster, the Roman Catholic Bishop, is a duplicitous social climber. There is no place for him in Castle Croom. Eyrebury's schools cause havoc — fighting, expulsions, denunciations. No English landlord can sort out the Protestant-Catholic question. Nor can he be sure whom to invite to the Castle. As for the peasantry, when the genteel Miss Winter thought of them, we are told, 'the words, Hottentots, wild Indians and Savages, were repeatedly on the tip of her tongue, yet they were gulped down, for fear of giving offence'.[5]

The class structure of Ireland seems less gradually pyramidal than that of England, where one can imagine any slope from the poorest at the base up through lower middle class, middle class, upper middle class and so on. In Ireland the massive base was poor and Catholic, and only the top tenth was Protestant and prosperous. Religion was a clear indication of prosperity and class. The Established Church of Ireland was the church of the Ascendancy at prayer, that is, of a tiny minority, but it had the right to collect tithes from the Catholic majority. (The Protestant Archbishop of Dublin was the highest paid Archbishop in the world until the disestablishment of the Church of Ireland in 1869.) Within Protestantism there were gradations and shades of opinion: strong Evangelical tendencies inside the Church of Ireland; vehement Presbyterianism in Ulster (personified in Carleton's wicked Yallow Sam in 'The Poor Scholar' (1833); Calvinistic Methodism in Dublin (caricatured in Charles Maturin's *Women, or Pour et Contre*, 1818). But they were perceived en masse from without as Protestants pure and simple — or not so pure and far from simple. And they were perceived as alien from the native race, whether like Eyrebury they had just arrived, or like others they had lived in the country for centuries.

This difference in kind, in race, in look, in feature, is constantly brought before us in fiction. In the Banim brothers' *The Croppy, A Tale of the Irish Rebellion* (1828), for example, we meet the beautiful Eliza Hartley in graceful pose:

Through her whole position there was a play of the curving line, so much esteemed by artists, perfected and rendered fascinating to any observer . . . by embracing in its progress through the figure, those tender undulations that characterise maiden beauty.[6]

Very different from the pert, busily-tripping peasant Kitty. This could of course merely be a class difference; the point is that in the Irish novel religion and class are indices of each other.

Differences between Catholic and Protestant are not confined to opposite ends of the social spectrum. The Catholic peasantry of *The Croppy* despise the looks of their Protestant counterparts:

Much jeering remark might be heard from them as they descanted on the unsoldierlike appearance of 'the Shoneens,' 'Johnnys' — a term of derision applied to the lower class of the opposite persuasion, who had been planted, by certain landed proprietors, among the native peasantry, as, in some degree, an antidote to the amazing fructification of Catholism. Even to the inexperienced eye, the bungling and slovenly attempts at martial appearance of many of these poor men, were quite visible, and the abhorring peasant would not forfeit an opportunity of allowing some of his hatred to ooze out in humoursome contempt. Mixed with bitter taunts, there might also be overheard a muttered threat, or perhaps a more steady remark upon the best manner of contending with such enemies.[7]

The constant tension of Catholic and Protestant, however painful in life, makes for powerful fiction, whether it be the 'party fight' between Protestant and Catholic as in Carleton's 'The Party Fight and Funeral' (1830); or in the spreading of dark opposing forces in agrarian vengeance gangs of Ribbonmen, Whiteboys, Shanavests, as in his 'Wildgoose Lodge'; or in the 'Confessions of a reformed Ribbonman' (1830), which latter makes explicit 'the secret grip of Ribbonism'. In 'The Hedge School' (1830), the hedge school master, on the gallows, admits: 'God forgive me, many a young crathur I enticed into the *Ribbon* business and now it's to end in *Hemp*'.

Carleton describes the party fight as almost a ritual, '*an integral part of an Irish peasant's education*':

In the northern parts of Ireland, where the population of the Catholics on the one side, and of Protestants and Dissenters on the other, is nearly equal, I have known the respective scholars of Catholic and Protestant schools to challenge each other, and meet half-way to do battle, in vindication of their respective creeds.[8]

The connection between religion and land is clear in this tale. 'The peasantry were almost to a man members of a widely-extending system of agrarian combination'; under the sinister name of 'Mat Midnight' they threaten flaying alive to anyone who rents a vacant farm. The Protestant Vesey Vengeance, undeterred, bids for it. The landlord warns him of the risk he is taking:

'Leave that to me, sir,' said Vengeance . . . 'if they annoy me, let them take care. . . I am a *true-blue*, sir — *a purple man* [These terms denote certain stages of initiation in the Orange system, explains Carleton] — have lots of fire-arms, and plenty of stout fellows in the parish ready and willing to back me; and, by the light of day! if they make or meddle with me or mine, we will hunt them in the face of the world, like so many mad dogs, out of the country: what are they but a pack of *ribles* [rebels], that would cut our throats, if they dared?'[9]

The connection between religion and law is spelt out by Carleton in *Valentine M'Clutchy, the Irish Agent* (1845):

Solomon M'Slime, the law agent, was a satisfactory proof of the ease with which religion and law may meet and aid each other in the heart and spirit of the same person . . . it would not be an easy task to find, among the several classes which compose society in general, anything so truly engaging, so morally stainless, so sweetly sanctimonious, so seductively comely, as is that pure and evangelical exhibition of human character, that is bound to be developed in a *religious* attorney. . . .

Solomon M'Slime was a man in whose heart the two principles kept their constant residence; indeed so beautifully were they blended, that his law might frequently be mistaken for religion, just as his religion, on the other hand, was often known to smack strongly of law.[10]

Protestantism is the way to get on in life:

'I am Head Agent; you are my deputy; Master of an Orange Lodge — a Magistrate, and write J.P. after my name — Captain and Paymaster in the Castle Cumber cavalry, and you Lieutenant; and though last, not least, thanks to my zeal and activity in the Protestant cause, I am at length a member of the Grand Panel of the county. Phil, my boy, there is nothing like religion and loyalty when well managed, but otherwise —'[11]

Religion is also intertwined with politics, and priests often incite to violence as in Eyre Evans Crowe's *The Northerns of Ninety-eight*, in *Yesterday in Ireland* (1829):

'Down with his palaver!' cried the priest of the Gorbals; 'we'll have no Union, but the Pope for ever, and down with heretics! You say the Orange mass, and that's enough for us'. . . .[12]

But now every passion within them was renewed, and hallowed as pious, by the bigot-preaching of their ecclesiastical leader.

'Death to the Orangeman — the black heretic to hell!' were cries that burst forth on every hand.[13]

Not all aggressive clergy are Catholic, however; even the virulently anti-Papist Charlotte Elizabeth Tonna's *Derry* (1833) records Protestant clerical aggression. She loathes Catholicism:

These pages but faintly delineate popery as it was, in Ireland; and what popery was, in its days of rampant domination, THAT POPERY IS, AND EVER WILL BE.[14]

But even her Letitia remarks: 'I do not like to hear of a fighting clergyman . . . and they say Mr Walker is one.'[15] The point-blank confrontation of Catholic and Protestant is apparent when after much bloodshed the convert Magrath answers the question:

'But, Magrath, wherein lies our security, if not in Papists defeated?'

'In Papists converted, Sir,' answered Magrath, energetically.

'Take the word of a Papist who came here to destroy his friends, and now goes forth with no wish but to save his enemies. You'll never enjoy the land till you've conquered it; you never will conquer it while Popery reigns. You may build palaces, and dwell in fenced cities, and laugh your enemies to scorn; but there's that concealed under the cabin roof which all your armies cannot overcome. You may hang, and shoot, and persecute, but destroy it you cannot; you may flatter and foster, and give it power, but your friend it will never be. Popery is the curse of God upon a land; and nothing can remove it but the blessing of God, made known in the gospel of Jesus Christ'.[16]

Thomas Moore's *The Memoirs of Captain Rock, Written by Himself* (1824) is less concerned with the blood and guts of Rockite attacks, more with the economics of Catholics and Protestants, especially the huge revenues of the Church of Ireland, but it spawned a number of Captain Rock and Whiteboy stories, varying from Mrs Hall's *The Whiteboy* (1845) to Eyre Evans Crowe's *The Carders* (1825) and Michael Banim's *Crohoore of the Billhook* (1825), the most bloodthirsty of them all.

Agrarian violence is caused by religion, and inflamed by its bitterness. Eyre Evans Crowe demonstrates its ugliness in *The Carders,* in his *Today in Ireland* (1825). Carders are Rockites, disruptive to society:

Treason certainly is a tempting crime to the members of an oppressed church, and of an ancient and fallen family. But for some reason or other, there is no country in Europe, except perhaps modern England, where rebellion is more vulgar or less blended with romance, than in Ireland.[17]

He wants a united Ireland, in the face of opposing, irreconcilable religious differences: of Protestant and Catholic. In *The Northerns of Ninety-eight* (1829), he expresses that wish, and the difficulty of achieving it:

'I had rather,' said Winter, 'teach them that they are all Irishmen and unite them in the same feelings and the same cause, the good of Ireland.'

'Fine! and why not teach them?'

'Religion forbids them to hear any voice but its own; religion, that source of hate and disunion, that true and only cause of man's degenerateness'.[18]

Later Winter says:

'You speak as an English-born, an English-nurtured, aristocrat, my friend. *I* feel as a *son* of Ireland, and feel too, that to the cruelty and obstinacy of England's religious fanaticism we owe the loss of every liberty'.[19]

Crowe shows United Irishmen, Orangemen, battle scenes; burnings, pitched heads, all the horrors. In battle, troops are undisciplined; no order is imposable, no glory achieved. The atrocity strain continued through the century: Kickham wrote his *Tales* in *The Celt*, starting in 1857; in these violence is shown from the Catholic-Nationalist side. He pursued this theme until his death in 1882; for him Catholicism is martyrdom, suffering, true nationalism.

The less horrific, more domestic aspect of the Catholic-Protestant divide shows an equally painful and destructive effect on society when a man and woman from each side are unfortunate enough to fall in love. Then the opposing orders clash against each other with the lovers caught at the point of impact between antagonistic families, social classes, religions, and possibly races as well. Not all authors are partisan, but all take for granted the mutually exclusive division into irreconcilable parties. It is here that the most compassionate novelists show the harm being done to the whole social structure of the country, and to individuals trapped within it. Novels of this kind include John Banim's *The Boyne Water* (1826), Michael Banim's *Father Connell* (1840) and Gerald Griffin's *Tracy's Ambition* (1829), where the strains of a 'mixed' marriage prove intolerable.

In John Banim's *The Nowlans* (1826), Catholic father and Protestant mother produce a confused and directionless daughter, a son who is a failed priest. The different directions in which friends or members of a family will go depending on religion is also taken for granted. Lady Morgan's *The O'Briens and the O'Flahertys* (1827), for example, explores the dramatic possibilities of religious wars, but also the different effects on people of Catholic and Protestant cultures. The Catholic foundling Shane is closer to nature, speaks Irish, has not been attenuated like the Anglo-Irish 'hero', his former foster-brother Murrough O'Brien.

The Catholic hero and heroine exist, but it is interesting to observe how often they are enshrined in history, not in current society. Lady Morgan is the great exponent of the genus, as in *O'Donnel: A National Tale* (1814), or *Florence Macarthy: an Irish Tale* (1818); and of course her *Wild Irish Girl* (1806), Glorvina herself, is a Catholic, mysterious, talented, romantic. Lady Morgan lifts Catholicism out of provincial Ireland and into the wider world of European high society. *The O'Briens and the O'Flahertys* orchestrates a flamboyant Catholicism, in which abbesses can be romantic as well as religious:

The fauteuil, on which the Abbess reclined, and the table that stood before her, were pictures in themselves. . . Her table was piled with volumes richly bound. . . A finely carved ebony crucifix stood before her. Her dress was a religious habit, with ample sleeves to the wrist, and confined by a girdle beneath the bust. The folds of her veil and *sogolo* were so arranged, as to give a strong resemblance to the bust of the *Vestale* in the capitol. Her countenance was rich in expression, passionate and intellectual, even in repose; it resembled the female heads of Correggio.[20]

And so on to her mobile features, transparent cheek, highly polished skin and Irish eyes. It can be seen that Lady Morgan enjoys presenting the visual accessories of Catholicism:

'But are nuns allowed to wander about this way?' asked Lady Knocklofty, yawning. . .

'Yes,' said Miss Maguire, 'one of the nuns of Galway is the toast of the county, and parades her veil and rosary every night on the Mall. To go into a nunnery here, is to take out a brevet of coquetry.'[21]

Lady Morgan hastily adds a footnote:

This is now no longer true. Through the influence of Protestant persecution, all Catholic institutions are daily acquiring new force (bigotry engendering bigotry), the Papist grows more papistical, as the Protestant becomes more proselytising.[22]

Nuns in fiction range from such exotic figures to the disturbing nun of Carleton's 'Lianhan Shee', exiled, wandering, destroyed by her liaison with a priest, carrying her nun's habit around in a burden on her back that makes the peasantry think she is a sinister fairy.

Both the romantic and the alien nun are peripheral to society, but priests, whether praised or reviled, are very much part of the fabric of society. Where they are worthy, they take part in active charity, in starting schools, visiting the sick, bringing comfort to the dying and the bereaved. It is the perspective on priests that gives away the author's views of Catholicism most blatantly. Carleton's early priests, whips and collecting plates in hand, are the scourge of their poor deluded parishioners. With the zeal of the convert and would-be converter, he shows them as vicious and cruel. In *Tales of Ireland*, they are anguished, sinful, macabre, spoilt.

He has a few good cooperative priests later, and some noble priestlings such as the Poor Scholar, but his standard priest is weighted down with whiskey bottles; and is greedy self-indulgent, preying on the superstitions of his parishioners.

For the Banims, however, the priest is a pillar of society. In *Father Connell* (1840), the priest is shown pondering how to build a schoolhouse, now that in the year 1780 'little ragged papists could at last go to school openly and legally, and shout as shrilly as any of their Protestant contemporaries, when let loose from its threshold'.[23] He decides (as 'private means he had none') to let them build a schoolhouse of stone gathered wherever they could find it. He buys fifty suits of clothes to distribute to his poor scholars, including sheepskin 'ma-as' described in loving detail. He buys stores for destitute women, deprives himself, takes part in the lives of his meanest parishioners. 'Active charity', says the narrator, like all other active things, when once put into motion, soon gains its goal. 'Father Connell had been saying and doing, and going backwards and forwards a good deal to say nothing of contriving and suffering a good deal.'[24] he is fully integrated into the life of his parish, dies presenting a petition for one of them to marry a Protestant girl, and is followed to his grave by thousands of village mourners.

One must of course separate individual priests and clergymen from the churches to which they belong; one would not use the odious Mr Elton or the bland Edmund Bertram as evidence for Jane Austen's views on the Church of England. Where Carleton attacks the Church of Rome, however, in his early works, it is clear that he is attacking the whole of the Catholic religion, addressing it directly for its power over the superstitious peasantry. In 'The Station' of 1829, confession is 'in every sense pernicious'; 'going to one's duty' is 'a corrupt and mistaken test . . . of Satan'; 'many ordinances of the Romish religion are on the side of man's depravity'; 'those who are most scrupulous in attending upon the ordinances of the Church . . . are really adding scale upon scale to the mental eye and, advancing day after day, into deeper darkness and greater error'.[25] By the time Carleton has mellowed a little, finished correcting, his individual priests may be weighted down with whiskey bottles ('Shane Fadh's Wedding', 1830), or turn into waltzing dandies (*The Squanders of Castle Squander*, 1852), but his direct attack on Catholicism is moderated to depicting priestly personalities, not principles.[26]

Gerald Griffin is the writer who best sees and avoids the binary system of Catholic/Protestant. He sees Catholic strong farmers as taking over from the absentee landlords. He also sees a stratification within Catholic society which is not apparent to Protestant writers, who lump Catholics together as Catholics lump Protestants. For him there are layers of prosperous farmers, middlemen, peasants. He acknowledges the divide between denominations, but his characters are set to bridge it, to go to college, to take a ruling part in society. The lovers in *The Collegians* (1828), the callous, comfortably-off Hardress Cregan and the vulnerable, poor, Eily O'Connor, whom he abandons, are both Catholics.

In *The Collegians*, Protestantism is 'the genteel religion'. Hepton Connolly, a Catholic, says to the Protestant Creagh, 'You have the whip hand of me . . . for I am a Papist. . . . A Papist, to fight a duel, requires and possesses the courage of a Protestant ten times over'. His reasoning is that duelling has been banned by the Council of Trent. So,

> 'A Protestant is allowed a wide discretionary range on most ethical, as well as theological, points of opinion. A poor Papist has none. . . . A Papist must be the braver man; for in addition to his chance of being shot through the brains on a frosty morning in this world (a cool prospect), it is no joke to be damned everlastingly in the next.'[27]

There is little sense of religion as a moral or spiritual force in most writers, but Griffin sees Catholicism as a social control. Hardress, the Catholic who goes to Trinity College, comes from the newly emergent powerful Catholic stock. His mother gives a ball which, we are given to understand, is ungenteel by comparison with an English ball, but over-stimulating to Hardress. Griffin takes the opportunity to point out the uses of Catholicism as a discipline; unlike Brittaine's Mr Leighton, he does see Catholicism as 'restraining vice':

> Our feelings are so much under the government of our habits, that a modern English family in the same rank might have denied the praise of *comfort* to that which in the unaccustomed eyes of Hardress wore the warmer hue of luxury; for he lived at a time when Irish gentlemen fostered a more substantial pride than at present; when appearances were apparently but little consulted, and the master of a mansion cared not how rude was the interior, or how ruinous the exterior of his dwelling, provided he could always maintain a loaded larder and a noisy board.[28]

The apparent luxury gets Hardress into a 'condition of peculiar and exquisite enthusiasm which made it susceptible of deep, dangerous, and indelible impressions.' Griffin reflects on the good sense of the Catholic Church:

> The wisdom of religion, in prescribing a strict and constant government of the senses, could not be more apparent than on an occasion like this, when their influence upon the reason because almost as potent and absorbing as that of an internal passion.[29]

Religion for Griffin is a code of practice, a guide in daily life, as he postulates in *The Christian Physiologist: Tales illustrative of the five senses* (1830):

> Religion, in Christian countries, has already made the mass of mankind familiar with all that is necessary or perhaps possible for them certainly to know of their moral nature. Her instructions may have been neglected but they are within the reach of almost all men, and for a fundamental portion of the education of the poorest.[30]

He seeks to 'add to that knowledge of his moral nature which his religious education supplies to the young Christian, and such a knowledge of his physiological existence, of the wonders of his own frame, as might assist him in the observance of his heavenly duties', and to make religion part of the framework of the everyday man and his life.

This ideological view of religion is exclusive to Griffin. Only he sees it as a benign part of the body, or of the body politic. To other authors it is a disruptive force. The most depressing thing about religion and society in nineteenth century Ireland as seen through her fiction is the hopelessness of reconciling Protestant and Catholic, and the harm done to society by that hopelessness.

THE WORD, THE LORE, AND THE SPIRIT: FOLK RELIGION AND THE SUPERNATURAL IN MODERN IRISH LITERATURE

DÁITHÍ Ó hÓGÁIN

In investigating the issue of religion in Irish folklore, a distinction is often drawn between what are described as pagan and Christian elements. This distinction is not entirely satisfactory, for it tends to dispense with the need for detailed research into the history of each particular item, and it does not place sufficient emphasis on shared ideas and habits between what seems 'pagan' and what seems 'Christian'. The phenomenological approach can only be brought to fruition by analysing the consciousness which lies behind the customs, the beliefs, and the stories. Since consciousness is the very stuff of creative literature, the occurrence of religious folklore in such literature invites the folklore scholar to take account of what it has to offer. In this, folklorists are returning the compliment to creative writers, who have already done their own evaluation of folklore before they included it in their work.

The Folk Life:

At the dawn of the 19th century, Maria Edgeworth provided a conscious treatment of oral tradition in her novel *Castle Rackrent*, both within its text and in the copious notes which she appended to it[1] The novel takes the form of a chronicle written by a retainer of the big house, called Thady Quirk, and Maria gives an authentic colouring to this character by having him express a traditional outlook. He boasts, for instance, that his employers have an ancient Gaelic lineage, being 'related to the Kings of Ireland', and that the banshee was heard to cry before a death occurred in the family. This is one of the most celebrated, as well as most exclusive, otherworld motifs of Gaelic tradition.[2] Maria glosses Thady's remarks by explaining, quite accurately, that 'the banshee is a species of aristocratic fairy, who in the shape of a little hideous old woman has been known to appear, and heard to sing in a mournful supernatural voice under the windows of great houses, to warn the family that some of them are soon to die'. Thady is also typical of Irish folk culture in his belief in the fairy world. He refers to how his employer, Sir Murtagh Rackrent, 'dug up a fairy-mount against my advice, and had no luck afterwards'. This is a very frequent motif in Irish folk legend, as it was believed that the dwellings of the *sí* beings should not be interfered with.[3]

Thady conforms to popular superstition in other ways also. For example, he starts writing his memoirs on a Monday, in accordance with the folk tendency to lay special stress on the initial day of the working-week. In her glossary, the author explains this by stating that 'no great undertaking can be auspiciously commenced in Ireland on any morning but Monday morning'. The more usual Irish folk belief is that Monday is an unlucky day to commence something, but in superstitions generally it is the image which is basic and the interpretation can be either positive or negative. Another striking aspect of Irish traditional life was the custom of keening the dead, and the author works this too into Thady's narrative. In describing the funeral of Sir Patrick Rackrent he exclaims: 'Then such a fine whillaluh! You might have heard it to the farthest end of the county. . .' Wailing over the corpse was regarded as a necessary way of showing respect for the dead until well into the nineteenth century, and so established was the custom that women who were noted for their special prowess at keening were often engaged professionally for this purpose.[4] Again, in her notes, Maria gives a good deal of detail on this and other folk beliefs and practices concerning the waking of the dead.[5]

Edgeworth's main achievement in folklore terms was to overcome the external viewpoint in which her landlord background placed her and, in so far as relevant to her purpose, to give a genuine picture of Irish popular culture. William Carleton was in a much more advantageous position, for he was fully of the people whose inheritance this lore was. Accordingly, we find his short stories and novels full of details of the ordinary lives of the people, of their attitudes and ideas, and of the ways in which they whiled away the evenings. Yet it is ironic that while Edgeworth moved towards the genuine folk culture, Carleton tended to move away and much of his work is marred by deliberate attempts to distance himself from it. He often looked, or affected to look, on the lives of the people with a jaundiced eye, but this does not negate the accuracy of his actual reporting of cultural detail. We may take as an example of this a passage in his short story *Tubber Derg, or the Red Well,* in which he castigated 'certain opinions floating among the lower classes in Ireland' and being spread, he claimed, by beggars. He meant by this the many messianic prophecies which were current in folklore, but his initial cynicism trails off into the telling of an authentic folk narrative:

> Then there was *Beal-derg,* and several others of the fierce old Milesian chiefs, who along with their armies lay in an enchanted sleep, all ready to awake and take a part in the delivery of their country. 'Sure such a man' and they would name him, in the time of the mendicant's grandfather, was once going to a fair to sell a horse — well and good; the time was the dawn of morning, a little before daylight; he met a man who undertook to purchase his horse; they agreed upon the price, and the seller of him followed the buyer into a Rath, where he found a range of horses, each with an armed soldier asleep by his side, ready to spring upon him if awoke. The purchaser cautioned the owner of the horse, as they were about to enter the subterraneous dwelling, against touching either horse or man; but the countryman happening to stumble, inadvertently laid his hand upon a sleeping soldier, who immediately leaped up, drew his sword, and asked '*wuil anam inh?*' Is the time in it? Is the time arrived? To which the horse-dealer of the Rath replies, '*ha niel. Gho dhee collhow areesht*'. No, go to sleep again. Upon this, the soldier immediately sank down in his former position, and unbroken sleep reigned throughout the cave.[6]

Carleton numbers this among 'fictions concocted by vagrant mendicants', whereas in fact it was a popular legend with widespread provenance in Ireland, and of a type to be found throughout Europe.[7] Nevertheless, his is one of the fullest and most informative of the many recorded versions, and shows his attention to detail and to atmosphere, even citing some of the words from the spoken Ulster dialect of Irish.[8]

Space does not permit us to continue quoting samples of folk life and belief in 19th century creative writers, but the important point is that their purpose was to give colouring and social setting to their work. With the emergence of the movement of 'literary revival', however, a more analytic use of such materials can be discerned. To writers like Lady Gregory and W. B. Yeats the whole paraphernalia of popular tradition, combining use of language with the folk mentality, was a means of expressing a definite artistic perspective. Their objective is encapsulated in the well known words of advice given by Yeats to J. M. Synge in 1898: 'Give up Paris . . . Go to the Aran Islands. Live there as if you were one of the people themselves; express a life that has never found expression'.[9] Yeats himself was an avid collector of folklore, culling material from Carleton and earlier writers, noting material from his conversations with Lady Gregory and Douglas Hyde, and doing an amount of field-collecting himself. Like George Russell, James Stephens, and others he was particularly interested in fairy belief, and in some at least of his writings he gives such beliefs a status approaching to that of theology. This is somewhat out of joint with the folk mentality, which managed to keep the Christian view of the otherworld apart from other simultaneously held ideas.[10] Yeats' tendency to force mystical and even occult perspectives onto the lore led inevitably to some distortion, a distortion which of course contributed to the insights gained by him on the independent plane of creative art. The raw material which he used came from good sources, and it is easy enough to trace the influence of his own interpretative idiosyncracies anterior to his final productions in poetry, prose, and drama.

In the case of Synge, the notes and observations which that author made in Galway, Kerry, and Wicklow provided plenty of raw material for his drama, as well as clear guidelines for the study of his sources. The interest in death-lore shown by Maria Edgeworth, for instance, is more than matched in Synge's great tragic drama *Riders to the Sea*. This uses the practice of lamentation with high dramatic effect, not only as a motif in the play, but in the whole action of the human spirit which cries in the face of cruel destiny. Here we can see the artistic purpose for the use of folklore in the 'revival' movement, for to Synge keening is no curious custom to be observed and described, but is internalised in the depths of the human personality. As Synge wrote elsewhere: 'In this cry of pain the inner consciousness of the people seems to lay itself bare for an instant . . . they shriek with pitiable despair before the horror of the fate to which they all are doomed'.[11] The actual custom of keening had come down from remote antiquity, despite being vehemently opposed by the clergy, who regarded it as a negation of the promise of a Christian afterlife.[12] It obviously fulfilled an important psychological function for the relatives of the dead, and in this vital and basic respect the practice is vindicated by the playwright's use of it.

This is not the only issue on which Synge clarifies folk emotion. For instance, whereas to Carleton the figure of the mendicant friar was a cynical and calculating one, Synge in his play *The Well of the Saints* portrays such a figure in a benevolent light and thus accords with the popular mind, which had most affection for this type of ecclesiastic. Synge's friar, with miraculous power, restores sight to a blind married couple, but a deeper dimension is given to the narrative by having them disappointed in seeing how each other really are, and they blind themselves again. This strange twist to the plot has some warranty in Irish folklore, as some religious stories have been collected which associate eye-sight with an occasion of sin and counterpoise it with the innocence of those who are blind.[13] Synge's most famous treatment of folk material is, of course, in *The Playboy of the Western World*, based on a traditional account which he had heard in Aran of a young man who had injured his father in a quarrel and was sheltered from the law by local people until he managed to escape to America.[14] In the play, however, Synge engages in acute distortion of both speech and actions, thus giving an instance of a writer recreating folk culture for quite independent artistic purposes. The lack of moral perspective which the characters show is far from the situation portrayed in the oral source, which had the locals acting out of sympathy for a desolate young man rather than for an act of patricide. Furthermore the idiom is deliberately exaggerated in this play,[15] and the whole atmosphere has a tantalising charm quite foreign to the controlled aesthetics of folk narrative.

The intensification of folk culture into high tragedy or enigmatic comedy by the writers of the Revival seemed strangely out of focus to Patrick Kavanagh, whose background in the post-Gaelic rural society of Monaghan was at odds with such perspectives. In a newspaper article which he wrote in 1939 he stated very trenchant views on the question of collecting and studying folklore. 'Not only is this stuff culturally useless, it is definitely harmful,' he said. 'We cannot live on memory. Not all the remembered beauty of last year can compensate for the stupidity and vulgarity that is this year's harvest'.[16] In this Kavanagh was expressing a trend which is noticeable in the development of Irish literature through the twentieth century — that is, a general replacing, as a means of expressing the human dilemma, of folkloric imagery with social data. It is a natural development, given the decline in the vigour of living folklore and the increasing urbanisation of Irish society. Yet Kavanagh himself could strongly feel the tugging of tradition. In his long poem The *Great Hunger* he compliments peasant life:

> There is the source from which all cultures rise,
> And all religions,
> There is the pool in which the poet dips
> And the musician.

His work is replete with the immediate and minor data which can give rise to oral narrative, and the types of characters he shows us are typical bearers of tradition. Yet his emphasis is elsewhere, on the impressionistic elements in situation and place:

> Lot's wife would not be salt if she had been
> Incurious as my black hills that are happy,
> When dawn whitens Glassdrummond chapel.[17]

We can say that the sense of place has generally been substituted for the culture of place, a quality well exhibited by the work of Máirtín Ó Direáin, one of the leading poets in Irish. The poetry of Ó Direáin, whose relatives of an earlier generation had provided source material for Synge on Aran, consists of highly evocative pen-pictures of the actual life of, on the one hand, the elemental western island, and on the other hand drab but throbbing Dublin. However, the artistic use of background cultural material was not entirely discarded. In a vein not dissimilar to that of Kavanagh, the leading prose-writer in Irish, Máirtín Ó Cadhain, once declared, 'I have really made very little use of this thing which would be called folklore'.[18] Ó Cadhain was, however, steeped in the folk culture of his native Galway Gaeltacht, and the exceedingly rich and embracing quality of his writing is soundly based on oral style and metaphor. One of the finest of his short stories, 'An Strainséara', has as its subject the mental desolation of a childless woman.[19] The narrative is highly psychoanalytic, but the base-note throughout is the folk custom which has left her stillborn babies buried in the non-consecrated ground of a boundary ditch. The rationale for this widespread custom was the making of the limbo of non-baptism synonymous with the spatial lack of identity of a boundary.[20]

The Folklore Plots:

Returning to *Castle Rackrent*, we find there one clear example of a folk anecdote which has been used by Maria Edgeworth in that novel. She tells us that Sir Condy Rackrent resorted to subterfuge in order to secure extra votes at an election. The returning officers required that each voter swear on oath that they had freehold on which to stand, and the wily Sir Condy 'sent out for a couple of cleaves-full of the sods of his farm of Gulteeshinnagh, and as soon as the sods came into town he set each man upon his sod, and so then ever after, you know they could fairly swear they had been upon the ground.' This is an adapted version of a story which had been current in Ireland for several centuries. It is catalogued as no. 1590 in the index of international folktales compiled by Antti Aarne and Stith Thompson,[21] who summarise the standard form as 'with earth from his own property in his shoes, the man swears when he is on his neighbour's land, that he is on his own'. The use of the folktale in a social context is not greatly out of line with reality, for Irish folk wisdom contained several tricks to avoid moral culpability in swearing short of the truth.[22]

Gerald Griffin's handling of oral narrative was less studied, and he gave some folktales as direct conversation pieces by his characters. For instance, a story told in *Tales of the Munster Festivals*, published in 1827, is a version of an anecdote which has been current in western Europe since the Middle Ages and which is given the type-number 1186 in Aarne-Thompson. It is a story of social protest, couched in a humorous vein, and has the devil snatch away a tyrant figure who has been cursed by one of his victims 'from the heart'. Internationally, the tyrant is usually a magistrate, but in Ireland he is either a bailiff or, as in Griffin's version, a tithe-proctor.[23] Griffin has deliberately altered the plot in some regards. His tithe-proctor has changed his profession to that of a doctor, clearly an echo from a reading of the Faust legend which here reflects the author's more theological attitude. Similarly, the devil comes from a fairy rath, which is an over-orthodox Christian equation of different otherworld contexts; and the curse put on the proctor/doctor is stated to be sinful, which contradicts the spirit of the folktale. On the level of style, Griffin decorates the conversation between the characters in order to impress the readers with the quaintness of Hiberno-English, and this wordiness also alters the effect of the narrative, without infusing any extra dimensions to it.

When Carleton took plots from folklore, he tended to present them in forms faithful to those in which he had heard them. He often has folktales told by characters so as to illustrate their own personality. This is the context for a religious story told by a wandering cleric in *The Poor Scholar*.[24] A woman who has lived a remarkably selfish life acquired a holy scapular on the day before she died. Her sister, a pious woman, prays to the Virgin Mary that the condition of the departed be revealed to her. Accordingly, the dead woman appears to her and describes how she has attained heaven. She had travelled alone on a road which divided into three parts — towards heaven, hell, and purgatory — but the Virgin had come on the scene and saved her from falling into hell by covering a perilous breach with the scapular. She had later got a view of her husband in hell. He had led a wicked life, but had once given alms to a poor scholar and had as reward been given a green sod under his feet in alleviation of his pain. This is in fact a version of a frequent Irish combination of two international tale types, Aarne-

Thompson nos. 470 (Friends in Life and Death) and 471 (The Bridge to the Other World).[25] Carleton's bias is clear — the teller of the story being a cleric who stands to gain from alms-giving — but the narrative situation has an incidental historical truth, for many such religious folktales were invented and spread by preachers.[26]

Carleton sometimes shows more sophistication by employing echoes from folk plots for evocative effect and thereby improving artistic communication with his readers. For example, in his story *The Lianhan Shee,* involvement with a paramour drives a conscience-racked priest to suicide.[27] To traditional Catholic society, the breaking of the vow of celibacy by a priest was one of the most execrable acts; and Carleton here takes full advantage of this dramatic potential in the folk mind and, in describing the last moments of this unfortunate man, he deftly introduces imagery from a folktale. Imagining that he sees a sign in the fireplace, the priest throws himself onto it, exclaiming: 'The immolation! I shall be saved, yet so as by fire. It is for this my hair has become white — the sublime warning for my sacrifice! The colour of ashes! — white — white! It is so! I will sacrifice my body in material fire, to save my soul from that which is eternal!' Carleton records in a footnote the tale to which he owed this striking idea. It concerns a friar who had contracted himself to the devil but was saved by having himself decimated with a hatchet. Known throughout Europe, and of strong provenance in Ireland, this is Aarne-Thompson no. 756B.

A related, but more lighthearted folktale, gave Carleton the opportunity to demonstrate how he could bridge the gap between folklore and literature by skilful use of words alone. This is Aarne-Thompson no. 330. It concerns a blacksmith who gives alms to a beggar and is granted three wishes as reward. He uses the wishes in an apparently foolish manner, and later when in abject poverty sells his soul to the devil. He outwits the devil, however, by use of the magical properties he has obtained through the wishes; and when he dies can gain admittance to neither heaven or hell. So he becomes a perpetual wanderer and is known as Will-o'-the-Wisp, a folk interpretation of the glowing light phenomenon known as ignus fatuus. Carleton again keeps to the exact oral plot, except to introduce some psychological subtleties and many witty twists to the conversations. It is interesting to compare this telling with the novel, based on the same folktale, written a half-century later by Fr. Peadar Ó Laoire. This, entitled *Séadna,* is regarded as the first full novel to be written in Irish.[28] Ó Laoire was also a consummate artist with words, and there are several fine descriptive passages in the novel. He fails in two respects, however, by comparison with Carleton's less ambitious undertaking. Firstly, he over-extends his narrative and forces it into uneasy union with realistic social data; and secondly, he treats the adventure with an excess of tragic seriousness. Carleton avoids such difficulties by keeping cleverly close to the oral format and treating the story as a comedy, which was the usual folk attitude to it.

W. B. Yeats tried similar motifs with deadly serious feeling in his very first play, *The Countess Cathleen*. Cathleen is a noblewoman who does her utmost to aid the starving people in a time of famine. When all her resources are exhausted, demons come to purchase souls in return for food, but she saves the people by selling her own soul at a high price. She dies soon after signing the infernal contract, but is saved by the angels, for 'the Light of Lights looks always on the motive, not the deed'. Yeats's source for the plot was 'what professed to be a collection of Irish folklore in an Irish newspaper', but the original was a story published in Paris but claimed to have been collected in Co. Cork.[29] If something like it was in fact current in Cork lore, the French recorder of it is likely to have confused a standard-type religious folktale with some aspects of local history. Reading in his source that 'the sale of this soul, so adorable in its charity, was declared null by the Lord', Yeats gave his play an ending which conforms to a conclusion given to several Irish religious folktales of the kind. These folktales have the victim's soul ascend to heaven in the form of a white dove.[30] We are reminded of the praise for Cathleen which Yeats puts into the mouth of one of the rescued peasants — 'she was the great white lily of the world' — a good instance of the aesthetic concurrence which often comes to light when literary is collated with oral art.

In Carleton's case, strained censuring of popular lifestyles and attitudes has clouded his perspective and often damaged his art; and the other major defect in his work is lack of inventiveness in terms of plot. Folk belief offers genuine human reactions to the environment, and the plot-structures of oral stories have been honed and strengthened by long transmission. It is therefore of particular interest to observe Carleton at his best, as at those times when he allowed folklore to carry some of the heavy burdens of rationale and structure for him, and thus give his vigorous style a full rein. That vigour is well demonstrated in another folk story which he retold and embellished. It is called *Moll Roe's Marriage; or, the Pudding Bewitched,*[31] and the dual nature of its title reflects the combination of two different narratives which we can accept as having been in his immediate oral source. These two narratives are a migratory legend (listed under motif C94.1.1 by Stith Thompson)[32] and folktale no. 2025 (a humorous children's story which describes a fleeing pancake) in the Aarne-Thompson catalogue. A pudding has been substituted for the pancake, but this latter narrative is not of basic importance here as it has been merely grafted on to the migratory legend. That legend derives from mediaeval Continental sources, and versions of it have been found by folklorists in different parts of Ireland. On the Continent, it tells of how a priest or other holy man punished irreverent dancers by miraculously rendering them unable to cease until he decided to release them from his power.[33] Some Irish versions put a folk magician in the place of a priest,[34] and it is clear that Carleton had heard the legend in this form. A residue from the more standard form may, however, be deciphered in that clergymen are given the leading opposite role of the dancers. Carleton describes how a Catholic girl marries a Presbyterian. The Presbyterian minister performs the ceremony, and clergymen of all local denominations are invited to the wedding breakfast. The bride's uncle, however, disapproves of this arrangement and, by secreting a charm in their food, he sets all four clergymen (the Catholic priest as well as the three other ministers) dancing hilariously. The plot allows good scope for the author's wit and descriptive skills. A lay onlooker, for instance, is made to remark to the untypically rollicking reverends: 'Whirroo, gintlemen, the fun's in yez afther all — whish! more power to yez!' Well might Carleton say, in introducing the story, 'it is utterly impossible for anyone but an Irishman fully to comprehend the extravagance to which the spirit of Irish humour is often carried'.

Yeats was a great admirer of the folklore in Carleton, and it may well be that a recollection of this comical text contributed to a curious scene which is the setting for his play *The Dreaming of the Bones*. This play was his most successful attempt at the technique of Japanese Noh-drama, to which Yeats aspired. It is written in a patriotic vein, and tells of how a young rebel, on the run after the 1916 Rising, meets the ghosts of Diarmuid Mac Murchadha and the lady Dearbhfhorgaill, whose love-affair in the twelfth century was the immediate cause of Ireland's long subjection to the sister-isle. The ghostly lovers are stranded on a lonely windswept mountain, and they are doomed to dance continually but never to touch. The plot Yeats got from a Japanese folk-play, but the unceasing dance is his own contribution. We are told that Diarmuid and Dearbhfhorgaill are 'but shadows, hovering between a thorn-tree and a stone' as they do 'penance for a passionate sin'. Irish folk stories often portray the state of Purgatory as that of souls suffering in some bleak and desolate part of the actual landscape;[35] and other folkloric elements also are employed in the play. Reference is made, for example, to the belief that those born at midnight can see spirits,[36] and to the belief that spirits are banished by the crowing of a cock born in March.[37] In this as in much of Yeats' writing, all perspectives which he perceived as mystical are raw material for creating atmosphere and action at once. He explained in his notes that 'the conception of the play is derived from the world-wide belief that the dead dream back, for a certain time, through the more personal thoughts and deeds of life',[38] and how close this quasi-moralising is to folk narrative is clear from a later comment of his: 'We may see at certain times and in certain houses old murders acted over again, and in certain fields dead huntsmen riding with horse and hound, or ancient armies fighting above bones or ashes'.[39]

What has been said so far shows that Irish storytellers and writers have found the lore associated with religion to be of enduring appeal – whether that appeal be idealistic, or daunting, or humorous. This triad of creative functions came together in the rather odd but effective novel which was the most successful work of James Stephens. *The Crock of Gold* was first published in 1912, and is shot through with aspects of fairy lore and of gleanings from mediaeval Irish mythological tracts much after the manner of Yeats. But Stephens goes even further than Yeats in ascribing religious status to his medley of traditional beliefs about the otherworld, having as the novel's climax a great troop of Celtic divinities descending on Dublin. They do so to save a philosopher from the gallows, a fate ordained for him by the cruel and mundane upholders of modern society. The diffuse and somewhat disjointed structure of the novel owes nothing to folklore, but elements from one particular folktale are scattered throughout and are used by Stephens to give some of its baroque appeal to the book. The folktale, listed as type no. 950 in Aarne-Thompson, was known from antiquity and popular throughout much of the world. It tells of how two brothers robbed the well-protected treasury of a great magnate and how one was caught, but the other by his wile escaped all efforts to discover him and eventually married the magnate's daughter. Irish versions[40] show certain marked peculiarities. The thieves, for instance, are described as being the sons of a wise man, called the *barrscológ* ('supreme scholar'), and we are told that Aristotle answered three difficult questions for them and prophesied that one of them would someday get *croch gheal Bhaile*

Átha Cliath ('the bright gallows of Dublin'). The treasury which they raid is that of the mayor of Dublin, and the prophecy is fulfilled in an unexpected way when the successful thief marries that mayor's daughter, who has the unusual name of Croch and is fair-haired. This Irish ecotype of the international folktale is hardly more than a few centuries old, for the *barrscológ* is a borrowing from a verse-text, common in tradition from the eighteenth century on, which has such a character give poetic advice to his son.[41] Stephens seems to have had this in mind when he put many maxims of advice into the mouths of the two philosophers, one of whom dies and the other becomes the hero of the book and is saved from the gallows in Dublin.

Although wise men and wise women proliferate in Irish folklore, philosophy as a profession is quite rare in that context. In fact, it is almost confined to the most famous of all practitioners, Aristotle himself, whose name had percolated through to ordinary speech from learned — and probably clerical — sources.[42] For a culture which regarded knowledge as almost synonymous with sacredness, it is not surprising to find that the name of that archetypal wise man, once known, was in frequent demand in the realm of story. Aristotle is not mentioned in Stephens' book, but we are significantly told that the two philosophers could answer 'the three questions which nobody had ever been able to answer'. The treasure, too, from the folktale is found in the novel, and it is the reason why the hero comes so near to being hanged, but Stephens has somewhat awkwardly introduced an extraneous motif from Irish folklore i.e. the treasure-trove of a leprechaun,[43] as part of the process of eclipsing the folktale plot. It is worth noting also that, in order to generate the mystical energy which leads to the triumph of the Celtic gods, the author borrows copiously from other oral as well as literary sources. Thus he refers three times to the resurgence of the divine people, the Tuatha Dé Danann,[44] in terms of the messianic folk legend which we have already encountered in Carleton. 'The horses had trampled in their sleep and the sleepers had turned on their sides', and we are further told that this occurred in the 'Cave of the Sleepers'. The imagery here is from the folk legend, and when Stephens tells us that this cave was the dwelling of the god Aonghus he is deliberately joining it to material from a literary setting. A similar convergence is instanced by the travelling to Dublin of the divine company, after the manner of the trooping fairies (*slua sí*) of folklore.[45]

Synge's play, *In the Shadow of the Glen,* is directly based on an oral tale which was quite common in Ireland. This concerns how a tramp gets lodgings in a house where a young wife is waking her elderly husband. During the night, the tramp is surprised to find that the woman entertains a lover, but the husband is merely pretending to be dead, and accordingly the 'corpse' jumps up, and expels his wife and her lover from the house. Synge collected the tale from oral tradition on the Aran Islands,[46] but he situates his play in Co. Wicklow. He follows the plot accurately until the ending, when he has the tramp take the woman's part, and she goes away with him in preference to both her husband and her cowardly lover. The sympathies involved in the original plot are thus reversed, and the moral point of the folktale is rejected. Synge has used the folk narrative structure, but he has infused a romantic spirit into it which he saw as more suitable to his artistic vision. That vision is developed right through the play by metaphorical speech which shows the contrast between the dull and constrained life of the woman Nora Burke and the rambling and adventurous life she can lead with the tramp.

The Poet Idealised

The artistic purpose does not always clash with folk attitudes in modern Irish writing. Yeats, whether depending on popular Christian data or on occult fantasy, could shape his sources and his purpose into one commanding edifice. This is particularly true of his patriotic writings. We have seen how, on the imagistic level, he tended to identify religious lore with the cause of resurgent nationalism. The lore, however, was far removed from dogmatic or denominational matters, and in this Yeats presages the general attitude of 20th century Irish writers towards religion. It is the idealistic impulse of religion which has appeal, whereas there is a general hostility to the more formalised aspect. Religion, as such, becomes one among several means of expressing man's higher instincts.

The poetry and prose of Pádraic Pearse provide several illustrations of this attitude. For him, the image of saviour refers to both spiritual purity and social regeneration, and he carried this to its logical conclusion in his own sacrifice in 1916. His short stories in Irish portray a folk whose great love is the suffering and liberating Christ, a reading of the folk mind which can be vindicated by a study of apocryphal Christian legends in Irish oral tradition. Legends of Jesus' death were especially popular, and in these the Saviour often shares in the imagery of patriotic folk heroes.[47] Thus, when Pearse describes himself as coming 'of the seed of the people, the people that sorrow' he is connecting popular tradition with 'God the unforgetting, the dear God that loves the peoples for whom he died naked, suffering shame'. In portraying himself as a spokesman for the culture, Pearse makes a reference which has wide implications viz. 'I that have vision and prophecy and the gift of fiery speech'.[48] The allusion is not just to political messianism, but also — and perhaps even more so — to the age-old power and status of the poet in Irish society. The Gaelic poet was believed to have special access to the otherworld, and to have mystical knowledge of past, present, and future.[49] Such ideas survived in folklore into this century, and many legends portrayed poets as verbal champions of the people whose satires were feared by the partisans of haughtiness, greed, and oppression.[50]

Images of the traditional Gaelic poets provided much raw material for the personae of Yeats. On the one hand, there were the picaresque folk legends concerning the 18th century Eoghan Rua Ó Súilleabháin,[51] which Yeats had read in print and out of which he forged as an aspect of himself the rakish and wizard-like figure of Red Hanrahan. On the other hand, there was the figure of the sage-poet, buffeted by a cruel change in circumstances and by the destruction of an old and noble civilisation. Yeats expresses this vehemently in *The Curse of Cromwell*:

The lovers and the dancers are beaten into the clay,
And the tall men and the swordsmen and the horsemen, where are they?
And there is an old beggar wandering in his pride —
His fathers served their fathers before Christ was crucified

The imagery here derives from the work of Aogán Ó Rathaille (1670–1726), whose memory survived strongly in Munster lore and from one of whose poems the last line here is taken ('Na flatha fá raibh mo shean roimh éag do Chríost').[52] Accounts of southern poets like Ó Rathaille, Ó Súilleabháin, and Liam Ó hIfearnáin 'the Blind' were available to Yeats in print; and he was struck by the fact that their favourite compositional genre was the *aisling* (vision poem) in which they encountered the female spirit of their country. Ireland as a woman is one of the most persistent themes in the country's culture, deriving from ancient myth of the earth-goddess through mediaeval symbolism of kingship down to modern concepts of the goddess of liberty. Ireland's changing fortunes have long been accommodated by the paradox that she can appear as a beautiful young woman or an ugly old crone. This paradox is related to, and may originally have sprung from, the widespread folklore motif which has a loathsome hag transformed to a lovely maiden by the kiss of a hero.[53] The best-known of Yeats's patriotic dramas, *Cathleen Ni Houlihan*, is based directly on this tradition, and the inspiration and title come from an aisling of Liam Dall Ó hIfearnáin,[54] in whose role of composer Yeats substitutes himself. By writing the play he is the hero who gives the kiss of transformation, and by writing it also he is the visionary poet who mediates for his people. Thus the dual complex of martial and verbal hero, so pronounced in Gaelic tradition, is here as elsewhere expropriated by Yeats to himself.[55] In the play, a poor old woman intrudes on a household which is full of gaiety in preparation for a wedding. She complains that her land has been taken from her and claims mysteriously that many have died. Eventually the prospective bridegroom leaves with her and joins the French army in the rising of 1798. A witness to this is asked has he seen 'an old woman going down the path?' and replies: 'I did not, but I saw a young girl, and she had the walk of a queen'. The structure of the play is quite static and the import rather ambiguous, but Yeats's point is not so much philosophical as to show how heroism has a tragic dignity of its own. It questions the equilibrium between the material world and the ideal and as such touches on the phenomenon of religion.

Art, like religion and folk narrative, involves a superseding of the ordinary environment, and it is not surprising to find all three perspectives mingling in an Ireland of unprecedented literary and political development. The prospect of rapid transformation had, of course, little appeal to Irish ecclesiastical authorities anxious to secure approval within the status quo, but transformation was clearly related to the element of transcendence. In varying degrees and often in quite distinct directions, modern Irish writers have seen themselves as instrumental in achieving transcendence. To Irish folklore, the poet is the artist par excellence, the 'king of all trades',[56] and thus his traditional imagery provides ready-made personae for this strong theme in modern Irish literature. Some writers have deliberately adopted such personae, others — given the metastructure in which art functions in all human society — have coincidentally accorded with them, and it is not always easy to distinguish between adaptation and accord. James Stephens, who probably represents both elements, saw the duty of the poet as being 'to intensify life' and held that he 'must have the seeing eye, the comprehending brain, the sympathetic heart'.[57] In *The Crock of Gold*, he uses the following formula to rationalise the act of composing: 'Thoughts come from God. . . . The head moulds the thought into the form of words, then it is borne and sounded on the air which has been already in the secret kingdoms of the body'.[58] This is quite close to the anatomy of poetry as found in the imagery of folk narrative, which has either head or heart as the source of the art, a special poetic vein as its channel in the body, and the especially lithe tongue of the poet as its shaper and launcher onto the world.[59] Contrariwise, James Joyce was adamant in his rejection of traditional portrayals, and in *Ulysses* hits out directly at the supposed magical powers of the old poets.[60] Yet in *Finnegans Wake* he shows ambiguity towards the mythic seer-warrior Fionn Mac Cumhaill, whom he has as a personification of Dublin in its aggravating but, one suspects, in its appealing aspect also.

The great advocate of the folk perspective on the figure of the writer was Daniel Corkery, who in 1925 published *The Hidden Ireland*, a colourful study of eighteenth century Gaelic poets. The book's drift owes something to Yeats's vision, but Corkery was a good scholar of his subject and his account is based directly on the literary texts. In several parts of the book he adds a new ingredient to literary criticism, folk legends of the poets which he weaves into his discourse with the intention of giving a fuller picture of their significance. The over-all impression which emerges is that of the poet as a down-to-earth character who passes into an alternative and ideal world at the point of composition. Corkery himself was a composer — a writer of novels and short stories — but these creative works of his only rarely make use of folklore. Although not the best known of his productions, one particular short story, 'Solace', is significant since it constitutes an attempt to carry his interpretation of Gaelic tradition over into the sphere of art.[61] It describes a poet of the eighteenth century whose family has become impoverished, but within whose mind a splendid song grows as he lies in bed at night. His wife watches as 'the poet's eyes were different: in them was an ever-increasing glow, but it was the heat of great energy of creation, not of anger'. Throwing all caution to the wind, he gets up and slaughters their last remaining cow and next day spreads the word far and wide that a great bardic session is to be held in his house. The author's information on the semi-ritualistic custom of composing in the dark and on the convocation of the poets came from both literary and folklore sources,[62] which he again uses in a complementary manner. Corkery commended Gaelic literature for three 'classical' traits which he saw in it — religion, nationality, and the land — preoccupations which indeed can be distinguished also in Irish folk legend; but his strong influence on writers such as Frank O'Connor, Seán Ó Faoláin, and Liam O'Flaherty worked itself out rather in social realism than in traditional modes. It is significant that while O'Flaherty in one of his novels, *Land*, made use of three folk-hero types — 'the soldier, the poet, and the monk represent what is finest in man' — he subjected this attitude to rigorous criticism in his later works.

Patrick Kavanagh, like Joyce, was sceptical, regarding the folk portrayal of the poet as being external to himself and consequently rejecting it. For him, poetry was no stream of tradition but was 'the breath of young life and the cry of elemental beings',[63] and he wished to be 'by Man, not God, inspired'.[64] He valued the personal consciousness of the ordinary people rather than their collective unconscious manifested in narrative. 'These men,' he says, 'know God the Father in a tree: the Holy Spirit is the rising sap, and Christ will be the green leaves that will come at Easter from the sealed and guarded tomb'.[65] Yet folklore gave status to the poet, and Kavanagh was pleased to see himself in the time-honoured role when it coincided with his personality. In 'The Hero' he portrays himself as a 'poet-king' who disappoints his public by giving them only satire when they desire praise. Folklore represented poetry as composed of the opposites, praise and satire, and due to the greater dramatic potential of the latter it was given by far the greater stress.[66] Although he jibes at Corkery's tableaux by stating of Eoghan Rua Ó Súilleabháin that he was 'in the front rank of the ten thousand Irish poets of his day',[67] he nevertheless shares a good deal of common feeling with the same Eoghan Rua. For the 18th century Munsterman was, also, like Kavanagh in 'If Ever You Go to Dublin Town', 'dangerous', 'eccentric', 'slothful', 'a nice man' and 'a lone one'.

The questions of tradition, religion, and social setting in Irish literature were central to the work of Austin Clarke. Though he tended to set his sights further back than recent folklore, back to the mediaeval literature, he was aware like Yeats that there were many shared elements in both these sources. He also bordered on the realm of folklore in the historical and geographical dimensions which he gave to his work. On the question of religion, his sustained criticism of clerical high-handedness has several correspondences to sentiments expressed in folk legends, and this can be thematic as well as instinctive. A good example is furnished by the poem 'The Happy Saint', which personalises the contest between straightjacketed and emotive forms of religion. St. Enda of the Aran Islands symbolises the latter form, and the poem describes how he was eventually brought low by 'the old, the sly ones' who were praying that he should die. The plot here is Clarke's own invention, but rivalry between saints was very much part of Irish hagiographical lore.[68] Clarke makes direct use of a folk legend, which coincided with his own feeling, in 'How Covetousness Came into the Church'. This describes how Christ was more charitable to a bandit than to a beggar. St. Peter questioned this, but later discovered that the bandit was a generous fellow whereas the beggar was a miser whose clothes were loaded with silver. Peter is told by Christ to throw that silver into a lake, but he retains some and his Master laments this bad precedent.[69] Clarke calls for a religion without smugness or hypocrisy, and elsewhere he uses the traditions of various Gaelic poets to represent the dignity of those wanderers of the spirit who 'hated cant'.[70] His skilful style enabled the various streams of tradition and of personal experience to flow into each other. In 'The Son of Lir', to quote an apt example, he shows how effectively he can synchronise his own practice of bicycle-touring with the travels of the poets of old, by culling imagery from the sixteenth century popular literary text *Eachtra an Cheithearnaigh Chaoilriabhaigh:*[71]

> Last night in the house of Red Hugh
> I jumbled, I juggled, I danced,
> To-day on a fife I was stopping the music
> For women in Skye and soon after
> I talked with poor men in Cantyre.
> I sprawl in blue rags and bad shoes
> By the fire of a small king in Leinster,
> I will play for his ease or I won't. . .

One other work with relevance to this discussion is the long poem in Irish by Seán Ó Ríordáin, entitled 'Oileán agus Oileán Eile', published in that writer's collection of 1952, *Eireaball Spideoige*. Ó Ríordáin, like Daniel Corkery, was a Corkman, and in this composition he fulfilled many of the latter's aspirations for combining the received tradition with the creative impulse. Influenced also by the work of Gerard Manley Hopkins, Ó Ríordáin was inclined to regard the acute personal struggle of making verse with the struggle for spiritual integrity. In this poem, he goes to a favourite centre of folk pilgrimage, the lake-island of Gougane Barra, in order to find truth by listening to the thoughts of St. Finbar in the pious atmosphere there. He declares that he has long been astray in the words of worldliness, and he now seeks mystical echoes within himself — echoes of complicated saintliness, for 'there is nobody alive who has not been granted an island'. A pilgrimage, however, is too fleeting, and he finds no lasting solution to his problem except the rhetorical statement that 'my mind is bent with a question' (*m'aigne cromtha le ceist*). This has several reverberations, and the unanswered question has many forms, including not only the relationship of the individual artist to his community, but also the aesthetic balance between literary and oral achievement.

GHOSTS IN ANGLO-IRISH LITERATURE

PETER DENMAN

The ghost story, considered as a genre of narrative prose fiction rather than just an element of folklore, occupies a prominent space in the tradition of Anglo-Irish writing, but its significance within that tradition is difficult to determine. During the course of what is arguably the most distinguished work in Anglo-Irish literature an attempt is made to redefine what is arguably the most distinguished work in English as a ghost story. In the National Library scene in *Ulysses* Stephen Dedalus would have it 'that *Hamlet* is a ghoststory'.

> What is a ghost? Stephen said with tingling energy. One who has faded into impalpability through death, through absence, through change of manners.

By this account, a ghost is an emblem of loss, an absence marked in the tangible living world. Ghost stories become the literature of deprivation. In the context of Stephen's own situation, mourning his dead mother and searching for a surrogate father figure, such an attitude is understandable; as a gloss on the nature of ghost stories in general it requires some modification.

More typically, the ghost is an unsettling presence which intrudes into the empirical world without warrant or status. It may be that it is called into its uncertain being to compensate for some felt absence. This is the case with the most remarkable Anglo-Irish ghost stories of the twentieth century, those by Elizabeth Bowen which were collected as *The Demon Lover and Other Stories* (1945). Written and published in London during the war years, these stories are characterised by a lack of temporal or spatial certainty. The eponymous piece tells how a married women goes in dread to a London house, keeping a pact with a lover killed twenty-five years before in the Great War; after an uneventful sojourn in the house, she quits it in some relief, hails and enters a taxi, and only as it is moving off does the driver turn to show his face. . .

In 'The Happy Autumn Fields' the setting moves between a peaceful rural Victorian (Irish?) setting and blitzed London. Bowen wrote, in the 'Post-script' to the collected stories, that the hallucinations in them are not a peril; nor are the stories studies of mental peril. The hallucinations are an unconscious, instinctive saving resort on the part of the characters; life, mechanised by the constraints of war-time and emotionally torn and attenuated by the changed circumstances, had to complete itself in some way. Dreams and fantasies compensated for the desiccation of experience in war-time civilian life. These 'resistance-fantasies', the redemptive illusory worlds which they offer, and their ghosts, are certainties which, whether they be hostile or not, fill the vacuum surrounding the uncertain human protagonists so as to counteract fear by fear and stress by stress, in Bowen's phrase.[1] By this account also, ghosts are to be seen as springing from a sense of deprivation, but they are not the impalpable absences that Stephen Dedalus conjures. Bowen's ghost transcends the waning inadequacies of experience; it is other, unreal, but absolute. It is insusceptible to relativism.

There has been a ghost fiction of sorts in Anglo-Irish literature since the early nineteenth century, following the decline of Gothicism. The Irish Gothic mode is represented most notably by Maturin's *Melmoth the Wanderer* (1820), which stands as the culmination and effective end-point of the Gothic novel in English literature generally, just as surely as Walpole's *The Castle of Otranto* (1764) signalled its start. Apart from *The Fatal Revenge* (1807), also by Maturin, there are some more restrained examples of 'Irish Gothic' in the manner of Ann Radcliffe: Regina Maria Roche's *The Children of the Abbey* (1796), Lady Morgan's *The Wild Irish Girl* (1806) and Lady Caroline Lamb's *Glenarvon* (1816). One of the defining characteristics of the Gothic mode is exoticism, and in the three last-named the Irish setting is presented as being as strange and unsettling to the protagonists as ever was Southern Europe in Mrs Radcliffe's novels. Any suggestion of the supernatural in these works is incidental to the novels' exploration of sensibility. In the ghost story proper the supernatural manifestation is integral and central to the narrative, and the ghost irrupts into a setting which is presented as real and familiar.

Ghost stories drawing on Irish material begin to appear in the 1820s. The collection and publication of folk material by Thomas Crofton Croker reminded the literary public of a living tradition of supernatural lore. In 1825 John Banim's early short novel, *The Fetches,* took a series of supernatural events as its basis and used a specifically Irish belief and setting. A fetch, or wraith as it is more usually known in England, is the apparition of some living person, generally presaging that person's imminent death. In effect it is a variant of that better-known Irish harbinger of death, the banshee; as a ghost figure it points forward ominously to death rather than appearing after it as a revenant. The Banims looked to Walter Scott as their model when writing *Tales of the O'Hara Family*, and it is tempting to account for *The Fetches*, and for early Irish supernatural fiction generally, as a Romantic phenomenon stemming from Scott's literary success and the recovered awareness of folk beliefs and popular tradition. But the use of folklore is only one element of *The Fetches*; there are also elements of a codified spiritual investigation, and of rational thinking about the causes of apparently supernatural manifestations. The novel centres on the love of Anna and the student Tresham. He has been delving into continental occultism, and outlines an account of supernatural visitations, according to which, as Anna enthusiastically recounts it to her sister,

> they come and go, over and around us, and are with us and present to us in our blindness! — that the air, and the shadows of the air, and the recesses, and the depths of space, teem with the busy and mysterious denizens of another world! — while to the eye, made dim by the gross mind of our latter days, there has ceased to be given the seeing power of the days that are gone; though, if the primitive spirit could be reinstated within — and there is a way, dear sister, to bring that to pass — it would see, and hear, and understand, in a total freedom from vulgar fear, . . . and elevate man's soul, even while pent up in man's body, to an approach towards the intelligence of angels! (Ch 3).

Against this transcendentalist optimism there is the opinion of Dr Butler, the sceptical physician who asserts emphatically that ghosts and fetches are products of a diseased mind. Between them Tresham and Butler dramatise the early nineteenth-century arguments concerning hallucinations and kindred manifestations. On the one hand there were the Rosicrucian esotericism and the spiritualism of such as Swedenborg; on the other the materialist-based theories explaining apparitions on physiological grounds; prominent among the latter were John Ferriar's *Essay Towards a Theory of Apparitions* (1815) and Samuel Hibbert's *Sketches of the Philosophy of Apparitions* (1824). Both authors were graduates of Edinburgh's medical school, and each offered a rational explanation of apparitions. In Hibbert's words, 'apparitions are nothing more than ideas, or the recollected images of the mind, which have been rendered more vivid than actual impressions'. The attempt at methodological rigour evident in these books, especially Hibbert's, distinguishes them from contemporary works such as Scott's *Letters on Demonology* (1830) which is, in the manner of Croker, a compendious account of superstition and practice.

The Fetches was developed from one of the papers Banim contributed to the *Literary Register* under the serial title 'Revelations of the Dead-Alive'. These were observations on contemporary manners supposedly written by one who was able to enter into prolonged trance-like states during which he attained a sort of clairvoyance, with his consciousness leaving the confines of his body. This uncertain and unattached state may have corresponded with the condition of being Irish in London, observing and noting the social behaviour of those around him. While in London during the 1820s, Banim was one of a group of expatriate literary Irishmen, a leading member of which was William Maginn. A little-known book, *Tales of Military Life* (1829), which has been attributed to Maginn, contains a two-volume story in which the action moves from the Emmet rebellion in Dublin to the Peninsular Wars.[2] There is a remarkable instance of an apparition in it, explained away by a doctor who cites the contemporary hypotheses as outlined by Hibbert.

From Banim to Bowen there is a continued linkage between ghostly fiction and expatriate authorship. Ghosts claim attention because they transcend the contingencies of time and place — they appear when or where reason says they cannot. It might be argued that this essential dislocation, with its crossing of boundaries, repeats the historical experience of some Irish authors. The most notable Irish writer of supernatural fiction, Sheridan Le Fanu, spent his life in Dublin; however, he lived his later years in such a manner as to gain the reputation of a recluse, an internal exile in his own city.

Sheridan Le Fanu's stories began appearing in the *Dublin University Magazine* in the late 1830s, and for the next thirty-five years he was the most consistent and accomplished practitioner of supernatural fiction in English. During that time the temper and material of Le Fanu's stories and novels varied considerably, not least because his career spanned the emergence of spiritualism as a fad of the late nineteenth century. This brought about a change in social attitudes to the supernatural, and consequently in supernatural fiction. In addition, Le Fanu was an adherent of Swedenborgianism, a system of belief which colours much of his work and lends it an air of spirituality. Nevertheless, his emergence has its origins in the more pragmatic world of periodical writing during the 1820s and 1830s.

Between 1821 and 1838 *Blackwood's Edinburgh Magazine* published a number of short stories by various authors. They were so distinctive in style and subject-matter that the labels '*Blackwood's* fiction' was attached to them, not altogether admiringly. The stories centred on characters in extreme situations of danger or imminent death, and described their sensations with minutely observed detail. In concentrating on the psychology of stress and terror there was ample opportunity for the suggestion of hallucinatory apparitions as control of the mind and senses was lost. Many of these stories were by Samuel Warren, appearing under the serial title 'Passages from the Diary of a Late Physician' between 1830 and 1837. A number of these introduced ghostly manifestations and then offered explanations for them which were physiological and materialist — Warren, like both Ferriar and Hibbert, had studied medicine at Edinburgh.

'*Blackwood's* fiction' exhibited at once the characteristics of both sensation story and case history. These were the pieces which were parodied by Poe in his 'How to Write a *Blackwood's* Article',[3] but also imitated by him in the *Tales of Mystery and Imagination.*' As it happened, two Irish writers were among the earliest and latest contributors to the *Blackwood's* stories: William Maginn, author of 'The Man in the Bell' (November, 1821), and Samuel Ferguson, whose 'The Involuntary Experimentalist' appeared in October 1837. Ferguson was also among the earliest and most prominent writers for the *Dublin University Magazine*, which had been founded in 1833 in direct emulation of *Blackwood's*. The Dublin periodical adopted the same format and style as its Scottish model, and even took a nickname, 'Dea', after the fashion of 'Maga'. One of the respects in which it followed *Blackwood's* was the prominence it gave to fiction, and in 1838 Le Fanu commenced his career with the publication in its pages of that series of stories which appeared posthumously in book form as *The Purcell Papers* (1880). Like Warren's 'Passages from the Diary of a Late Physician', these were stories of varied experience linked by the presence of a narrative persona — in this instance Father Francis Purcell, a Catholic country priest, 'one of the old school, a race now nearly extinct — whose habits were from many causes more refined, and whose tastes more literary than those of the alumni of Maynooth'. Just as Warren's narrator, being a physician, had intimate access to people at moments of suffering and fear, so Le Fanu's priest can enter into the world of his parishioners at moments of spiritual crisis. Among Le Fanu's Purcell stories are 'Passage in the Secret History of an Irish Countess', (an early version of *Uncle Silas* and with a title reminiscent of Warren), and 'The Drunkard's Dream', which, incidentally a warning against strong liquor, is centred on a premonitory vision of hell and has a strong physiological basis. This latter is as extreme as anything in *Blackwood's*, with an agonised sick-bed, a revivified corpse, and a violent death, while the supernatural is suggested without being explicitly accepted. Other stories use the supernatural more definitely, as for instance in the prologue to 'A Chapter in the History of a Tyrone Family' which tells of a ghostly coach heard drawing up outside a house at night, but with nothing whatsoever visible to the inhabitants when they go to greet the arrivals. The supernaturalism which is added to the *Blackwood's* strain of extreme sense-experience derives from folklore. For example, the very first of Le Fanu's stories, 'The Ghost and the Bonesetter', begins with remarks supplied by the supposed editor of Father Purcell's papers outlining beliefs and customs surrounding funeral practices which could have come straight from the pages of Croker. They serve to give an Irish cast to Le Fanu's work, but are incidental to the specifically supernatural elements of his fiction.

Le Fanu's reliance on Irish folklore is most prominent in the three pieces which he contributed late in life in 1869 and 1870 to *All the Year Round*: 'The Child that Went with the Fairies', 'The White Cat of Drumgonniol' and 'Stories of Lough Guir'. For the most part his use of the supernatural is based on the Swedenborgian system of belief; the eighteenth-century mystic's emphasis on the omnipresence of spirits accorded well with nineteenth-century spiritualism. Nevertheless, the early nineteenth-century materialist theories continued to play a part even in Le Fanu's later stories.

Physiological factors figure strikingly in 'Green Tea' (1869) an account of a learned clergyman who, perhaps as a result of overindulgence in green tea to keep him awake over his books, is plagued by the persistent apparition of a small black monkey. He eventually consults Martin Hesselius, a doctor, who undertakes to cure him. Hesselius is a 'psychic doctor' of a type frequent in supernatural fiction, from Warren's *Diary of a Late Physician* to Bram Stoker's *Dracula* (Van Helsing) and Algernon Blackwood's John Silence stories. Before the curative treatment can commence the strain on the Reverend Jennings becomes too great and he is found lying dead, a pool of blood and a razor by his side. The similarities to one of the stories in Warren's Diary, 'The Spectral Dog', are numerous, and in some respects so marked that one is led to the conclusion that Le Fanu retained a memory of Warren's story, even at this late stage in his career. In each story the two principal characters are a clergyman and a physician, who are protagonist and narrator respectively. In each instance the apparition takes the form of an animal — a fairly unusual occurrence in supernatural fiction. Like Warren, Le Fanu refers to the early nineteenth-century theories of apparitions:

I have read, of course, as everyone has, something about 'spectral illusions', as you physicians term the phenomena of such cases.

It is suggested that the cause of each apparition is dietary, and there are incidents common to both stories. Mr Jennings first sees his apparition while travelling in an omnibus; the protagonist of Warren's story, on first noticing the dog, boards a passenger coach in the hope of escaping it, but is no sooner seated inside than he finds the dog at his feet. Mr Jennings first becomes aware of the immateriality of the monkey when he stretches out his umbrella to poke at it.

It remained immovable — up to it — *through* it. For though it, and back and forward it passed, without the slightest resistance.

This reproduces an incident in which Warren's protagonist

poked about his walking-stick, and moved it repeatedly through and through the form of the phantom; but there it continued — indivisible impalpable — in short, as much a dog as ever, and yet stick traversing the form in every direction, from the tail to the tip of the nose!

As regards the specifically supernatural aspect of the story, Le Fanu adds an extra dimension to it. When Mr Jennings admits to taking infusions of green tea, it emerges that he does so to sustain him in his work on a Casaubon-like survey of pagan religion. This immediately raises the possibility of some occult spiritual force come to plague him, a possibility that is enhanced by the strong presence of Swedenborgian teaching in the story. When Hesselius first visits Jennings he finds volumes of Swedenborg's *Arcana Caeloesta* lying open in the clergyman's library, with certain passages underlined and annotated. Several passages are quoted at some length, bringing Swedenborg's teachings into the text. For instance:

When man's interior sight is opened, which is that of the spirit, then there appear things of another life, which cannot possibly be made visible to the bodily sight.

Similar doctrines, set within a medical framework, are referred to by Dr Hesselius after the discovery of Mr Jennings' body.

By various abuses, among which the habitual use of green tea is one, this [neuro-cerebral] fluid may be affected as to its quality, but it is more frequently disturbed as to equilibrium. This fluid being that which we have in common with spirits, a congestion found upon the masses of brain or nerve connected with the interior sense, forms a surface unduly exposed, on which disembodied spirits may operate: communication is thus more or less effectively established.

This passage shows the eventual culmination and synthesis of the two attitudes to the supernatural observed in *The Fetches*. With his talk of an inner eye capable of 'seeing' into the spirit world through the medium of a circulating fluid, Hesselius inclines towards the transcendental approach to supernatural phenomena, an approach prepared for by the earlier allusions to Swedenborg and pagan religious. But in stressing also his work on the mechanisms of the brain, and discussing the physiological effects of a dietary stimulant such as green tea, he admits the possibility of a materialist explanation of the apparition. Thus, the ambiguity of Mr Jennings' experience — was he, or was he not, plagued by a small black monkey-figure? — is enhanced by the ambivalence of the seemingly matter-of-fact summing up.

The folk-motif which Le Fanu used most effectively in his fiction was not taken from Irish folklore at all. 'Carmilla' (1872), along with Bram Stoker's *Dracula*, stands as one of the most notable vampire stories of the nineteenth century. As an element of fiction, the vampire is a variation of the revenantal ghost. It too offers an image of death outlived, but manifests itself as a tangible and actively predatory body rather than as an insubstantial spirit. The vampire has practically no folklore associations in Ireland. Montague Summers, in his account of *The Vampire in Europe* (1929), finds only one isolated and unattributed story relating to a Norman warlord in Waterford. The exotic locales of *Carmilla* and *Dracula* make for part of their significance in Anglo-Irish fiction, for in the remote castles and extensive estates of Styria and Transylvania was found an imagined territory equivalent to the world of nineteenth-century Ireland, hereditary and alienated. Carmilla herself is a cypher, her name an anagrammatised version of Mircalla and Millarca; her nature is similarly changeable. At the end of the story this most physical of revenants remains in the memory of the narrator as a potent symbol of absence, one of the few to concur with Stephen's dictum quoted above:

To this hour the image of Carmilla returns to memory with ambiguous alternations – sometimes the playful, languid, beautiful girl; sometimes the writhing fiend I saw in the ruined church; and often from a reverie I have started, fancying I heard the light step of Carmilla at the drawing-room door.

A more native element of Irish folklore, the banshee, figures remarkably little in Irish fiction. Banim's fetches are allied to it, as is the figure of the 'washer at the ford' introduced by Ferguson into his long narrative poem *Congal* (1872). Le Fanu gives a brief anecdotal account of a banshee culled from a source in County Limerick in his 'Stories of Lough Guir' (1870), but the most effective use of the motif is in Charlotte Riddell's 'The Banshee's Warning' (1894). Riddell (1832–1906) was born in Carrickfergus but spent her prolific novel-writing career in England; 'The Banshee's Warning' is set in London, and concerns an Irish surgeon who finds he has to operate on his dying illegitimate son. Mrs Riddell is more concerned with the moral weight of her story than with its supernatural effects.

By the turn of the century the Victorian ghost story had established itself as a genre. The Irish ghost story, notwithstanding the prominence of Le Fanu as a practitioner, had been assimilated into the English tradition, and recent critical assessments of the form have not gainsaid this. For instance, Peter Penzoldt in his psychologically based account of *The Supernatural in Fiction* (1952) takes Le Fanu as the starting point, as do Julia Briggs in *Night Visitors: The Rise and Fall of the English Ghost Story* (1977) and Jack Sullivan in *Elegant Nightmares: The English Ghost Story from Le Fanu to Blackwood* (1980). None of these writers, Swiss, English and American respectively, consider Le Fanu's work to be identifiably Irish in any way.

And in truth, taking them as supernatural stories, there are no real grounds on which to argue for a specifically Irish supernatural fiction; there are only Irish writers of supernatural fiction. Oscar Wilde's 'The Canterville Ghost' gently parodies the form. Shane Leslie wrote several ghost stories, of which the best is 'The Diplomatist's Story', beginning with the same phenomenon of the ghostly carriage that Le Fanu had used in his 'Chapter in the History of a Tyrone Family' but integrating it into the plot. Yeats essayed the form frequently in *The Secret Rose* (1897) and *Stories of Red Hanrahan* (1913), but not always successfully, for his symbolism is inappropriately intrusive. The novels and stories of Lord Dunsany tend more to fantasy, and belong with the work of James Stephens and Flann O'Brien in that the overdetermined and ostensibly realistic setting associated with the ghost story proper is absent.

The forerunner of these Irish fantasists is Fitzjames O'Brien (1828–1862), a shorter-lived contemporary of Le Fanu. Born in County Cork, he commenced publishing in *The Nation*, where a poem of his attracted scathing comment from the editor Gavan Duffy. Nothing daunted, he continued offering pieces to Dublin periodicals, including the *Dublin University Magazine*, until his emigration to New York in 1851. There he eked out a living as a writer for the remainder of the decade, fought as an officer on the Union side in the American Civil War, and died of wounds in 1862. Among the stories written in New York, 'The Wondersmith' is true fantasy, but 'The Diamond Lens' and 'What Was It?' both centre on inhuman presences. In the former, a beautiful microscopic figure is observed through a remarkable diamond lens; 'What Was It?' is the story of an invisible intruder whose shape is discovered only through a cast made after rendering it unconscious with chloroform.[4]

Early in 'The Diamond Lens' there is a description of a spiritualist seance at which the narrator receives instructions on how to construct the lens. This is one of the earliest descriptions in fiction of a seance. The medium's name, Mrs Vulpes, is a Latinate pun on the name of the Fox sisters who arrived in New York in 1850 to commence seances at Barnum's Hotel. This was just two years after reports of the mysterious rappings in the Fox household in northern New York State had set in train the craze for spiritualism which swept first through the east coast of America and soon through Europe.

Spiritualism is more remarkable as a social than as a supernatural phenomenon. With its emphasis on the seance, it fostered a group attitude to the ghostly. Its avowed aim was a contact and communion with the spirits of the dead. The endeavour took place at a meeting, with much holding of hands and a dark intimacy which contrasts strongly with the isolation and menace of the fictional supernatural. The ghost story, with its lonely protagonist confronting the inhuman in an atmosphere of pity (perhaps) and terror (certainly) may even aspire to the tragic; spiritualism, with its history of confusions, deceits and communal solidarity would be irredeemably comic were it not for the credulous assent invested in it by so many.

During the nineteenth century the most notable Irish enthusiast for spiritualism was the Earl of Dunraven, who was one of those present on the occasion that Daniel Dunglas Home (Browning's 'Mr Sludge, the Medium') apparently levitated out of a window in Baker Street: Dunraven left an account of *Experiences in Spiritualism with Mr D. D. Home* (1870). In the early twentieth century W. J. Crawford investigated the mediumistic claims of the Goligher family in Belfast, and Yeats's long involvement with the occult has been documented elsewhere.[5] In Dublin, Sir William Barrett, former Professor of Physics at the Royal College of Science, had been a founder member and President of the Society for Psychical Research and had published books *On Psychical Research* (1911), *On Swedenborg* (1912), and *On the Threshold of the Unseen* (1917). A friend of his, Mrs Travers Smith, the daughter of Edward Dowden, experimented over a number of years with automatism; in the course of her book *Voices from the Void* she tells of messages from Hugh Lane, drowned in the *Lusitania* sinking.

This is the society in which Yeats sets his play *The Words Upon the Window-pane* (1930). Dr Trench, President of the Dublin Spiritualist Association claims to have met Lord Dunraven in his younger days, and knows Swedenborg's teachings. The evocation of the ghosts of Swift and Vanessa through the mouth of the medium Mrs Henderson is a powerful dramatisation of the insubstantial. The central image of the play's title, with words written on the light, suggests the mediumistic contact with 'the other side'; the window glass is at once the barrier and the means of access to the higher, wider world beyond the contingencies of the mundane room in which the seance takes place. In a very different setting, Synge's *The Playboy of the Western World* (1907) is also based on a revenantal structure; the reappearance of Old Mahon, supposedly dead, is only too physical for Christy and Pegeen Mike. He returns to demonstrate that the real cannot be transcended; the western world is no other world.

Short prose fiction is the typical haunt of the literary ghost, but it also figures prominently in twentieth-century Irish poetry. Homer's ghost comes whispering to Kavanagh's ear, Plato's ghost sings 'What then?' to Yeats, the ghosts of those shot on Bloody Sunday in Derry speak to Kinsella, and in 'Station Island' Heaney confronts a succession of ghostly presences from his personal or literary background.[6] As supernatural manifestations these are all conventional; their appearance is subordinate to the overall effect of the poems, which seek not to narrate a supernatural event but to explore the human and social relations of the poet. Their function is to allow figures from the past — Homer, Plato, dead victims of violence, — to become present. The act of memory is dramatised, and the ghost utters from a dead past, minatory or monitory as the case may be. The past which produces these revenants requires something of the supernatural to make it present again.

It is worth recalling that the lyric which stands at the head of the Anglo-Irish poetic tradition, Ferguson's 'The Fairy Thorn', is a poem of the supernatural, and one of the finest such in English. Its theme anticipates that of Le Fanu's story 'The Child That Went With The Fairies', as the girls hear their companion drawn into the otherworld.

> Thus clasped and prostrate all, with their heads together bowed,
>   Soft o'er their bosoms beating — the only human sound —
> They hear the silky footsteps of the silent fairy crowd,
>   Like a river in the air gliding round.
>
> No scream can any raise, nor prayer can they say,
>   But wild, wild, the terror of the speechless three —
> For they feel fair Anna Grace drawn speechlessly away,
>   By whom they dare not look to see.

'The Fairy Thorn', and its intended companion-piece 'The Fairy Well', could draw on the still-living folklore of early nineteenth-century Ireland. They inaugurated a lyrical mood which was passed on to Allingham, AE, Yeats, and the 'Celtic Twilight' poets, most notably in Yeats's poem 'The Stolen Child', published in the year of Ferguson's death, 1886.

> Come away, O human child!
> To the waters and the wild
> With a faery, hand in hand,
> For the world's more full of weeping than you can understand.

The waters and the wild offered here by the faery are permanencies which will compensate for the lost imperfections of human feeling and comprehension. In Ferguson's poem, Anna Grace passes from human ken; the concluding stanzas concentrate on the three girls left behind. They are left 'ghostly' and 'desolate', but whether this is at the loss of their companion or at missing out on her supernatural translation is unstated. It is they who are left sorrowing and dwindling towards death, as emotionally torn and impoverished as any of Elizabeth Bowen's protagonists in *The Demon Lover*.

The title story of that collection, which served as the preferred starting point for this essay, is also derived from folklore, as the title's reference to the ballad of the same name (Child 243) reminds us. The ballad begins with an exchange between a woman and her former lover who has just returned from a long sea-voyage. She is now married to another, but agrees to go away with him to his magnificent home overseas. Once embarked, however, she is overtaken by remorse, whereupon her lover reveals himself as a demon. Characteristically, the ballad concentrates on the final part of her story; Bowen is more concerned to establish the atmosphere leading up to the final climatic moment of abduction and revelation. But it too is a story of abduction into another world, just as are the poems by Ferguson and Yeats. Each can be read as metaphor of expatriation.

The wavering and uncertain rhythms of Ferguson and his followers are not more wavering and uncertain than the boundaries between the natural and the supernatural as they are drawn in literature. At times, the supernatural appears as faery, offering an alternative and possibly more attractive world into which humans can pass; at times it appears as a ghostly intrusion into our own place and time, requiring something of us, if only recognition.

SHAW AND CREATIVE EVOLUTION

A. M. GIBBS

I

Shaw was deeply interested in religion, and religious subjects are a major preoccupation in his writings.[1] Whilst still at school, he told an understandably rather startled friend, Edward McNulty, that his ambition in life was to 'start a new religion'.[2] This ambitious plan was announced again in a letter to F. H. Evans in 1895: 'I want to write a big book of devotion for modern people, bringing all the truths latent in the old religious dogmas into contact with real life — a gospel of Shawianity in fact'.[3] The first instalment of the 'big book' was *Man and Superman* (1903). Shaw described the play as 'a dramatic parable of Creative Evolution',[4] and frequently referred to the third act, 'Don Juan in Hell', as a statement of his creed. He developed his ideas about Creative Evolution in various religious speeches delivered in the first two decades of the twentieth-century and produced his most extensive exploration of evolutionary themes at the end of that period, in the Preface and five plays of *Back to Methuselah: A Metabiological Pentateuch* (1921). A minor, but important, later work, the prose tale *The Adventures of the Black Girl in her Search for God* (1933) is also primarily concerned with evolutionary themes in relation to religion. In this essay I shall argue that whilst it is possible to see in Shaw's writings a reasonably consistent, affirmative and optimistic creed which by a not too violent extension of the term can be called religious, his beliefs are counterbalanced consistently by satirical and sceptical impulses which seem at times almost completely to overwhelm the positive thrust of his ideas. The same Faustian young man who told Edward McNulty that he intended to found a new religion was also a disciple of Mephistopheles, whose image he painted in water colour on the whitewashed walls of his bedroom as 'the patron saint of sceptics and deriders'.[5] Shaw's ideas about the Life Force and the Superman have at least as strong an affinity with Swiftian radical satire as with neo-Lamarckian theories of evolution. I use the term radical satire here to describe satire which attacks the entire human species rather than the vices and follies of individuals and particular groups. Rochester's *Satire Against Mankind* and Swift's *Gulliver's Travels* are examples of the type I have in mind.

The household at the aptly named childhood home of the future exponent of Creative Evolution, 1 Hatch Street,[6] Dublin, would have provided a natural breeding ground for conflicting attitudes towards religion. In the house, the young Shaw was exposed to Protestant and Catholic orthodoxy, free-thinking and spiritualism. The Shaws were Protestant, but many of Mrs Shaw's maternal duties were shared by an Irish Catholic nurse who, according to Shaw, never put him to bed without sprinkling him with Holy Water.[7] Shaw's father is recorded by his son as having concluded a serious eulogy of the Bible by remarking that 'even the worst enemy of religion could say no worse of it than that it was the damndest parcel of lies ever written'.[8] His mother was deeply interested in spiritualism, and the Shaws were the owners of the first planchette (a device for recording spirit messages) imported into Ireland.[9] In an interview published in 1929 Shaw recalls that he cheated at one of his mother's seances, an offence about which he had earlier expressed repentant feelings in a letter to the leading spiritualist, Sir Oliver Lodge.[10] If he was sceptical about spiritualism, he was actively hostile towards the official Shaw family religion of Protestantism. Although some of his later religious views might be described as broadly Protestant in character, Shaw was fiercely critical of the Irish Protestantism of his youth. As far as the Protestant gentry was concerned, he thought Ireland the 'most irreligious country in the world'. Irish Protestantism, he said, was not a religion but 'a side in political factions, a class prejudice'.[11]

Shaw referred to Creative Evolution as the religion of the twentieth-century. But as Julian B. Kaye has remarked 'from our vantage point it looks very much like the religion of the nineteenth'.[12] The most important sources of Shaw's ideas about Creative Evolution were the evolutionary theory of the pre-Darwinian naturalist Lamarck and the anti-Darwinian writings on evolution of Samuel Butler. These debts are clearly acknowledged in Shaw's Preface to *Back to Methuselah*. The wider context of Shaw's ideas can be found in the broad tradition of Romantic and post-Romantic responses to the undermining of religion by, on the one hand, the perception of intellectual weaknesses, naive credulity and absurdities in orthodox religious teachings, and, on the other hand, by mechanistic philosophical systems and scientific materialism. In the Romantic period William Blake characterised the conventinal image of the Christian God as 'Nobodaddy', ridiculed the idea of Christ as meek and mild and railed against the philosophical writings of Bacon, Locke and Newton. Shelley rejected orthodox Christianity but influenced Shaw with his conception of God as an immanent power in the universe.[13] Schopenhauer's concept of the will in *The World as Will and Idea*, which Shaw read in 1887, contributed substantially to the Shavian synthesis of ideas about Creative Evolution.[14] Shaw was also almost certainly influenced by Auguste Comte and the religion of humanity developed in his *Système de Politique Positive* (1851–4) as well as by John Stuart Mill's utilitarian arguments in *Three Essays on Religion* (1874).[15] All of the major Victorian writers sought in different ways to reaffirm religious and spiritual values in the later nineteenth-century context of disintegrating creeds and increasing materialism. Shaw's ideas on religion clearly belong to the *zeitgeist* in this respect, however much his style and accent may differ from writers such as Carlyle, Arnold, Ruskin and Tennyson. When Carlyle's Teufelsdröckh speaks in *Sartor Resartus* of embodying 'the divine Spirit of . . . Religion in a new Mythus, in a new vehicle and vesture',[16] he might very well have been describing Shaw's design in developing his 'new religion' of Creative Evolution. Shaw's strategy was to be an attempt to marry a mythus of science with a mythus of religion. What was needed, in Shaw's view, was 'the revival of religion on a scientific basis'.[17] Although Nietzsche and Bergson contributed important concepts to Shaw's writing on Creative Evolution – the notions of the Superman and the *élan vital* and the term 'Creative Evolution' (Bergson's 'L'Évolution Creatrice') – the essential shape of his ideas about the subject had been formed, in the matrices of nineteenth-century debates on evolution and religion, before he came into contact with those writers.

Jean-Baptiste de Lamarck's major work, *Philosophie Zoologique* was published in 1809. In this work, following leads provided by his fellow countryman Buffon, Lamarck rejected the idea of fixed species and argued that living things evolve because of their need to adapt to environmental circumstances. Lamarck's account of the process by which evolutionary change occurs is now generally regarded as invalid in two main respects. His most often quoted example of evolutionary change is his account of the way in which the giraffe gained its long neck. The giraffe feeds mainly on acacia leaves. Lamarck thought that, over a long period of time, an originally short-necked species of mammal developed a long neck because of its constant need to strain upwards in order to reach the foliage. This theory was later memorably, if not quite correctly, summarised in verse by Lord Neaves:

> A deer with a neck that was longer by half
> Than the rest of its family's (try not to laugh)
> By stretching and stretching became a Giraffe
> Which nobody can deny.

Lamarck's theory depends on an assumption, now known to be false, that characteristics acquired by a parent, for example, unusual muscular development because of a particular activity such as weight-lifting, can be inherited by its offspring. Lamarck also thought that the pattern of evolutionary change was always from simpler to more complex organisms. It is now known that although evolution does sometimes follow that pattern, by far the most common evolutionary events are what G. L. Stebbins describes as 'adaptive radiations at one particular level of complexity'.[18]

Modern evolutionary theory is, of course, primarily based on the principle of natural selection advanced by Charles Darwin in *The Origin of Species* (1859). Darwin's theory rests on the assumption that all living things are engaged in a struggle for existence. Within all species, variations between individuals occur. Some variations are neutral in their effect, but others confer an advantage in that they enable the bearers to adapt more successfully to their ecological niche, and thus have a greater chance of survival:

> variations, however slight and from whatever cause proceeding, if they be in any degree profitable to the individuals of a species, in their infinitely complex relations to other organic beings and to their physical conditions of life, will tend to the preservation of such individuals, and will generally be inherited by the offspring.[19]

Darwin was unaware of the pioneering work in the field of genetics of his contemporary, Mendel, and of the mechanisms of heredity. Nevertheless his theory has remained a basic foundation of modern study of evolution.

Although they were widely acclaimed and accepted, Darwin's theories had many opponents in the second half of the nineteenth-century, amongst them the author of *Erewhon* and *The Way of All Flesh*, Samuel Butler. In a series of works published during Shaw's early years in London, *Life and Habit* (1878), *Evolution, Old and New* (1879), *Unconscious Memory* (1880) and *Luck or Cunning*? (1887), Butler put forward his ideas on evolution and conducted an increasingly acrimonious attack on Darwin. Butler was unable to accept the idea that volition, effort, intelligence, and cunning play no part in the processes of evolution. Darwin's theories, he claimed, involved 'the pitchforking . . . of mind out of the universe'.[20] Butler's ideas owed much to the pre-Darwinian evolutionists, Erasmus Darwin and Lamarck. He argued that creatures respond to their needs by sustained efforts which eventually become unconscious habits. The process of heredity by which such habits are passed on is a mode of memory.[21] The accidents of evolution, Butler maintained, could not happen to or be taken advantage of by any creature which was not, as he put it in phrasing which calls to mind some of Gilbert and Sullivan's older female characters, 'zealously trying to make the most of itself'.[22] Butler's protest against the idea of a world of 'chance and blindness'[23] brings us very close to the spirit of Shaw's critique of Darwinism in the Preface to *Back to Methuselah*. In the conclusion to a chapter on 'The Teleological Evolution of Organism' in *Evolution, Old and New*, Butler wrote:

> I should be sorry to believe that I am a pessimist. Which, I would ask, is the pessimist? He who sees love of beauty, design, steadfastness of purpose, intelligence, courage, and every quality to which success has assigned the name of 'worth', as having drawn the pattern of every leaf and organ now and in all past time, or he who sees nothing in the world of nature but a chapter of accidents.[24]

This passage is closely echoed by Shaw in a comparison of the Lamarckian and Darwinian theories:

> as compared to the open-eyed intelligent wanting and trying of Lamarck, the Darwinian process may be described as a chapter of accidents. . . . There is a hideous fatalism about it, a ghastly and damnable reduction of beauty and intelligence, of strength and purpose, of honor and aspiration, to such casually picturesque changes as an avalanche may make in a mountain landscape, or a railway accident in a human figure.[25]

Shaw seems also to have been closely indebted to Butler in the notion that thought is the origin of physical form. 'The votary of Creative Evolution', Shaw writes in the 1944 Postscript to *Back to Methuselah* 'goes back to the old and very pregnant lesson that in the beginning was the Thought; and the Thought was with God; and the Thought *was* God, the Thought being what the Greeks meant by 'the Word'. He believes in the thought made flesh as the first step in the main process of Creative Evolution'.[26]

In the concluding paragraph of *Luck or Cunning*?, Butler declares that 'bodily form may be almost regarded as idea and memory in a solidified state. . . Action arises from, and through, opinion. Opinion from, and through hypothesis. "Hypothesis", as the derivation of the word itself shows, is singularly near akin to "underlying and only in part knowable, substratum"; and what is that but "God" translated from the language of Moses into that of Mr Herbert Spencer?'[27] Both Shaw and Butler see God as being continuous with the created world: 'God is in all His creatures, He in them and they in Him'.[28]

Shaw's approach to Darwinism in his major essay on Creative Evolution, the Preface to *Back to Methuselah*, is more circumspect and concessive than might at first appear. He acknowledges that Darwin accounted for a great many of the phenomena of natural history and that Darwinism is not finally refutable[29]. In its eloquent reminders of what Darwinism leaves out of account and its general analysis of the way in which Darwinian theory helped to foster ruthlessly exploitative political and economic theories and systems, Shaw's Preface is an impressive, and at times magisterial, piece of writing. Insofar as it purports to be an explanation of organic transformation, Shaw's account of Creative Evolution is decidedly weakened by the fact that he nailed his flag so firmly to the mast of Lamarckian and neo-Lamarckian theory. But this weakness becomes less significant if we extend the definition of evolution to include human cultural evolution as well as natural organic transformation. A creature which a century ago was unable to fly can now take journeys to the moon and back. Computers can perform many mechanical functions of the brain far more quickly and more efficiently than the brain itself. Human genetic engineering is, in scientific terms at least, an achievable goal; and it would be rash to rule out the possibility that developments in biology, gerontology and surgery may one day make possible dramatic extensions to the normal human life span. In the sphere of cultural evolution neo-Lamarckian accounts of the causes of evolutionary change, in terms of intelligence, creative effort, desire and purpose, regain validity. Shaw's ideas about Creative Evolution are not essentially undermined by the fact that they are in some senses 'unscientific'. A more serious question about the value of Creative Evolution as a religion is that, unlike the most widely practised traditional religions, it does not, *in itself*, provide a clear code of ethics.

II

Leaving aside the complications of dramatic contexts, and the

sceptical and pessimistic thought which is an almost invariable accompaniment of Shaw's religious affirmations, his 'new religion' of Creative Evolution can be summarised as follows:
The universe is driven by an intelligent, purposive force, the Life Force, which is working towards higher forms of life and consciousness through the processes of evolution. The godhead is not a complete and perfect entity but an evolving phenomenon. (In one of his religious speeches, Shaw explicitly identifies God with the evolutionary process itself.)[30] The purpose of human life is to contribute to the evolution of the godhead. God is will and we are the hands and brains of God:[31] 'we and our father are one . . . the kingdom of heaven is within us'.[32] The teleological goal of the evolutionary process and human cooperation with it is variously described by Shaw. In Act Three of *Man and Superman*, Don Juan speaks of the 'working within [him] of Life's incessant aspiration to higher organization, wider, deeper, intenser self-consciousness, and clearer self-understanding'.[33] In a speech delivered in 1912, Shaw said that there 'need be no end' to the process, but he envisages 'the production of some being, some person if you like, who will be strong and wise, with a mind capable of comprehending the whole universe and with powers capable of executing its entire will – in other words, an omnipotent and benevolent God'.[34] A recurrent feature of Shaw's accounts of the goal of Creative Evolution is the notion of gaining greater self-consciousness and self-understanding. But a rather different emphasis is found in one of Don Juan's speeches in Act Three of *Man and Superman* in which he declares: 'I sing not arms and the hero, but the philosophic man . . . who seeks in contemplation to discover the inner will of the world, in invention, to discover the means of fulfilling that will, and in action to do that will by the so-discovered means'.[35] The Shavian Superman, in this account, is similar to Plato's philosopher-king, the contemplative man of action.

There is no reason to doubt the seriousness and sincerity of Shaw's belief in his creed of Creative Evolution. It had profound consequences for Shaw's work from 1903, and the ideas which go to make up the creed are part of what gives Shaw's writings and his outlook on life their peculiar stamp. Without such a creed the following passage in the Epistle Dedicatory of *Man and Superman*, which contains, for many, something of the quintessence of Shavianism, could not have been written:

> This is the true joy in life, the being used for a purpose recognized by yourself as a mighty one; the being thoroughly worn out before you are thrown on the scrap heap; the being a force of Nature instead of a feverish

little clod of ailments and grievances complaining that the world will not devote itself to making you happy.[36]

Yet for all the buoyancy of spirit and sense of purpose which passages such as this convey, it is impossible to make a study of Shaw's religious ideas without becoming aware not only of the powerfully satirical and pessimistic contexts in which the ideas are expressed, but also of the way in which the ideas themselves become part of the rhetoric of satire. Moreover, when in *Back to Methuselah* Shaw actually creates fictional images of highly evolved human beings of the future, they seem to be endowed with many more repellent than attractive features.

'I do not know whether you have any illusions left on the subject of education, progress, and so forth. I have none'.[37] These words in the Epistle Dedicatory to *Man and Superman* set the tone of much of the writing there and in the two other sections of the whole work most relevant to the present discussion, Act Three and the appended Revolutionist's Handbook. The Epistle and Handbook present a view of Democracy as a completely failed political system. Burke's 'swinish multitude' has displaced the old selectively bred ruling aristocracy and the land is now misruled by 'college passmen . . . well groomed monocular Algys and Bobbies . . . cricketers to whom age brings golf instead of wisdom'.[38] In the Revolutionist's Handbook the invective against mankind becomes even more severe. Man in his present state of evolution is seen as incapable of progress. Each attempt at civilisation is followed by rapid and disastrous backward slidings into destructive savagery, and each high point of civilisation is 'but a pinnacle to which a few people cling in giddy terror above an abyss of squalor'.[39] When at the end of this diatribe the author of the Revolutionist's Handbook declares that we must eliminate the Yahoo, and goes on to make extravagant proposals for the creation of either a State Department of Evolution or perhaps a private society or chartered company 'for the improvement of the human live stock'[40] the spirit of the author of *Gulliver's Travels* and *A Modest Proposal* seems close at hand. The true function of the modest proposals at the end of the Revolutionist's Handbook seems to be not so much serious advocacy of Creative Evolution as a means of amplifying the preceding expressions of despair about, and condemnation of, man in his present state.

The invective of the Epistle Dedicatory and The Revolutionist's Handbook is paralleled in various speeches in Act Three of *Man and Superman*. Shaw tends to use Don Juan and the Devil almost interchangeably as critics of human folly; but he gives to the Devil what is probably the most sustained condemnation of the human species in all of Shaw's works. In the speech which begins 'And is Man any the less destroying himself for all this boasted brain of his', Shaw has the Devil argue that Man's inventive energies have been most successfully deployed not in the service of life but in the service of death. In the evolutionary scale he is the most successful of all predators, the cruellest of the animals and 'the most destructive of the destroyers'.[41]

The three-act comedy which surrounds the Dream of Hell in *Man and Superman* also contributes to the deflation of Tanner's ideas about the Life Force. I have argued elsewhere that Tanner suffers only a partial defeat in the play, and that the comic structure can be seen to embody an affirmation of the values Tanner stands for over those represented by Octavius and others.[42] Yet it must be admitted that Tanner is often presented as a comically isolated, impotent figure, and that his prodigious talk has little or no effect on the flow of events which carry him at the end of the play to his reluctantly accepted doom of marriage with Ann Whitefield. In the last act of the play Tanner's grand ideas about the Life Force are reduced to a joke by Ann's comment on the term: 'I don't understand in the least: it sounds like the Life Guards'.[43]

Evolutionary themes are sounded briefly but significantly in the highly charged atmosphere of the last act of *Heartbreak House*, again with an accompaniment of satire. At the beginning of the act a mysterious drumming noise is heard in the night sky, which Hector interprets as 'Heaven's threatening growl of disgust at us useless futile creatures'. He goes on to declare that 'one of two things must happen':

> Either out of that darkness some new creation will come to supplant us as we have supplanted the animals, or the heavens will fall in thunder and destroy us.[44]

If Hector's description of the inhabitants of *Heartbreak House* as 'useless, dangerous' and deserving of abolition[45] calls to mind passages in *Gulliver's Travels* such as the King of Brobdingnag's final assessment of the human race, even more clearly reminiscent of Swift is Lady Utterword's retort to Hector that the only thing needed to make her father's dwelling a 'sensible, healthy, pleasant house' is the presence of horses.[46] In Lady Utterword's view the virtues of Swift's Houyhnhnms seem to be transferred to horse-owners, or, as she describes them, the Equestrian Class:

> Go anywhere in England where there are natural wholesome, contented and really nice people; and what do you always find? That the stables are the real centre of the household.[47]

In the preface to *Heartbreak House* Shaw makes explicit reference to Swift's portrayal of man as 'a Yahoo rebuked by the superior virtue of the horse'.[48]

The mood of anger and frustration which appears in many passages of the dialogue in *Heartbreak House* found further expression in Shaw's next major dramatic work, *Back to Methuselah*. *Heartbreak House* was written during World War I. After writing the play, but before he wrote the Preface, Shaw accepted an invitation to visit the war front in France. There he saw signposts pointing to townships that had been blasted off the face of the earth by more advanced versions of the diabolical engines which his Devil had referred to in *Man and Superman*, devastated landscapes and, amongst other horrors, a headless corpse lying by the roadside.[49] In January 1918, the son of Stella Campbell, the woman with whom Shaw had what was probably the most intense of his several extra-marital love affairs, was killed in action. The work of Shakespeare's angry ape and Swift's Yahoo could never before, in Shaw's lifetime, have seemed to be more clearly in evidence. The sources of the spirit of *saeva indignatio* which underlie the themes of Creation Evolution in *Back to Methuselah* are easy to locate. He began writing the play in March 1918.[50]

In *Back to Methuselah* the ideas about Creative Evolution and the fantasy of a return to the enormous life-spans attributed to Methuselah and the other patriarchs in the Book of Genesis are inextricably intertwined with critical reflection on contemporary history and the failure of political institutions. Shaw's Serpent in Part I, who turns out to be a female expert in language and theories of Creative Evolution, tells Eve that the origin of creation is imagination:

> You imagine what you desire; you will what you imagine; and at last you create what you will.[51]

She conveys to Eve the secret of sexual reproduction. But the first scion we meet — Abel does not appear in the play — is Cain, an archetype of the macho, bellicose male, a bogus Superman, who later (in Part IV) evolves into a cartoon-like portrait of Napoleon. Cain is the master of a sluttish wife, Lua, for whom he kills animals in order to provide her with fur clothing and inspire her admiration. His dreams of conquest supply a nightmarish and fiercely ironic reflection of the history of the time at which Shaw's play was being written, and a powerfully negative interpretation of the meaning of the Life Force:

> Think of that! All those multitudes of men fighting, fighting, killing, killing! The four rivers running with blood! The shouts of triumph! The howls of rage! the curses of despair! the shrieks of torment! That will be life indeed: life lived to the very marrow: burning, overwhelming life.[52]

Shaw's Cain seems very much like a fictional descendant of the naïve Gulliver who tries to impress the King of Brobdingnag with his enthusiastic and graphic accounts of human achievements in the arts of warfare.[53] War is again a major theme in Part Two of *Back to Methuselah*, where we see caricatures of Britain's wartime leaders, Lloyd George and Asquith, feebly defending their involvement in the war, and being told that they would go down in history as members of a group of statesmen and monarchs of Europe who all but succeeded in wrecking its civilisation and did succeed in wiping out millions of its inhabitants. The rationale for going 'back to Methuselah' is that, with their present lifespan, men and women never reach sufficient maturity to be able to govern themselves successfully: the First World War provided a ready proof of the existence of the problem at least.

Edmund Wilson found the final vision of the future in *Back to Methusaleh* to be of the bleakest and most desolating description',[54] and indeed there is much in the last play of the cycle, and elsewhere, which gives rise to such responses. Yet it would be wrong to suggest that Wilson's terms adequately convey the spirit of the whole work. Particularly in the last three plays, extravagant comic fantasy is a major ingredient. Moreover, for a work notorious for its utterly sexless, Stuldbrug-like He-Ancient and She-Ancient, who have lost all interest in anything but contemplation, *Back to Methuselah* contains a surprising number of erotic images. Some of the scenes are reminiscent of rather risque revue sketches. In Part Three an attractive black woman, identified as the Minister of Health, is accidentally discovered on the large screen of the President's tele-visual equipment in her bedroom, dressed only in her underwear. She is quite unembarrassed, and later calls up on the same device to tell the President she is available for an afternoon's dalliance. In the next play the Elderly Gentleman is guarded by a spunky young woman called Zoo who is dressed in a silk tunic and sandals, *'wearing little else except a cap with the number 2 on it in gold'*.[55] In Part Five, which is set in the year 31,920 AD, a pretty seventeen-year-old girl is born out of a giant egg on stage, and appears draped *in 'a few filaments of spare albumen'*, before being washed and dressed by attendant youths and maidens.[56] In Part Two the ex-Prime Minister, Lubin, openly flirts with the skimpily dressed Savvy, whose name stands for Savage. The visual imagery in the play often seems to have the effect of conducting a comically subversive argument against the philosophical and ascetic themes.

Back to Methuselah is a prime example of the way in which Shaw's complex creative imagination refuses to allow his plays unambiguously to demonstrate the theories advanced in the prefaces. The first of the longlivers who appear in the work, the Archbishop and Mrs Lutestring in Part Three, are benevolent and venerable enough. But the further Shaw takes us down the track of the future the more ambiguous and dialectical his projection of human evolution becomes. Part IV, *Tragedy of an Elderly Gentleman*, is set in Galway Bay in the year 3000 AD. The Elderly Gentleman, a shortliver, has come on a pilgrimage to Ireland, now occupied by a supposedly superior race of longlivers. The Elderly Gentleman figure is certainly deployed by Shaw for satire on old-fashioned snobbery, national and imperial loyalties, and sentimentality. Shaw was irritated when he discovered that the actor playing the Elderly Gentleman in the first production in New York had been made up in such a way as to give him a Shavian appearance.[57] Yet in some ways the Elderly Gentleman is a touching and dignified figure who engages more sympathy than the longlivers at whose hands he is finally exterminated with discouragement. His custodians, Zoo, and her male counterpart, Zozim, adumbrate some of the figures in the dystopian society of Huxley's *Brave New World*. They seem exemplary products of the very forces of scientific materialism of which Shaw complains in the Preface. They speak without images and metaphors and react with a robot-like rejection, as incomprehensible, of terms such as 'impertinence', 'insult', 'improper', 'civilised', 'decencies', 'moral sense' and 'marriage'. In one of his speeches the Elderly Gentleman curses the invention of long life, and defends his normal humanity in a way which threatens to bring the entire house of cards of *Back to Methuselah*, as an embodiment of a religious and philosophical creed, to the ground:

> I accept my three score and ten years. If they are filled with usefulness, with justice, with mercy, with good-will: if they are the lifetime of a soul that never loses its honor and a brain that never loses its eagerness, they are enough for me, because these things are infinite and eternal, and can make ten of my years as long as thirty of yours.[58]

In the final play of the cycle, *As Far as Thought Can Reach*, Shaw's comedic and dramatic impulses again prevent us from seeing his longlivers as simple projections of ideal goals of human evolution. His dome-headed, completely hairless Ancients, who wander about with their eyes closed, preoccupied with their thoughts and bumping into dancing youths and maidens, can hardly be received without a smile at their exceptionally dessicated appearance, preternatural detachment and their total lack of interest in pleasure, 'this dancing and singing and mating'.[59] The complaint of one of the young men, Strephon, about the rapid ageing and maturing process in this brave new world may well accord with an audience's feelings about the dubious advantages of being a He or She-Ancient.

What is the use [he asks] of being born if we have to decay into unnatural, heartless, loveless, joyless monsters in four short-years?[60]

The Ancients certainly have their moments of powerful authority and curtly delivered wisdom: 'Life is not meant to be easy, my child; but take courage: it can be delightful'.[61] But Strephon's question and the severity of the Ancients' characterisation clearly create further tensions in Shaw's exploration of evolutionary themes in the last play of the cycle. In Parts II and III, the comic idea of going back to Methuselah functions happily as a satirical device which dramatises the folly and immaturity of man in his present state. But Shaw's portrayal of the longlivers frequently raises the question as to whether we are being offered a utopian or dystopian vision. When at the end of the last play Lilith predicts further evolution of humanity into a 'vortex freed from matter' and a 'whirlpool in pure intelligence',[62] it seems that the satirist's problems are finally to be solved by the cancellation of the species.[63]

Shaw wrote the prose tale *The Adventures of the Black Girl in Her Search for God* when he was held up for five weeks in South Africa after a motor-car accident early in 1932. Essentially the tale is an exploration in the form of a fable of the idea of God as an evolving phenomenon. Armed with a knobkerry, for smashing idols, and a powerful curiosity, the black girl sets off into the African forest to find the true God. She meets a succession of Gods who represent an ascending scale of sophistication in human conceptions of the divine. She first meets the vengeful Lord of Hosts of the early books of the Old Testament who enjoys human and animal sacrifices and demands a freshly slain virgin. He is followed by the Gods of Job and Micah and then by a gentle 'conjurer' who represents Christ. With the latter she has a long discussion about the doctrine of love, which she can't swallow because there are a lot of people, including members of her own family she doesn't like and she sees love as an objectionable form of possession. Later on she meets Mahomet, whose attitude towards women is brought under close critical scrutiny. Eventually the black girl meets Voltaire tending his garden. Voltaire advises her that it is rather dangerous and presumptuous for humans to want to come face to face with God. If God were coming down the road, Voltaire says, he would hide, lest God 'put his foot on me and squelch me, as I would squelch any venomous little thing that broke my commandments'.[64] The black girl finally settles down in the Voltairean garden with a red-headed Irishman who sums up the story, and Shaw's views on Creative Evolution, by saying of God:

> My own belief is that he's not all that he sets up to be. He's not properly made and finished yet. There's somethin in us that's dhrivin at him, and somethin out of us that's dhrivin at him: that's certain; and the only other thing that's certain is that the somethin makes plenty of mistakes in thryin to get there.[65]

The figure of the black girl is an example of an increasing tendency in Shaw's later writings, encouraged no doubt by the world tours he undertook with Charlotte in the early 1930s, to see the black and oriental races as supplying possible sources of optimism about the future of humanity. The black girl regards the whites whom she meets as 'heathens and savages' whose most wonderful creations are their guns.[66] A white ethnologist whom the black girl encounters in her travels declares that 'the next great civilisation will be a black civilisation. The white man is played out'.[67] Negritude, or more generally an idealisation of coloured races, in Shaw's later works takes the place of his earlier jesting fantasies of eugenics and extreme longevity, not simply as a focus of optimism but as a weapon in his critique of the West.

CATHOLICISM IN THE CULTURE OF THE NEW IRELAND
CANON SHEEHAN AND DANIEL CORKERY

RUTH FLEISCHMANN

'The intellect of Ireland is irreligious', wrote Yeats in 1926 during a campaign organised with success by the Christian Brothers of Dublin to have an English paper banned because it contained 'devilish literature' and 'an insult to God'. The 'insult' was a medieval Christmas carol called 'The Cherry Tree', of which Douglas Hyde had found an Irish version in Connacht, a profoundly religious poem, a literary masterpiece, and the most famous carol in the English language.[1]

This kind of incident is probably what is most readily associated with the title of the present essay. With the setting up of the censorship board, the subsequent banning of the best works produced by Irish writers, and the establishment of a new 'murder-machine' in Irish education, the influence of the Catholic church in the Irish Free State proved to be a major obstacle to the cultural development of the country.

The partition of Ireland in 1920 and the establishment of two denominational sectarian states put an end to the twenty-five years of discussion of the nation's dual culture and the possibility of the peaceful and mutually stimulating co-existence of the two traditions. The territorial division made legislative provision for tolerance and equality superfluous in both states, and although in the South leading Anglo-Irish figures attained high office in government, they were unable to halt the march towards a Catholic state. The depressing results of what we tend to imagine as a heroic epoch of Irish history, the poor and petty states born of the 'terrible beauty' of Irish nationalism in which green croziers and orange drumsticks were wielded with such stunting and stultifying power, all this has made it each to condemn the narrowness and difficult to see, or to want to see, its origins. All our sympathies go to the Anglo-Irish writers and scholars who made the case for a tolerant new state that would vigorously promote a culture derived from the dual heritage; and their arguments are still so distressingly relevant today that there would seem to be little point in studying their opponents.

Yet there is much to be learnt from them. To understand the immense difficulty of the task of reconstruction one must turn to the writers of Irish Catholic background and study what colonialism does to the self-awareness of the colonized. This cannot be studied in the writings of the Anglo-Irish: their discovery of the hidden Ireland at their door-step was an enrichment, an additional world to be explored,[2] whereas the Catholics were struggling to establish one in which they could at all come to terms with themselves. Two Catholic responses to the pressing needs of the times will be discussed in the following: that of the priest and novelist, Canon Sheehan (1852–1913), who at the age of forty-two began a literary career in order to counteract the influence of the Anglo-Irish writers of the Revival and to advocate a Catholic New Ireland; and that of Daniel Corkery (1878–1964), teacher and writer, who spent his life working to define, encourage and contribute to a national culture in which the Irish language, nationalism and religion would be essential elements.

These were the three big issues of the time, the nets from which Joyce fled to Europe. Of the three, religion was the least discussed and the most divisive. Douglas Hyde, after a night drinking poteen as a young man in 1883, had a dream in which he, his Conscience and Reason discoursed with representatives of various religions and with a Mr Nogod. The latter argued:

> Religion is only another name for party. Religion and politics are the two sources of nearly all the quarrels social and domestic, the two great causes of all the strife and embittered feelings of the world, the two fruitful springs of pain and cruelty and heart-scald all over this earth, and of the two religion does the most harm. Can you deny it?[3]

Many of Hyde's Anglo-Irish friends would no doubt have sympathized with this view. Some Catholic nationalists involved in the Gaelic League, such as the journalist D. P. Moran, would certainly have shared his feelings about politics, whether nationalist or unionist. But most Catholics would probably have regarded the harsh comment on religion as applying only to Protestantism.

The political face of Protestantism was as familiar to Irish Catholics as its spiritual one was unknown to them. The trouble Elizabethan conquistadores went to in order to prove that the Irish were not 'either Papist, nor Protestant' but rather 'atheists or infidels', their customs barbarous, their way of life an abomination[4] was understood as being politically motivated, because the English involved in the bloody wars needed to be able to think of themselves as civilizers and as honorable gentlemen. The pious sentiment expressed by Edward Barkely during the expedition to subdue Ulster: 'How godly a dede it is to overthrowe so wicked a race. . . I thinke there cannot be a greater sacrifyce to God'[5] would have been regarded as typical of colonial hypocrisy — landrobbers masquerading as religious crusaders. The Penal Laws were seen as an economic and political attack on the propertied Irish rather than as an attempt to save their souls, and the change of religion demanded as a declaration of political allegiance rather than one of faith. Irish Catholics only came to know the aggressive nationalist aspect of Protestantism; the democratic features which so appealed to the Scots and English could, of course, never have become apparent to those subjected in their name.[6] Most Catholics were aware only of the spiritual side of their own religion and unaware of its political aspect. They failed to understand the deep-seated reserve which even the most nationally-minded Irish Protestants bore towards Catholicism, the church of the Inquisition, of anti-Semitism, of papal infallibility, the authoritarian enemy of liberalism, secularism and science; and they took Anglo-Irish distaste for it to be a relict of the old contempt of the Ascendancy for the religion of its serfs.

In countries where peoples of different tribal origins had been politically united under colonial rule, a common religion differing from that of the colonizer could provide the essential unity of culture. In Ireland, where a leading section of the nationalist movement was of Ascendancy origin, the part religion could play in the nationalist ideology was limited. Catholicism nonetheless remained a powerful source of nationalism. It was the only area where colonialism had never prevailed and the first in which colonial laws had to be repealed. As the Irish language declined, Catholicism became the main distinctive feature of the Irish as a nation.

So if religion was, though a powerful, a divisive force, what then was the basis of Irish nationality? This question constituted a great dilemma, one we do not always readily see today. Our impression of the period of the Revival is that it was one of great political promise, given the dismantling of the colonial features of British rule, from the disestablishment of the Church of Ireland in 1868 to the land reform of 1903, with Home Rule clearly visible on the horizon. We are so dazzled by the achievements in the cultural field that we tend to overlook the sense of dismay that pervades the writings of many of the leading figures in the movement regarding the distressing paradoxes they were faced with. In his famous speech 'On the Necessity of De-Anglicising Ireland' of 1892, Douglas Hyde describes Ireland's plight as being that it was 'ceasing to be Irish without becoming English'; that it 'continues to clamour for recognition as a distinct nationality; and at the same time throws away with both hands what would make it so'; and that 'the old bricks that lasted eighteen hundred years are destroyed; we must now set to bake new ones, if we can, on other ground and of other clay'.[7]

The journalist, D. P. Moran, shared Hyde's belief that unless the Irish language were revived political independence would come too late, as the essence of the nation would have been extinguished. He wrote in 1905 that Ireland was nationally distinct in 'her torpor and decay rather than her development'; that the Irish were now 'sulky West Britons' full of self-pitying indolence and moved only by a destructive spirit of impotent and sentimental hatred of Britain; and that if they continued to allow the national life to bleed out of them, all they would gain from independence would be the 'right to make laws for the corpse'.[8]

Irish nationalists disagreed strongly and often venomously over the national question, but, whether they considered the revival of Irish, or the creation of an Irish literature in English, or the development of a healthy economy, or the winning of Home Rule the vital issue, they were all agreed that Ireland urgently needed to be able to isolate herself culturally from the 'stronger and richer tradition' (Corkery)[9] as well as from the overwhelming economic pressure of Britain in order to salvage as much as possible from the wreckage and to begin the arduous task of reconstruction behind secure defences.

In Canon Sheehan's first novel of 1895 it is underlined that Irishmen must be weaned from their 'West-British ambitions and desire' and brought to concentrate on

> building up a great Catholic nation — Irish in its traditions, Irish in its sympathies, ay even narrow and insular so far that a wall of brass would be builded round the island to keep out British ideas and principles, and those fin de siècle fancies that are steadily undermining religion amongst us.[10]

The 'wall of brass' comes from Bishop Berkeley, whose *Querist* (1735) asks whether this might not be the condition necessary for prosperity to exist among the 'natives'. Not that the thinking of Berkeley, Swift or Molyneux on Ireland's economic problems will have been the reason for Canon Sheehan's adoption of the image, but their view of the Irish nation: just as they took it for granted that they, the Anglican Anglo-Irish, constituted 'the' nation, so Canon Sheehan now postulates the same position for Irish Catholics. It was for the Catholic middle classes who never read any of the Anglo-Irish writers that Canon Sheehan wrote ten novels between 1895 and 1913, very popular books that sold over 100,000 copies during his own lifetime alone, in which without ever mentioning his adversaries or their theories he systematically built up bulwarks against them in his readers' minds.

Yeats and Synge knew that the ancient oral culture of Ireland would disappear with the modernisation of rural life, that 'the fatal drip of printer's ink', 'the little tales one after another, day after day, in the books and newspapers' would drive the old stories out of the minds of the people, as Robin Flower was told on the Blaskets.[11] Canon Sheehan had similar fears with regard to their religious consciousness. Religion had prospered during the bad times and he was afraid that it might decline with the disappearance of great poverty. He therefore invariably plays down the question of land reform in his novels and allows the old-time rural Ireland to appear in a relatively mellow light. He disputed that rural Ireland needed development, or the theories of the Catholic nationalist Arthur Griffith, or the practical policies of the Congested Districts Board and of the Protestant democrat and unionist, Sir Horace Plunkett, who started one of his co-operative ventures in Doneraile the year the Canon became parish priest there. In the novels development schemes are organised by well-meaning priests, and they always fail because the people are not interested in them. The pastoral innovations, on the other hand, are successful and much appreciated.

Canon Sheehan suggests that what Moran and Plunkett deplore as the torpor and inertia of the people is in fact a positive feature: that it is indifference towards improving standards of living, but not indifference towards life. He maintains that this is an innate spirituality, the hallmark of the Irish, and what has prevented them from becoming English. He warns that the alternative to the people's inertia is not progress, but socialist or militant republican activity, with the people being misled by British, Freemason or Jewish agents.[12]

Criticism of the Catholic clergy is firmly and very discreetly refuted through the priest characters in the novels. Instead of the tough, grasping, ignorant, cute political priests of George Moore and so many others, we find men devoted to their people, generous to a fault and correspondingly impoverished, lovers of learning and men of culture who win the respect of the gentry in their parishes. Rural life is indeed shown to revolve around the priests, but only because the people wish it to do so.

Canon Sheehan's rural Ireland is enclosed by walls of poverty and lack of ambition. It is the world of the landlords and tenants, yet is free from unrest and agitation. The people seem to accept their lot as the will of God and to spend their lives gossiping, arguing, drinking — and praying. But this picture of a peaceful, patient and passive rural Ireland was a product of wishful thinking and a didactic exercise. Canon Sheehan did not share Hyde's and Moran's concern about the Irish language, but he too had grave misgivings about Ireland's future. He feared that his wall of brass might be built too late, that the people's religious world view might be eroded beyond repair before Home Rule came and that the church would never come to exercise in the new state the influence which the priests enjoyed in their parishes.

This influence was threatened by the articulate and militant labour movement of Connolly and Larkin. There was no trace of the deference to authority which Canon Sheehan's novels extol in James Connolly's discerning refutation of the Jesuits' sermons against socialism of 1910 and his spirited but courteous demonstration, supported by a wealth of evidence from Irish and church history, why 'he serves religion best who insists upon the clergy of the Catholic church taking their proper position as servants of the laity and abandoning their attempt to dominate the public, as they have long dominated the private life of their fellow Catholics'.[13]

Canon Sheehan believed that the influence of the church was also threatened, in a very different way, by the growing political and economic power of the Irish middle class. He watched with disgust, as did Connolly, Moran, AE and Yeats, the shameless scramble for position and patronage which the opening of local government to the Irish Party brought with it. The corruption and scurrilous faction-fighting within the party made him despair of the future and led him at the end of his life to a reassessment of the Fenians, who with their willingness to give up everything for the cause now stood out in such stark contrast to the political takers of the present. In the last novel, published posthumously in 1915, the Fenian returns home after ten years in prison for his part in the rising of 1867 to find himself lost in an Ireland that lives for money, and derided for his principles. He is killed by a drunken assailant at a political meeting of the parliamentary party. The blood sacrifice of his companions[14] has been in vain: they have found few admirers and no followers.

The outlook for religion was, Canon Sheehan feared, almost as bleak. Like Swift, he believed he was fighting a losing battle for his church.[15] He could not imagine that Catholicism would survive in a country obsessed by the pursuit of money. He doubted whether the church understood the seriousness of the threat posed by the modernisation of Irish life, and whether it would be capable of withstanding it, even if it did. It is therefore not surprising that the novels contain so many priest characters who feel they have failed to give the people the leadership and the service they need. This is by no means a mere didactic device: these figures are all partly self-portraits, and the inadequacies represented are deeply felt. Perhaps one of the most interesting aspects of Canon Sheehan's work is that it allows us to become aware of the great difficulty many of these priests had as men and as scholars in coming to terms with the narrowness and isolation they encountered in the rural parish and which as churchmen they felt obliged to foster in order to safeguard the religion of their people.

When in his attack on the Christian Brothers' 'Cherry Tree' carol campaign, Yeats described the intellect of Ireland as being irreligious, he said that Ireland had forgotten the only 'two men of religious genius' it had produced – John Scotus Erigena and Bishop Berkeley – and that for two hundred years no Irish writer had produced 'a solitary sentence that might be included in a reputable anthology of religious thought'.[16] Most of Canon Sheehan's writing on religion is kitsch, because his subject is not really religion at all: he is presenting ecclesiastical politics in the guise of religious truths and uses malleable, sentimental genre-pictures as his medium. One exceptional passage in an early novel shows what has thus been lost. It is a description of a funeral procession seen with the hostile eye of a young priest who is a stranger both to his people and to his past:

> He had protested often and preached against Irish funerals and Irish wakes. He could not understand the instinct that led people, at enormous expense and great waste of time, to bury their dead far away from home, sometimes on the side of a steep hill, sometimes in a well-covered inclosure in the midst of a meadow. It was with a certain feeling of impatience and disgust he headed these lonely processions of cars and horses and horsemen across the muddy and dusty roads, winding in and out in slow solemnity for fifteen or twenty miles, until at last they stopped; and the coffin was borne on men's shoulders across the wet field to where a ruined, moss-grown gable was almost covered with a forest of hemlocks or nettles. Then there was a long dreary search for the grave; and at last the poor remains were deposited under the shadow of the crumbling ruin, ivy-covered and

yielding to the slow corrosion of time, whilst the mourners departed, and thought no more of the silent slumberer beneath. Luke could not understand it. He preached against the waste of time involved, the numbers of farmers brought away from their daily work, the absurdity of separating husband from wife, in compliance with an absurd custom. He had never heard of the tradition that had come down unbroken for a thousand years — that there in that lonely abbey was the dust of a saint; and that he had promised on his deathbed that every one buried with him there should rise with him to a glorious resurrection. And these strange people looked askance at the new trim cemetery, laid out by the Board of Guardians, with its two chapels and its marble monuments erected over one or two of the Protestant dead. They preferred the crumbling walls, the nettles and hemlock, and the saint, and the abbey, and the resurrection.[17]

The hostile eye of the outsider records the decay into which this once powerful religious tradition has fallen: the obedience it still commands is half-blind, the purpose of the ritual but half-understood. That the people must defy the spiritual heir of the ancient monastic heritage in order to preserve the vestiges of its memory provides further ironic evidence of the degree of disintegration that has been reached. The priest assesses the customs of the community in terms of profit, thereby showing himself to be blind to his own tradition and to the loss its disappearance means. The loss is revealed in the glimpse of the new graveyard: a monument to the loneliness and barrenness of death attempting to ban decay through tidyness. In the old cemetery the 'poor remains' are deposited in the 'forest of hemlock and nettles' under the crumbling, overgrown walls, and forgotten. Yet out of this unpretentious image there emerges a hope of life, of resurrection, the strength of which lies in the roots it still has in the past and in the humility of its acceptance of neglect, oblivion and reabsorption into the natural cycle as the condition of a reawakening in the future.

From the double vision of the narrative stems the quality of this description of the Irish countryside, of the ruins of a long-destroyed culture hidden under a profusion of weeds, and of its precarious remaining hold on life through the memory of the people. Because Canon Sheehan looks at countryside, tradition and people through the eyes of an adversary, the anglicized young priest with his Benthamite indifference to the past, he must soberly register the decline of a local religious tradition. Here, however, he finds the evidence of the strength of the vanished culture and so he can convey a sense of the force it must once have had to survive for over a thousand years through the customs of the common people. No false hopes of revival are held out — the prospect, on the contrary, is that of imminent extinction. There is no lamentation: the loss is tersely demonstrated in the picture of the sterility which will replace it. Only because this death is faced, and decay accepted, can the great religious concept of hope in death emerge from this account of the meaning of the end of an old religious heritage. It is our loss that Canon Sheehan could not allow himself to make more frequent use of the eyes of his adversaries.

Canon Sheehan turned to novel-writing in order to give the people literature in which they could recognize themselves as Catholics, in which religion would appear as an integral part of their lives, and which would inculcate a sense of pride in their Catholicism. The need to counteract the people's feeling of shame about being Irish was a leitmotif of the writings of the time. Douglas Hyde wrote with bitterness of the destruction wrought by the Board of National Education in which Irish officials for decades collaborated in having 'schoolmasters who knew no Irish . . . appointed to teach pupils who knew no English'. The knowledge they had from home: their language, music, poems, Ossianic lays, stories and history were banned from the school curriculum; the result was that the children learnt 'to be ashamed of their own parents, ashamed of their own nationality, ashamed of their own names', ashamed of speaking a language which gave the average peasant a mastery of three to four thousand words in everyday usage.[18]

Daniel Corkery called the national consciousness 'a quaking sod'. He described the unsettling effect education had on the Irish child, in contrast to the English one, since what he read and studied did not 'focus the mind on his own people, teaching him the better to look about him, to understand both himself and his surroundings',[19] but presented the life of another people as that which was relevant and meaningful, while his own was ignored. The implicit lesson was that his own life, his world was not worth studying. The lack of literature, of Irish material to explain the child's world marked the beginning of 'overwhelming prestige of English culture in all Irish scholastic systems and therefore in Irish life generally'.[20]

Corkery, a primary schoolteacher, taught in Cork for twenty years under the British system. As a young man he encountered the chauvinist British attitudes exemplified in *Punch*, in Kipling's poems, and the Jingoism of the Anglo-Boer war. He will have been more familiar with contemptuous than with enthusiastic Anglo-Irish attitudes towards the Irish — contempt and hatred born of fear on the part of the landlords whose incomes were so sharply reduced after the land war. The Ascendancy's anger and dismay was by no means limited to the impoverished landed gentry of the west described by George Moore:[21] it could lead eminent Anglo-Irish scholars to virulent denunciations of Irish culture, as when the professor of Sanskrit and comparative philology at Trinity College in 1899 opposed the teaching of Irish in schools on the grounds that the language was a mere patois, and that both the ancient literature and the modern folklore were abominable, degrading and indecent.[22]

Corkery published his first book of short stories in 1916, when he was approaching his forties, and his *Hidden Ireland* in 1924, which Seán Ó Tuama says is one of the most important Irish books of the century.[23] He was a typical writer of the Irish Revival. In *The Hidden Ireland* he presents with the enthusiasm of the astonished and delighted discoverer eighteenth century Gaelic Munster's rich literary past. He made known to a wide audience the results of the research of the great Celtic philologists; his own striking comments on the poems and the fascinating accounts of the shattered world and the lives of the poets indeed achieved his aim of helping to save them from their 'second death': from the shame of being buried in 'the deep pit of contempt, reproach and forgetfulness'.[24]

But the discovery of the value of the destroyed culture came about through the study of the terrible story of its breaking, when 'a people cultured for fifteen hundred years' (Hyde) was reduced to 'a paralytic body where one part of it is dead or just dragged about by the other'.[25] The realisation, then, that — as Hyde puts it in the English dedication of his *Literary History* — 'Ireland has a past, has a history, has a literature' was inseparable from the realisation that Gaelic culture had not decayed and disappeared because of inherent weakness, but had been deliberately destroyed and its memory systematically obliterated in the schools. This made a particularly deep impact on those people who had been brought up to regard their own background as being hopelessly inadequate. But the pride in the riches of the past could easily bring with it blindness to the depletion of the present and to the irreparable damage done. Corkery, like Hyde, Pearse, Moran and all those who insisted on the urgency of saving the Irish language as the foundation of nationhood, remained keenly aware of the derelict condition of Irish culture and of the daunting nature of the task of reconstruction ahead.

Like almost all the writers of the Revival, Corkery believed that literature would play a vital part in the formation of the nation.

But he doubted whether the enormous pressure of English literary moulds and forms could ever be withstood, whether Ireland would ever succeed in producing a really independent literature, in creating its own forms for its own themes, as long as it had to make use of the language of English literature. The revival of Irish as the national language would guarantee an independent intellectual life because it would prevent the wholesale adoption of English models in every field of life. Of the immense difficulty of such a revival Corkery was all too conscious. He was therefore all the more concerned to define what was Irish literature in English and what was not.

He recommended that in their search for models, Irish writers should turn to Europe rather than to England, and in particular to the Russians, the two countries having much in common. He insisted that to be recognized as Irish writers, authors must write for the Irish public and not for foreign markets, that their work must be concerned with the specifically local rather than the cosmopolitan, and that, if a product of Irish life, it would necessarily treat of the three great forces which have formed that life: the religious consciousness of the people, nationality, and the land. He did not invent these issues: he came upon them in the popular literature of the nineteenth century, in the works of Davis, Mangan, Kickham, that 'submerged underworld of Anglo-Irish literature', mostly mediocre, never really good and yet the literature 'in which undereducated Ireland discovers its own image'.[26] He found these three forces in Irish history as the main obstacles to the conquest of the country,[27] and therefore the main targets of attack until the end of the eighteenth century, and the issues around which resistance crystallized in the nineteenth.

The land question he regarded as the least universal of the three, but felt that for a long time to come it would be a force behind Anglo-Irish literature 'as the freeing of the serfs lies behind Russian literature'. Nationalism, a force 'that wrecks as well as saves', he considered 'one of the deepest things in Irish life' which would find expression in true Anglo-Irish literature 'no matter what the nature of the expression may be, direct or indirect, heroic or grotesque, or perverse, but not alien-minded'. The religious consciousness of the people he believed was the most fundamental force 'vast', 'deep', 'even terrible' and so firmly entrenched that it permeated every aspect of life and should therefore do so too in literature 'as it does in the Greek plays — comedies as well as tragedies — or as it does in mediaeval art, grotesques and all'. He adds that perhaps 'only about Irish life can a really great sex novel be written in these days'[28]

Corkery excludes most Anglo-Irish writers from the category of Irish writers on the grounds that they ignore the central issue of the people's religion and dwell instead on the remainders of pagan beliefs. In so doing they were, he felt, continuing the Ascendancy tradition of presenting quaint native customs for the amusement of a foreign public rather than writing for the Irish as their own people. This is not the place to discuss whether writers can be divided into sheep and goats on this issue,[29] nor Corkery's rejection of Joyce and O'Casey and his reservation on this score about Synge, of whom he otherwise writes with admiration and perception. On account of his Catholic upbringing, and perhaps too his celibate life, he found alien and disturbing the gaudy, ribald and passionate aspects of the old culture which so fascinated Synge, and he filtered them just as thoroughly out of his own works as the Anglo-Irish writers excluded pietistic Catholicism from theirs.

Of greater interest here are the non-personal reasons for his insistance on the central importance of the religious consciousness of the people both in life and art. Those working for the de-Anglicisation of Ireland realised that Irish-Ireland had lost its once formidable powers of assimilation.[30] It was now the English element in the country which was assimilating the Gaelic. The Gaelic Leaguers could not become enthusiastic over the prospect of a new literature in English arising up out of the ashes of the older culture; they regarded it as an enrichment of English literature, but as irrelevant, if not damaging, to the cause of Irish. While Corkery did not take this extreme view, he too was reluctant to see the Anglo-Irish determine the cultural direction of the country. He, too, believed that unless Irish became the spoken language in a bilingual country the English element would predominate and ultimately undermine Irish independence. Or as Yeats has a fictitious Gaelic Leaguer phrase it: unless Irish became a living and 'disturbing intellectual force' the country would become like 'a dull school book', would face apathy and final absorption into the British Empire.[31]

Since the language had fallen into disuse, the main feature distinguishing the Irish from the English was their Catholicism. To Canon Sheehan the people's religion was an end unto itself; Corkery cherished it as the protector of the people's otherness, as a powerful insulating force. His analysis of the achievement of the early Irish church shows a similar tendency to regard religion as a means rather than as an end. What he underlines is the immense service the church rendered to pagan Gaelic civilisation. As Christianity did not come in the wake of a conquering imperial army, but established itself by convincing, it won the country's rulers and therefore adopted their language for teaching in the schools, Latin never supplanting the vernacular. And so the church's revolutionary innovation, the introduction of the art of writing, was employed in the service of the highly esteemed language and of literature, which was thus recorded and preserved. Again, in his discussion of Irish monasticism — which he says derived its inspiration from Egypt rather than from Rome — he emphasises that while it was the 'religious spirit' which drew scholars from all over Europe to the Irish schools, what they found there was 'another spirit which must have surprised them even more than the religious — the cult of native learning'.[32] In Ireland 'as far back as historic knowledge can reach, one national force has overshadowed and dominated all others. It has been the power of a great literary tradition'.[33]

The Irish language was the medium of this heritage; its most dangerous enemy the Benthamite utility and profit thinking which Corkery deplored in the middle classes and their politicians, especially Daniel O'Connell, who said of the language: 'I am sufficiently utilitarian not to regret its abandonment', and who, along with the Catholic church, did much to further that abandonment.[34] Like Canon Sheehan, Corkery regarded the Catholicism of the people as a bulwark against the competitive and money-orientated thinking and doing of modern society, and his hope was that as it was still strong, it might be tapped to supply the support and the enthusiasm needed for the strenuous task of restoring the language. This may be why he could not appreciate either Joyce or O'Casey with their dissections of the manifold, highly utilitarian uses to which the mantles of 'spirituality', 'idealism' and 'patriotism' could be put, although their works, as well as those of Synge and Yeats, correspond in so many respects to his own concept of what Irish national literature should be.

Replying to a reader's criticism of the importation of foreign ideas into Ireland through the co-operative movement, AE wrote in 1909: 'A nationality is great, distinguished, and individual in the best sense when all the world had been tributary to its greatness, when it has ransacked the earth for the best ideas and has fed its own life with them'.[35] His response is typical of the open, generous spirit of those Anglo-Irish who became involved in the Irish Revival. It is no wonder that such people had difficulty in understanding the susceptibilities of the Irish-Irelanders, their own consciousness — as Frantz Fanon said of French intellectuals facing an African cultural revival — sheltered by a culture that had already given proof of its existence and had never been contested.[36]

But how could the native Catholic Irish have been anything but rawly sensitive where England was concerned? The country had lain wide open to England since Tudor times with disastrous consequences. The middle class, which produced most of the nationalist leaders, had only just shaken off the contemptuous Ascendancy view of itself which it had long internalized, men successful in commerce making themselves 'respectable' by putting their sons into the professions as soon as they could afford to. The middle class was still despised by the landed gentry for being the mere trading class, and a small and modest one at that, and despised by the Anglo-Irish intellectuals as philistines, hucksters and gombeen men. Though the middle-class exploiters of the smallholders in the congested districts and of the urban poor well deserved the articulate contempt of Yeats, Plunkett, AE (and that of Pearse, James Stephens and Daniel Corkery during the Lock Out of 1913), it is no harm to remember that it was the landlord system which reduced smallholders to dependence on the gombeen men. Nor is it out of place to remember that the Anglo-Irish gentry did not only consist of Yeatses, Plunketts and Synges, but that the m jority were as obscurantist and as philistine as any shopkeeper, though with less excuse, never having been subjected to the state philistinism of the educational system the shopkeepers had to undergo.

On the other hand, the Irish middle class was not only made up of William Martin Murphy and Arthur Griffiths, with their limited nationalism and pro-Imperial leanings, their bullying anti-Semitism and sanctimonious Catholicism, their war on the Dublin trade unions and the most wretched workers of Europe. A large section of the middle class of rural Ireland was active in the movement of economic revival, in Sir Horace Plunkett's co-operative movement, which by 1920 had a thousand branches, a turnover of fourteen and a half million pounds, and involved nearly half a million people.[37] These dairy farmers, now owners of their holdings, most of them in Munster, had to contend with massive and unscrupulous opposition from the traders, middlemen and shopkeepers threatened by the co-ops.[38] It was in the dairy farm lands of Munster where the co-operative movement was most widespread that the IRA found greatest support during the Anglo-Irish war, and it was no coincidence that the Black and Tans singled out the co-ops and creameries for reprisals and destruction.[39]

We must not imagine, then, that the Anglo-Irish were as a whole as open towards the Catholic Irish as were their writers and reformers; nor that the Catholic middle class was always as limited as its conservative spokesmen and leaders. But the middle class had an overwhelming need to shut itself off after the centuries of enforced and debilitating openness to England. That was what Home Rule was all about, and independence even more so: the right to build walls behind which to reconstruct. This meant a return to the exclusiveness which marked the rule of the Ascendancy at the beginning of the colonial period, a completing of the circle. To give but one example: the rule of the Gaelic Athletic Association forbidding its members to play foreign games corresponded to a statue passed in Galway in 1527 forbidding loyal subjects to play Irish games.[40] The urgent need for seclusion in the field of economics, finance, language and culture could prevail when partition removed the necessity for compromise with the minority, and it provided the Catholic church with a broad basis for its policies of entrenchment. The establishment of church influence in every sphere of Irish life was the aim, nationalism the means employed, the secular culture was sacrificed as dangerous. Corkery's hopes were thus dashed: the Catholic church did not serve any culture, Gaelic or otherwise.

After the establishment of the Irish Free State, those writers who could not employ the Joycean recipé of exile, silence and cunning to deal with the issues of nationality, language and religion broached the themes with mordant satire, two of them in Irish. For, despite independence, the decline of the Irish-speaking areas of the country continued unabated, while politicians paid unceasing lip-service to the national language. In *An Béal Bocht* (*The Poor Mouth*) of 1941 Miles na gCopaleen presents, in caricature as gross as the pious fiction he denounces, the squalor of the poverty in the decaying Gaeltacht, a rural slum peopled by pigs, paupers and passing 'Gaeligores', and ruled by hunger, ignorance and alcohol. The themes of the land, religion and nationality are again treated in a similarly satirical vein in Mairtín O Cadhain's great novel of 1949, *Cré na Cille* (*The Clay of the Graveyard*). If Miles na gCopaleen's people inhabit wretched hovels on land that starves them and have not the smallest shred of culture any more, the only land left at the disposal of Ó Cadhain's rural community is that in the cemetery. Their consciousness, however, is as unquenchable as it is irreligious; and their speech remains, even in the graveyard, inexhaustible, malevolent, virtuose.

These works demonstrated with devastating clarity that the seclusion and enclosure which the country sought after independence had not laid the foundations for reconstruction but had brought stagnation and decay. AE once said that we become what we contemplate: nobly like what we love, and ignobly like what we hate.[41] It has been the tragedy of colonized peoples that they could not make themselves heard and understood in the world until they had adopted their master's voice and expressed their grievances in his terms; but by then they had become too close to what they were opposing to be able to break away from its field of gravity.

YEATS AND RELIGION

MITSUKO OHNO

For some poets and novelists, religion serves as the central theme for their work. For Yeats, it may be said that religion was an undercurrent, and not a mainstream, for if religion is something to be either accepted totally as truth or else rejected entirely, Yeats was too much a sceptic to uphold one faith alone. Religion for Yeats was like a natural phenomenon that requires scientific scrutiny, an object for his intellectual curiosity and analysis. What is more, the conclusion of his analysis does not seem to hold nearly as much significance as the searching process itself, for his works were generated through a process of searching, and his creative energy derived from inquiry. It may rather be said that religion, in the accepted sense, of a single faith, was not the utmost goal of his spiritual exploration, but it served his poetry, for what else did Yeats desire to accomplish but art?

In considering religion and Yeats, it is reasonable to start with his childhood experiences, as they seem exceedingly influential in the poet's development. Memories of childhood and youth contain obscure shadows and inexplicable fears as well as unnameable yearnings for any adult, whether brought up in the West or in the Orient. It is so much more so for an imaginative character such as Yeats, whose childhood was spent in a country richly endowed with myths and legends. Among factors that influenced Yeats's religious beliefs, we may assume that the tradition of folklore, superstition and the supernatural held among the Irish people certainly had a central significance. In 'Reveries over Childhood and Youth' Yeats describes his mystical experiences, some of which seem to be the results of innocent fascination by the unknown, and others quite intangible. Yeats recalls one such example:

> Once, too, I was driving with my grandmother a little after dark close to the Channel that runs for some five miles from Sligo to the sea, and my grandmother showed me the red light of an outward bound steamer and told me that my grandfather was on board, and that night in my sleep I screamed out and described the steamer's wreck.[1]

In fact, William Pollexfen's ship was wrecked, and Yeats's dream proved to him to be a foreboding. By writing thus, Yeats seems to suggest that he had a power akin to that of a visionary, though the premonition came to him only in a dream. Experiences like this recalled years after the event may not correspond exactly with the facts, but they do reflect a childhood disposition and sensitivity which later found literary expression in his work. Yeats's mystical inclination was enhanced as he grew older, and his interest broadened to take in mystical traditions in Europe and in the Orient. Contrary to the scientific and realistic trends of the times, Yeats was attracted to the occult, and eagerly studied the diverse beliefs and mythologies of the world. However, as Graham Hough points out: 'Yeats's heritage of beliefs, themes, myths and symbols is too various to be compressed within limits, and it is hard to find a single essential idea at the root of it'.[2] The aim of the present essay, therefore, is to trace the shift of his religious concepts and beliefs as they are reflected and illustrated in his writing, especially in his drama and prose writing, as they seem to show them more comprehensively than his poems.

Yeats wrote in *The Celtic Twilight* that among the country people in Sligo, where he had spent many youthful summers, there were people who saw faeries and banshees. The ancient villages were full of spirits and ghosts, and also full of people who claimed they had witnessed 'other-world creatures'. Even those who doubted Hell and ghosts believed, Yeats writes, in faeries; a woman says: 'Hell was an invention got up by the priest to keep people good'; and a man says: 'No matter what one doubts, one never doubts the faeries for they stand to reason'.[3] These views illustrate the state of the Christian faith among the people of rural Ireland. From what is disclosed in *The Celtic Twilight*, it is apparent that there existed a mixture of folk elements from the pre-Christian era and Christian orthodoxy. These mixed beliefs seem to have been widely accepted among the local people of Western Ireland, but in Yeats's work they are treated in such a way as to appeal to sophisticated readers in England and elsewhere as exotic and charming. By Yeats's time there had developed a taste for such material, where earlier they might have been shuffled off as merely crude and uncivilized.

The folk legends that Yeats introduced in *The Celtic Twilight* were later incorporated into a number of his poems and plays, a typical one being *The Land of Heart's Desire*. Like many children believed to be taken by faeries, the bride, having learned of them in a book, anticipates their call, and, despite her love for her husband, fails to resist their temptation. The balance between Christian faith and folk belief is a theme of the play. Yeats brings onto the stage the skirmish between the two forces and generates dramatic tension.

The result seems symbolic: the absence of the crucifix, the magic charm against the pagan lure, brings defeat to the Christians; while the faery world, represented by the innocent-looking child, wins. The soul of the young bride is lured out, leaving the mere shell of her physical body. The pre-Christian Irish myth has been revived by Yeats to symbolize the eternal longing of mortal man. The Christian faith is here strongly associated with the reality of daily life – the reality that one cannot remain young forever, nor can one escape one's doom to become old and cross with the wear and tear of life, while the Irish legends stand for man's eternal dream.

Man's dream and reality, or the dualism of hearth and wilderness represented later by the Blind Man and the Fool in *On Baile's Strand* in a more intricate way, are contrasted in the matching set of Irish legends and Christian faith, and the fantastical dramatization makes the former seem more attractive in contrast to the prosaic appeal of the latter.

The same theme appears in the poem 'The Stolen Child', in which the lure of faery land is melodious and enchanting:

> *Come away, O human child!*
> *To the waters and the wild*
> *With a faery, hand in hand,*
> *For the world's more full of weeping than you can understand.*

One thing that must have influenced the young Yeats in developing a preference for mysticism over orthodox Christianity and the predominant materialistic view on life needs to be mentioned, and that is his family background. Yeats's great-grandfather and grandfather on his father's side were rectors of the Church of Ireland, but Yeats himself was influenced more by his grandfather on his mother's side, William Pollexfen. Being an object of fear and admiration for the child, Pollexfen represented courage, passion, and manly dignity, as well as a mystical heritage. His father, John, was an agnostic and passed his thoughts on religion on to his son. Yeats reflects: 'My father's unbelief had set me thinking about the evidences of religion and I weighed the matter perpetually with great anxiety, for I did not think I could live without religion.'[4] In later years, Yeats was able to free himself from his father's abiding influence:

> It was only when I began to study psychical research and mystical philosophy that I broke away from my father's influence. He had been a follower of John Stuart Mill and so had never shared Rossetti's conviction that it mattered to nobody whether the sun went round the earth or the earth round the sun. But through this new research, this reaction from popular science, I had begun to feel that I had allies for my secret thought.[5]

Indeed, the positive and negative reactions to the family heritage are important clues to understanding the nature of Yeats's religious beliefs. Yeats was not so much against Christian religion in itself, but all his youthful experiences worked toward his departure from Christian orthodoxy, aided also by the nationalist cause in Ireland at the time. It is notable that, because of the psychological difficulties he had suffered with his father, Yeats resorted to the new religion in his youth, and found a new sphere for his art also.

Yeats's new fascination with psychical research was, itself, highly individual, for he sought the answers to his queries in his own way. Under George Russell's influence, Yeats became interested in theosophy and he founded the Dublin Hermetic Society. His interest grew, and, meeting Madame Blavatsky in 1887, he joined the Theosophical Society. However, when he entered the Hermetic Order of the Golden Dawn he persistently experimented with magic practice, and he was excommunicated from the Theosophical Society. Yeats's thoughts and experiments are described in his writings during these years. In the essay, 'Magic', he tells us about the practice and philosophy of magic as follows:

> I believe in three doctrines. . . These doctrines are:
> (1) That the borders of our mind are ever shifting, and that many minds can flow into one another, as it were, and create or reveal a single mind, a single energy.
> (2) That the borders of our memories are as shifting, and that our memories are a part of one great memory, the memory of Nature herself.
> (3) That this great mind and great memory can be evoked by symbols.[6]

These beliefs and doctrines are put to the test by Yeats, as described in the essays contained in 'Ideas of Good and Evil', but more candid and detailed explanations are given in his *Memoirs* later. These reveal that he was earnestly practising the evocation of 'lunar power', a magic power, and then trying to gather the Kabalistic interpretation of its symbolism.[7]

Indeed, Yeats's path in search of a new religion, though it was a personal course of exploration as we have seen, was not a solitary one, for it was also trodden by many others at the time. Yeats was at heart a solitary man, but his life seems to have been richly associated with men and women sharing his interest. These men and women, poets, artists, and writers, were supporters of spiritualism against popular science and materialism because they felt the latter were threats to the imagination, and their disillusionment with the general trend in favour of pragmatism led them to be attracted to mystical philosophy. With the nineteenth century approaching its end, there was a growing interest in magic, dreams, ghosts, spiritualism, mesmerism. And this occultism included Oriental philosophy and religion. The Western intellect was being attracted increasingly by Indian religion and Japanese art.

Although it bore much fruit as regards Kabalistic and symbolistic studies, the last decade of the nineteenth century did not seem to be a happy time for the poet, as his health deteriorated in these years and his love for Maud Gonne was a frustrating one. It was very fortunate for Yeats that he was introduced to Lady Gregory in 1896, when he was quite ill physically and emotionally. Under her guardianship and assistance he was able to recover his health and 'tolerable industry'. In such state of mind and physical condition, he had unusual dreams and visions that he found worth noting. In his *Memoirs* he records his own and his associates' dreams and visions, but the unusual dream that he describes in 'The Stirring of the Bones' seems significant:

> . . . an emotion never experienced before swept down upon me. I said, 'That is what the devout Christian feels, that is how he surrenders his will to the will of God.' I felt an extreme surprise for my whole imagination was preoccupied with the pagan mythology of ancient Ireland. . . . The next morning I awoke near dawn, to hear a voice saying, 'The love of God is infinite for every human soul because every human soul is unique; no other can satisfy the same need in God'.[8]

This was some time during 1897 and 1898, and the exuberance of his emotion is remarkable. Later in 1914 he recalls this particular time and experience in 'Swedenborg, Mediums, Desolate Places', and writes: 'I pieced together stray thoughts written out after questioning the familiar of a trance medium or automatic writer . . . and arranged the fragments into some pattern, till I believed myself the discoverer of a vast generalisation. . . . I lived in excitement . . . then one day I opened the *Spiritual Diary* of Swedenborg which I had not taken down for twenty years, and found all there, even certain thoughts I had not set on paper because they had seemed fantastic from the lack of some traditional foundation'.[9]

Out of this rediscovery of Swedenborg came further psychological effect on Yeats. He records in his *Memoirs* experiences that are very Swedenborgian, and it is sufficient to cite one such example to show the degree of influence Yeats received from the eighteenth century Swedish scholar. He saw a series of strange dreams in which he thought he was taken out of his body and into a world of light, and while in this light, which was also complete happiness, he was told he would now be shown the passage of the soul at its incarnation.[10] This quite obviously reflects the story of the Lord's manifestation to Swedenborg in April 1744, related in *The Journal of Dreams.*[11] As this manifestation marked the turning point for Swedenborg's Christian faith, so did Yeats's re-discovery of *The Spiritual Diary* for his religious explorations.

However, Yeats's excitement about this experience was not of an unqualified nature. He kept seeing visions and dreams in the following years, but he kept a critical eye on this extraordinary world. In the *Memoirs* he writes: 'I wished him [AE who had remarkable visions] to record all as Swedenborg had recorded, and submit his clairvoyance to certain tests. This seemed to him an impiety, and perhaps the turning towards it of the analytic intellect checked his gift, and he became extremely angry; and my insistence on understanding symbolically what he took for literal truth increased his anger'.[12] Yeats's sober attitude is impressive, and it is certain what he says here echoes what he wrote of those 'whose virtues are the definitions/ Of the analytic mind, can neither close/ The eye of the mind nor keep my tongue from speech'.[13]

In the last years of the 'fin de siècle' and the first decade of the new century, Yeats was much occupied with the Irish Literary Theatre. To reflect the visionary experiences that he recorded in detail in the *Memoirs,* he used the convention of dream-revelation in his drama. The plays that contain dreams are: *The Hour Glass,* published in 1903; *The Unicorn from the Stars,* which is the revised version of *Where There Is Nothing,* published in 1908; *The Only Jealousy of Emer* and *The Dreaming of the Bones,* published in 1919; and *The Herne's Egg,* published in 1935. He also used dream-like illusions and hallucinations in other plays.

Among the plays listed above, *The Unicorn from the Stars* attracts our attention, as it seems to represent some of the religious ideas Yeats held and the feelings he had at the time. In the notes, he writes that the play, being a revision of *Where There is Nothing* which was not satisfactory to himself, owes much to Lady Gregory, but he also acknowledges 'thoughts, points of view, and artistic aims which seem a part of my world'.[14] The hero, Martin, tells Father John after he recovers from his second unconsciousness

> Heaven is not what we have be-
> lieved it to be. It is not quiet, it is not singing and
> making music, and all strife at an end. I have seen it,
> I have been there. The lover still loves, but with a
> greater passion, and the rider still rides, but the
> horse goes like the wind and leaps the ridges, and
> the battle goes on always, always. That is the joy of
> Heaven, continual battle . . . we
> shall not come to that joy, that battle, till we have
> put out the senses, . . .

This world is the one described by Strindberg, in a note for his *Dream Play*, as one where 'Time and space do not exist'. Strindberg, too, had studied Swedenborg[15] and the idea of presenting the spiritual world, the world other than this visible one, by way of a dream, is an obviously attractive one for modern dramatists, concerned, as they often are, to depict complex mental and psychological states. But to actually do this effectively is not an easy task. Presenting the crucial moment when the unseen becomes seen, when the other world interferes with this one or vice versa, without appearing to be absurd or farcical, involves a number of requirements — an adequate theme, highly skilled handling of the subject matter so as to totally absorb the audience, and then the moment of revelation itself must be a moment of the highest dramatic intensity. Yeats aimed at this accomplishment but found it difficult to achieve. If we return again to the list of Yeats's plays using dreams, we notice that there is a gap of time between *The Unicorn from the Stars* and the next play. He confesses the difficulty he had in writing this play in the notes, and perhaps the reason for his not attempting another play of this type during these years may be that he did not wish to start such a play again until he felt sure he could control the various elements outlined above.

During these years, before the writing of *The Only Jealousy of Emer*, Yeats discovered the Japanese Noh play. Among the various elements of the Noh that attracted Yeats, was the solution it offered him to the problem of presenting ghosts on the stage. The traditional Japanese drama exemplified for him the model, as it were, for achieving the highest dramatic intensity at the moment of revelation through the dance and the chorus, making the two worlds merge before the eyes of the audience.

In the winter of 1913–14, Ezra Pound, who was then acting as Yeats's personal secretary, showed him the manuscript of the unfinished translations and studies of Noh by Ernest Fenollosa. Pound had been asked to complete and publish it by Fenollosa's widow, and they became quite engrossed in the unknown form of drama from the Orient. Yeats wrote in 'Swedenborg, Mediums, and Desolate Places': 'Nearly all that my fat old woman in Soho learns from her familiars is there in an unsurpassed lyric poetry and in strange and poignant fables once danced or sung in the houses of nobles'.[16] The reason why Yeats put his comments on Noh in the essay on Swedenborg is obvious: for Yeats, these two subjects belonged to the same flow of thought.

Out of this encounter came *'Noh' or Accomplishment*, published in 1916 with Yeats's introduction; and *At the Hawk's Well*, an experimental one-act play performed in the same year with the Japanese dancer, Michio Ito. Among the Noh plays that he had studied, Yeats was especially fascinated with the Mugen-Noh, the group of plays that deal with ghosts in purgatorial states. *The Dreaming of the Bones* can be regarded as the most faithful reproduction of the theme and style of Noh in this category. The young man fleeing after the rising at the Post Office meets at a desolate place a pair of local people, who then reveal to him their true identity and dance the climactic dance of enchantment. Like many Japanese Noh plays, the ghosts here present themselves before the young man's eyes in an attempt to seek consolation for their tormented souls from the living person. They are Dermot and Dervorgillagh, whose passion led to the Norman invasion of Ireland. Their souls have been roaming, seeking such consolation over hundreds of years, and to no avail. In place of the appeasing prayer by the travelling priest of the Noh drama, we see that the ghosts' wishes are not fulfilled, for in this play with a very contemporary Irish setting, the living refuse forgiveness to the betrayers' souls because of the national cause.

In this experimental play, Yeats succeeds in presenting both the living and the dead on the stage without resorting to the device of dream. The two local people turn to ghosts without changing costumes or masks before the eyes of the audience. This is an even simpler mode of metamorphosis from a living person to a spirit than is observed in the Noh convention, for in the latter the ghosts, after revealing their identity, usually disappear and then reappear in changed costumes. In Yeats's play the same metamorphic effect is achieved by their entranced and also entrancing dance, which makes the total aura that the stage emits highly charged with symbolism. As a dramatist Yeats seems to be fascinated with the dimension that dance can effect in drama, and this, aside from its lyric poetry, is the integral part of Noh's influence on Yeats.

Yeats's gains from the discovery of the Japanese drama, however, were more than the solutions to technical problems. The

Noh plays exemplified for Yeats not only the possible interface of the living and dead, but presented also, in an objective and concrete form, some of the ideas he had entertained about life after death. In 1914 he wrote: 'It is not uncommon for a ghost to come to a medium to discover some old earthly link to fit into a new chain. It wishes to meet a ghostly enemy to win pardon or to renew an old friendship. Our service to the dead is now narrowed to our prayers, but may be as wide as our imagination'.[17] This thinking owes much to the concrete images he found presented to his mind in the Noh. Yeats delighted in finding the concept of the interaction of the living and the dead in Noh, itself a reflection of the Buddhist thought with which he had had an affinity since his youth. His interest in the Orient revived, this time to the benefit of the dramatist as well, for now he knew that drama could be a vehicle for his religious views.

The Dreaming of the Bones thus may be regarded as a Noh play with Irish material, concerned with the theme of the interface between the living and the dead. Among other plays which were written under the influence of Noh, *At the Hawk's Well* is a play which shares with Noh the theme of man's longing for eternal life, but is not concerned with life after death, for here the conflict between man and the supernatural is the central issue. *The Only Jealousy of Emer* poses the question as to what 'our service to the dead' may be, where Emer's act of self-sacrifice calls the soul of the dead Cuchulain back. This concept is carried further in the last of his plays, *Purgatory*.

Before discussing the last play, however, we must mention the importance of the system of *A Vision* and its relation to Yeats's religion. Yeats found in Swedenborg what he sought as regards life after death, but as Graham Hough points out, 'What for Swedenborg, who is not a reincarnationist, is a final state, is for Yeats only the interval between death and rebirth'.[18] And Yeats found the answer, or rather a reinforcement for his premeditated view, in Buddhist thought through his exposure to Noh drama. The plays were to serve as his vehicles, but he felt they were not explicit enough in conveying the vast system of his concepts and beliefs. *A Vision* is not a product of mystical experience, but an attempt to construct a complex thought-system to shape time. It may be regarded as an invention of the poet's imagination, fired by the different but complementary systems of Swedenborg and Eastern religions. Yeats wrote in the preface to *The Ten Principal Upanishads*:

But now that *The Golden Bough* has made Christianity look modern and fragmentary we study Confucius with Ezra Pound, or like T. S. Eliot find in Christianity a convenient symbolism for some older or new thought . . .[19]

A Vision is a Yeatsian system of thought which is rooted not in the modern Christian faith but in the religions beyond the boundaries of sects and historical time.

In *Purgatory* we see two men and two ghosts alone on the stage and, in this one-act play, the interaction between the living and the dead is intensified, centering on the murder of the son. Despite the resolute and heroic act of murder by the Old Man, the dead are destined to relive the impassioned moment which was, to the eye of the Old Man, the source of their whole tragic fate. The Old Man realizes that the living cannot intervene in the sphere of the dead. Here again the familiar theme of the interface between the two worlds appears, but here the hope that the living may serve the dead through imagination seems totally shattered. Man is only granted a prayer to God:

O God,
Release my mother's soul from its dream!
Mankind can do no more. Appease
The misery of the living and the remorse of the dead.

And even this prayer does not sound quite effectual. As Sandra F. Siegel concludes: 'Yeats was sceptical . . . of the efficacy of the Old Man's prayer . . . The Old Man is neither the hero *A Vision* proclaims nor the spokesman for Yeats's "beliefs" but the parodic double of Yeats's own thought'.[20] This scepticism is linked to his sense that modern industrialised man may be excluded from wisdom as reflected in the introduction to *The Mandukya Upanishad* written in 1935:

I think it certain that Europeans, travelling the same way, enduring the same facts, saying the same prayers, would have received nothing but perhaps a few broken dreams. Bhagwan Shri Hamsa's evocation of 'the conscious', of 'the unconscious,' depended in part upon innumerable associations from childhood on, in part upon race-memory.[21]

This is an exceedingly pessimistic view to hold at the end of his long and strenuous exploration into the Eastern religions. And we know Yeats did not return to Christian orthodoxy either. Yeats's thinking was constant in the sense that he never stopped searching, discovering, and working upon what best suited his scheme.

Now that he is aware that his journey is approaching its end, he reflects: 'Players and painted stage took all my love / And not those things that they were emblems of.'

Thus reviewing his past aspirations, he now acknowledges that his poetry is not the incarnation of his religious thought, but the last resort for his soul.

It is not, however, in destitution of creative energy that he writes 'Now that my ladder's gone,/ I must lie down where all the ladders start,/ In the foul rag-and-bone shop of the heart.'

Yeats is merely saying that he will set out with renewed resolution for his religion, which is, as ever before in his life, his poetry.

JOYCE AND CATHOLICISM

EAMONN HUGHES

1. Introduction

I am a servant of two masters, Stephen said, an English and an Italian . . . and a third, Stephen said, there is who wants me for odd jobs. . . The imperial British state . . . and the holy Roman catholic and apostolic church.[1]

Stephen's famous description of himself as a trinitarian servant picks up, like so much of the opening section of *Ulysses*, from the closing pages of *A Portrait of the Artist as a Young Man*:

I will not serve that in which I no longer believe whether it call itself my home, my fatherland or my church.[2]

The purpose of this reference back to the earlier work is, literally, to put Stephen in his place, to show that he has been drawn back into the flow of Irish history. Stephen has been forced to recognise that his earlier defiance is not sustainable and his reformulation of the trinity of *A Portrait* into the more all-encompassing version in *Ulysses* signals both his own sense of the power of the forces ranged against him and the actual power wielded by those forces. Ignoring the other elements of the trinities I want to consider the differences between the phrases 'I will not serve' and 'I am a servant' in relation to the holy, Roman, catholic and apostolic church because these phrases represent the poles of Joyce's attitudes to Catholicism.

I do not intend to provide a reading of Joyce's work which glosses, say, the specific uses to which he put Catholic doctrines or which traces, for example, the formal correspondences between *A Portrait* and *Augustine's Confessions*.[3] Instead I want to consider the effects of Catholicism on Joyce's writing as a whole: how and in what ways Joyce could refuse to serve and remain a servant; how he could, as I shall phrase it, both deny and assent to Catholicism; and how and in what ways criticism can deal with Joyce and Catholicism. The scale of what I wish to do is best illustrated by considering the three distinct meanings of Catholicism in the phrase 'Joyce and Catholicism'. It can refer, as it usually does, to the conventional view of Joyce's redaction of Catholicism (famously, the entangled net, *AP*, p. 206); but it can also refer to the Catholic Church's own view of itself as a monolithic and absolutist structure (a seamless robe); and it can refer to the Catholicism contemporary with Joyce, that is, an institution subject to the forces of history (cloth cut to suit changing fashions). It is only by considering all these aspects of Catholicism that we can begin to understand the contradictions in Joyce's attitude to Catholicism, contradictions summed up in the dialectic of 'I will not serve' and 'I am a servant', a dialectic of denial and assent.

2. *Secular Culture and Critical Relativity*

Although this essay cannot pretend to offer a comprehensive review of the available literature on Joyce and Catholicism I wish to start with a very general retrospective of the problems in previous critical approaches not just because this will clear the ground but because it will also offer some insights into Joyce's attitudes to Catholicism and will enable us to tease out the full range of oppositions summed up in 'I will not serve' and 'I am a servant'.

> If we find a genius at all sympathetic, we tend to re-create him in our own image.[4]

These are the opening words of one of the first studies of Joyce and Catholicism and they paint a gloomy but largely accurate picture of the relativistic approaches of criticism to Joyce. This critical relativity has produced, as Morse's comment suggests, a number of 'Joyces'. At one extreme there is, for example, the Joyce whose use of Marian imagery in *Ulysses* is grounded in misogyny, at the other there is Joyce the deconstructive and proto-feminist Incarnator of the word.[5] The critical relativism which has produced these very different 'Joyces' is grounded in the severely limited engagement with the text that is allowed by the modes of criticism which have been dominant since Joyce's day.

Joyce's works were produced in time to find themselves subjected to the full blast of the New and practical criticisms, criticisms which circumscribed the reader's engagement with the text by denying the historical and worldly dimensions of the text. Similarly these criticisms deny their own history and yet a knowledge of that history is necessary if we are to appreciate why these criticisms cannot deal with the totality of Joyce's work. The need for such an appreciation is highlighted by conjoining Joyce and the totality that is Catholicism because these criticisms, while anti-historical, are yet secular in the sense that their object of study, literature, is a mode of discourse which, it is now well established, served increasingly as a replacement for religion. Terry Eagleton provides a useful summary:

> By the mid-Victorian period, this traditionally reliable, immensely powerful ideological form [religion] was in deep trouble. It was no longer winning the hearts and minds of the masses, and under the twin impacts of scientific discovery and social change its previous unquestioned dominance was in danger of evaporating. This was particularly worrying for the Victorian ruling class, because religion is for all kinds of reasons an extremely effective form of ideological control. Like all successful ideologies, it works much less by explicit concepts or formulated doctrines than by image, symbol, habit, ritual and mythology. It is affective and experiential, entwining itself with the deepest unconscious roots of the human subject; and any social ideology which is unable to engage with such deep-seated, a-rational fears and needs is unlikely to survive for very long. . . It is no wonder that the Victorian ruling class looked on the threatened dissolution of this ideological discourse with something less than equanimity. Fortunately, however, another, remarkably similar discourse lay to hand: English literature.[6]

Culture then, particularly literary culture, according to this argument, took over the *quondam* role of religion in the ideological ensemble and acted as a force for social cohesion by being a repository of 'the best knowledge and thought of the time and a true source, therefore, of sweetness and light'.[7] Literature, in other words replaced religion as an authoritative and validating source of moral principles and values at just that point when religion, specifically Christianity, was weakened by the forces of rationality. Christianity, while no longer powerful in itself, yet remained as a particular *locus* of values within the now dominant category of culture. The newly secularised culture could, however, no longer credit its values to Christianity, which now had no greater status than that of myth; nor, at the other extreme, could the ideological function of culture and its values be sustained if their true source was openly acknowledged; if, that is, they were seen to be merely the values of bourgeois morality.

This was where criticism had a part to play. The function of criticism in the ideological ensemble was to promote the values embedded in culture. Although humanistic and secular this criticism was centred on the abstract category of 'the moral', or, better, 'the spiritual'. This is to say that it both denied the existence of a transcendant authority and contradictorily suggested that literature had, if read aright, access to 'higher' truths. The methodology adopted by this criticism was largely exegetical, which again suggested that its object was a series of sacred texts containing 'received' truths and untroubled by history or the exigencies of human experience.

This brief sketch of a long and sometimes turbulent process necessarily contains many elisions and foreshortenings. It does, however, have two important consequences for a consideration of Joyce and Catholicism. We must remember that Joyce himself was partly a product of the intellectual processes which constitute this history. His image of the artist as a priest of the imagination chimes with the details of this history of secularisation and is explained as much by this secularisation as by Joyce's own personal history. However, while this shared history explains certain of Joyce's images and goes some way to accounting for his 'I will not serve' it leaves out of account the fact that Joyce was also, more so, a product of a society which resisted the process of secularisation. Unlike many of his critics Joyce was therefore keenly aware of religion, specifically Catholicism, as a still vital force in regard to both society and culture. This fact diminishes the importance of the intellectual history common to both Joyce and dominant contemporary critical practices by showing that Joyce was the product of more than one set of determinants.

Despite the continuing dominance of Catholicism in Ireland, much criticism of Joyce insists on rendering it as a variant on a Christianity in decline which has become merely a source of cultural myths. In such readings of Joyce the elements of Catholicism, stripped of their potency, are available to him in the same way, and to the same ends, that Greek myth is available, i.e. as a source of structuring metaphors. In this view Joyce's achievement was 'to convert Christianity from a dogma to a system of metaphors'.[8] Those metaphors are in their turn free-floating, rescued by Joyce from the constraints of Christianity, and available for critics to interpret almost at will.

In summary, such criticism can explain, and find support for itself in 'I will not serve'. The phrase is taken as either an end in itself, Joyce's declaration of artistic independence, or as the beginning of a new mode of consciousness which has its end in the perceived links between Stephen, Bloom and Molly. That most interpretations of these links are vitiated by sentimentality or by its obverse, cynicism, is attributable to the inability of such criticism to define Joyce in other than negative terms ('Non serviam' is almost certainly the most often quoted phrase from Joyce's writings). In the absence of affirmative terms criticism displays a rampant relativism and Joyce's works become a mirror to the various vanities of a secular criticism which elevates his works to the level of sacred texts to endorse those vanities. That Stephen also says 'I am a servant' is a contradiction with which most critics choose not to cope preferring to ignore Stephen and Joyce's testament to the power of Catholicism.

3. *Ideology and Determination*

What is needed is an account of Joyce and Catholicism which can comprehend Joyce's dual heritage as the product of both an age of secularisation and a society which retained what F. S. L. Lyons has called 'a dumb attachment to a Church which in most Englishmen inspired an almost instinctive revulsion'.[9] Only an account which does this can hope to confront successfully the contradictions between 'I will not serve' (intellectual history) and 'I am a servant' (social determinants). However, such an account faces a number of obstacles not the least of which is the lack of analytical concepts which can be applied to Catholicism.[10]

The obvious starting point is therefore to return to Eagleton, take up his point about religion as ideology and test it against Irish social and cultural history. Ideology is, however, a coarse-grained concept and needs to be further refined if it is to cope with the complexities of a long established church. For religion to function ideologically it must be a trans-social phenomenon, it must, in E. P. Thompson's words, have a 'dual role as the religion of both the exploiter and the exploited'.[11] Thompson is writing about a different religion and different circumstances but the reasons he adduces for the success of Methodism in England between 1790 and 1830 are, in the absence of a comparable analysis of Catholicism, a good summary of the components of religion as ideology. There are, according to Thompson, three reasons for the success of religion: briefly, direct indoctrination into religious beliefs, the sense of community fostered by shared values, and the consolatory and affective aspects of religious practices — what Thompson calls 'the chiliasm of the defeated and the hopeless'.[12] An analysis of religion as ideology thus yields an unholy trinity: the Church Terrorist, the Church Populist and the Church Opiate.

This analysis can, it seems, be easily adapted to an examination of Joyce and Catholicism: the sermon of *A Portrait* is indoctrination, Stephen's sense of loneliness at the end of *A Portrait* and at the beginning of *Ulysses* is set against the community offered by Catholicism, and when Bloom passes through Mass in 'The Lotus-

Eaters' he and Joyce both regard religion as an opiate. However easily this mode of analysis can be adapted to Joyce it does not exhaust the possibilities of Catholicism in Joyce's work. In part this is because it fails to account for the internationalist aspects of Catholicism as a religion which transcended States and Nations. More importantly, however, viewing Catholicism as a religious ideology runs into difficulties on the issue of it being shared by exploited and exploiter. In this case religion was not shared. During most of this period, as Miller has pointed out, the Catholic Church was not an institution of the British State but was pitched between that State and the Irish Nation in such a way that it could often wield direct political (rather than ideological) power.[13] As a consequence of this position the Church was both subversive of the ideology of the British State and a source of political cohesion in the Irish Nation. For it to be contained by an ideological analysis would require that we ignore these ambivalences, retreat from the specifics of both Irish and international Catholicism, and regard Catholicism once again as simply a variant on Christianity in decline. To do this would be to put ourselves in the position of seeing a simplistic significance in the coincidence 'that in the year of Joyce's *hegira* (1904), Max Weber commenced publication of *The Protestant Ethic and the Spirit of Capitalism*',[14] and thereby reduce the complexities and specifities of Catholicism to undifferentiated religion.

Catholicism considered as ideology is not then particularised enough. There is a second shortcoming which relates to the concept of ideology itself: it can account for the operation of determinants upon the individual, the interpellation of the subject,[15] but what it cannot do is to account for the self-determined actions of the individual. Individual cognition, under the dispensation of ideology, is always turned into misrecognition, and Catholicism, in this analysis, becomes again just the entangling nets of a society. Ideological analysis can thus, like secular liberal criticism, explain only one of our two phrases. 'I am a servant' is now rendered as resigned recognition of the impossibility of ever flying by (i.e. escaping) those nets. Once again the Joycean dialectic of Catholicism is reduced to a negative polarity. Stephen's phrase 'flying by' is ambivalent referring to both denial (escape) and assent ('flying by' = 'flying with', i.e. using the nets as wings).[16]

Where secular criticism released Joyce into the realm of an infinite relativity by defining his attitude to Catholicism in negative terms (I will not serve), ideological analysis results in a view of Joyce as being so determined by Catholicism that he has not even the freedom of denial. In the one case the nets are all too easily escaped, in the other they are impossible to escape. In both instances 'flying by' is reduced to the possibility or impossibility of escape and denial, and the sense of assent is lost. In neither instance do we get any sense of Catholicism as a rich and complex part of Joyce's mind and work.

I began this chapter by stating that Joyce had a dialectical attitude towards Catholicism and I have been concerned so far both to test various forms of criticism against that dialectic and to use those criticisms to tease out the features of that dialectic as compacted into two phrases. If these phrases represent a true dialectic than every possibility at one pole must be answered by its opposite at the other pole. Each mode of analysis that I have so far considered has broken at a point where dialectical interaction ceases when each type of criticism moves inevitably to one pole or the other. This has always been at the point of denial or negation. No form of criticism has yet been able to move beyond this to its opposite of assent and affirmation. The failing of previous approaches to the question of Joyce and Catholicism is that they have not been able to comprehend the possibility that an individual can recognise the limits of a particular system and yet find freedom within those limits by assenting to that system. However, the dialectical logic of Joyce's work requires that Stephen's Non serviam will always be answered by Molly's Yes. It may help to clarify matters if at this point I list the features we have uncovered grouped under Stephen's two phrases.

I will not serve	I am a servant
secularity	religion
intellectual determinants	social determinants
free will	indoctrination
loneliness	community
understanding	consolation
denial	assent
freedom	faith

I am conscious that the assertion that Joyce assented to Catholicism is unsubstantiated except by the necessity of having assent to balance denial. In the remainder of this chapter I propose to outline the object and form of Joyce's assent but there are three points that I wish to make here as a form of temporary substantiation.

The first has to do with Joyce's economy; his insistence on making full use of all the materials he had to hand. The complexity of his work is founded on this economy, the idea that every element had to function as fully as possible. *Finnegans Wake* carries this economy to its furthest extent by making each word serve as several words and by making one language function as though it were several. To say that Joyce in some way assented to Catholicism is in line with this economy; it is simply the most parsimonious explanation of the centrality of Catholicism in Joyce's work. The thing itself, in other words, is its own explanation obviating the need to reconstruct it as a system of metaphors, or as an imposed centre of power in order to understand it. Assent allows us to see Joyce and Catholicism with nothing intermediate. Denial, the other and necessary pole of the dialectic, as a critical touchstone, tends to place Joyce outside Catholicism and serves thereby either to reduce or to mystify it. If we say that Joyce assented to Catholicism we must see him within Catholicism as a mode of experience and Catholicism as a mode of consciousness. This means that he and his work (including his denials) can best be understood in Catholic terms and by means of Catholic concepts.

The second point is best made by Thomas McGreevy:

> The deep-rooted Catholicism of *Ulysses* was what most upset the pastiche Catholicism of many fashionable critics in England. The enthusiastic converts who discover the surface beauties of Catholicism . . . tend always to be shocked by the more profound 'regular' Catholicism of Ireland.[17]

McGreevy's comments, chauvinistic and almost bigotted, are meant to shock; they stand now, as they did in 1929, as a rebuff equally to those who would render Joyce's Catholicism as a pleasing set of metaphors or who would suggest that Catholicism was simply something that Joyce had denied and escaped from. McGreevy's comments have a more than salutary value, however. If Joyce did not actually supervise each essay in *Our Exagmination*, the collection does have his *nihil obstat* in that he was 'more or less directing [the writers] what line of research to follow'.[18] Joyce is thus, even if at one remove, pointing his critics to the specific reality of Irish Catholicism as a means of understanding his work.

The final point concerns the placing of the phrase 'I am a servant' in *Ulysses*. It comes during Stephen's conversation with Haines, just after Stephen has described himself as a 'horrible example of free thought' to which Haines naively replies:

> After all I should think you are able to free yourself. You are your own master it seems to me. (*U*, p. 17)

'Free thought' is usually taken to mean rationalist and secularist, and as such contradicts Stephen's 'I am a servant'. However, the two phrases play off each other. Free thought may not necessarily refer to secular rationalism — it can equally mean free will and would then suggest that Stephen, having freed his thought, has yet remained in service by choice. (Since free thought is associated with his conversation with Haines about belief in God we need not concern ourselves here with the consequences of that freedom for Stephen's remarks on the British Empire and Ireland.) These ambiguities reveal a mode of thought that the Englishman Haines is unable to understand:

> Either you believe or you don't, isn't it? Personally I couldn't stomach the idea of a personal God. (*U*, p. 17)[19]

Similar ambiguities also colour Stephen's earlier conversation with Cranly. 'I will not serve' is *not* the complete denial it appears to be, qualified as it is by the phrase 'that in which I no longer believe'. So even when Stephen is making what received wisdom claims as his credo he cannot escape ambivalence. His refusal to serve is conditional on not believing but he appears to be unable to make a plain statement of disbelief. When Cranly challenges him: 'if you feel sure our religion is false' Stephen immediately responds: 'I am not at all sure of it', and when Cranly appears satisfied Stephen is 'struck by his tone of closure [and] reopens[s] the discussion at once.' (*AP*, p. 247) Both conversations are also marked by emotion; Stephen's pure intellect is touched by Cranly's 'elder's affection' (*AP*, p. 251) and even by his sense that the hapless Haines is 'not all unkind', (*U*, p. 17). The ambivalences here, and the rare intrusion of emotion on the intellect of Stephen, are controlled by Joyce's dialectical fear of closure. This must be kept in mind while considering the object and forms of Joyce's assent.

4. *Catholicism: Ireland . . . the Universe.*

To elaborate the form of Joyce's assent to Catholicism we must encounter the reality of the object of that assent, the 'holy Roman catholic and apostolic church' in all its variousness and complexity. The received view of the Irish Catholic Church at this period is that it was 'too authoritarian, too apt to induce fatalism in the devout, too ready to divert scant economic resources into unnecessary church building . . . on the whole repressive'.[20] George Moore, in his story 'Homesickness', presents the Irish 'accepting the priest's opinion without question. And their pathetic submission was the submission of a primitive people clinging to religious authority'.[21]

This is the image of the Irish as, in Simon Dedalus' words, 'a priestridden Godforsaken race!' (*AP*, p. 39). In turn, in this view, the Irish Church itself is in thrall to the central authority of Rome which operates in absolutist terms.

Doctrinally, that is in its own absolutist terms, there are 'four marks by which we may know her: she is One — she is Holy — she is catholic — she is Apostolic.' The Church is united in belief and practices, offers access to the transcendant, 'subsists in all ages, teaches all nations', and claims an unbroken succession going back to the time of Christ.[22] The Church is, that is to say, a totality incorporating human history and offering complete integration to humanity. It should go without saying that the Church could also lay claim to a long intellectual history. In temporal, but still broad terms doctrine underpinned the structure of the Church. This structure, although nominally hierarchical, is diffuse. Each part of the Church is (in doctrinal terms has to be) whole in itself and capable of offering teaching, communion and access to transcendance (*cf* Thompson's indoctrination, community and chiliasm). The Church, despite its hierarchies, is not one concentrated centre and a widespread periphery or series of peripheries; it is rather a series of centres all relative to each other. 'Ireland, Europe, the World, the Universe' (*AP*, pp. 15–16), to take the young Stephen's effort at locating himself, are all centres. Because each part of the Church, no matter where it is located and regardless of the size of its domains, can and must claim access to the central doctrines the Church is a decentred totality. On its own terms the Church provides dizzying and shifting perspectives of time and space, through the Communion of Saints which links the living and the dead; it provides the comfort of an identity, which can be predicated both on the qualities of the local Church and on the qualities of the Universal Church; and it provides a measure of the worth of each individual through the concept of free will and because it teaches that each individual soul is both unique and contains within itself, in the Augustinian categories of memory, will and understanding, an image of the Trinity. The Church is a rich and complex object simply to deny.

In a broad historical perspective the Church contemporary with Joyce appears at first to be somewhat less difficult to deny. Throughout the nineteenth and into the beginning of the twentieth century the Church as a whole faced a series of crises and challenges from the increasingly powerful secular movements. The aftermath of the French Revolution brought in a series of challenges to the Church's temporal power.[23] These challenges took various forms and resulted in a series of encyclicals and other pronouncements directed at each source of crisis. These sources were summarised by Pius IX, 'the prisoner in the Vatican', in his 'Syllabus of Errors' (1864) in which he gives guidance and rulings on the relations between the Church and the State, on rationalism and on socialism among other things. In 1891 'Rerum Novarum' ('The Condition of Labour') provided the first documentation of the Church's social teachings, teachings restated and reformulated forty years later in 'Quadregisimo Anno' (On Reconstructing the Social Order). In between came further warnings about the dangers of socialism, 'Graves de Communi' (1901 – 'Christian Democracy'), and 'Pascendi Dominici Gregis' (1907) on the internal challenge of theological modernism.[24]

As David Miller has pointed out the Irish Church was not immune to the effects of these challenges:

> Churchmen were keenly aware . . . of the difficulties of the Catholic Church in various continental countries, where substantial segments of the working classes were abstaining from their religious duties and where the State, in several cases, was depriving the Church of more and more of her privileges.[25]

The Irish hierarchy's decisions on how it conducted its relations with both State and Nation had to be taken in the light of this broader, crisis-ridden context. This was especially so after the mid-nineteenth century when the ultramontanist party led by Archbishop (later Cardinal) Cullen became dominant.[26] However, the actuality of the Church's difficulty on the Continent was felt in different ways by the Irish Church. Precisely because of its ambivalent placing between the State and the Nation its struggle was not to retain power and privileges but to gain and consolidate them. In order to do this it had to negotiate with the State but could not afford to compromise itself for fear of losing the immaterial but important privileges it held from the Nation. As Miller puts it:

> The Church therefore continued to seek the proximate realisation of her social ideals and to protect and extend her vital interests primarily through her relations with the State, though the course of those relations would inevitably have important consequences for her relations with the Nation as well.[27]

As to the specific challenges of modernism from within and socialism from without, these too had to be dealt with on the Irish Church's own terms. Modernism in the form of various young intellectuals (lay and clerical) such as the journalist W. P. Ryan, the priest and novelist Gerald O'Donovan, and Walter MacDonald, professor of theology at Maynooth, was successfully if ironically stifled. The irony lies in the Irish Church's concern with education and the fact that it was people like these (and, for that matter Joyce) who were among the first generations of what might be called indigenous Irish Catholic intellectuals; Irish Catholicism was not intellectually rich enough to be able to squander such talents.[28]

Socialism which had been a worry to the Irish Church from the mid-nineteenth century was also successfully handled. Since the socialist challenge was to do with the Church's external relations, rather than its internal ones as was the case with modernism, it was not as easy to stifle. However, by the time Irish socialism found its ablest theoretician in James Connolly the Irish Church was so powerful within the Nation to which, rather than the State, Connolly was appealing, that he had to consider the 'distinctive position of the Catholic Church as the symbol of an oppressed nationality'. The Church's power in this instance derives from its very lack of institutionalised power, from, that is, its claim to be a part of the Nation. Consequently, Connolly had to recognise that to be a Catholic was to be, in some unresolved way, rebellious. 'Any attempt to resolve this led Connolly into a consideration of the degree of compatibility between Socialist and Catholic claims'.[29] Connolly's major text on this issue is *Labour, Nationality and Religion* (1910) in which, in response to Father Kane's Lenten Discourses in Gardiner Street Church, Connolly attempts to set the Church to rights rather than to overthrow it, showing himself to be as much a modernist as a socialist. Summing up Connolly's views on Catholicism in Ireland Bernard Ransom has stated:

> He regarded Irish adherence to Catholicity . . . as more than an episode in Church history or religious development. He saw it as an important moment in the development of a unique Irish consciousness, of the *idea* of Irish nationality. To be specific, Connolly stressed the importance of Catholicity as a value system opposed to the Protestant ethic of Ireland's English overlords and to the nascent ideals of capitalism implicit in the Protestant Reformation itself.[30]

The Irish Church could thus enforce its opinions and teachings either by direct force or by the indirect pressure available to it as an inescapable fact of Irish experience. In this way of dealing with crises it also showed its own individual and independent character despite its ultramontanist tendencies. Indeed, in spite of these tendencies, the Irish Church was helped by Rome's difficulties to maintain its independence. It was not unknown for the Irish bishops, both before and after Cullen's ascendancy, to flout Papal rescripts when it appeared to them that the Irish situation warranted it. In regard to both the British State and the Vatican, as Oliver MacDonagh has noted, the Irish Church displayed a mixture of conformity and defiance;[31] in doing so *vis a vis* Rome, however, the Irish Church was also turning this ambivalence inwards because of the Church's structure.

The ambivalence of the Irish Church is nowhere more marked than in its major project during Joyce's childhood and young manhood, its attempts to establish *de jure* denominational education in Ireland and to found a Catholic University. In pursuing this aim the Church was following its own supranational interests as well as attending to the needs of Ireland. However, the means by which the aim was pursued were controlled by national considerations; it was thus to 'the vital interests of his own institution, the *Irish* Catholic Church' that Archbishop Walsh attended even when this meant jeopardising English Catholic interests.[32] This ambivalence was then carried even further when the project began to be successful; as I noted above, many Irish Catholic intellectuals, precisely those which this education system was, presumably, designed to produce, were suppressed by the Church. It is not sufficient to attribute this to the Church's repressiveness however. We should ask instead why the Church behaved in this way and here again we return to the correspondence between Catholicism and Irishness which Connolly encountered. We must recognise that many of the qualities of the Irish Church were derived not from Catholicism *per se* but from the fact that Catholicism was the medium through which Irishness was often expressed. Terence Brown has noted that the Irish Church was a national Church in that it drew its bishops from its priests and its priests from its people. Those priests were trained at Maynooth and if the education they received there was anti-intellectual and sexually prudish this was a confirmation of their Irish rural values rather than indoctrination into new values.[33] In these introspective circumstances the wonder is not that the Church was often repressive but that it persisted in its efforts to establish a full Catholic education system for the laity which produced troublesome intellectuals, not the least of whom was Joyce. In Maynooth and the proposed Catholic University therefore the Church fostered both conformity and defiance.

Here we need to turn again to the fact of the Irish Church as part of an international body. In this too, the Irish Church satisfied the needs of Ireland while pursuing its own ends. The *Imperium Romanorum* provided a means by which early twentieth century

Irish nationalism could satisfy its internationalist tendencies. The Irish Church functioned that is, alongside the nation overseas, as a counterweight to the British Empire.[34] This can be understood in relation to education if we consider that, as Seamus Deane has said, 'Catholicism granted [Joyce] an awareness of the European tradition from which he was in other respects separated'.[35] In other words, because of its ambivalence, the Church could provide access to intellectual traditions which could go far beyond what was available to its own priests but which were traditions to which the Church could nonetheless lay claim. It was by virtue of those intellectual traditions that the Church, despite its many forms and its numerous contradictions and ambivalences, could still sustain itself as an integrated totality. It is in the light of this complexity and integrity that we must judge Joyce's attitudes towards Catholicism.

In a recent and important essay Richard Kearney has stated that 'We [the Irish] must reclaim the idea of ourselves' and, surveying a collection of essays designed to do so, suggests that the Irish mind shows that 'meaning is not only determined by a logic that centralises and censors but also by a logic which disseminates' and that 'in contradistinction to the orthodox dualist logic of *either/or*, the Irish mind may be seen to favour a more dialectical logic of *both/and*'[36] (cf Haines' 'Either you believe or you don't, isn't it'). Irish Catholicism is, it seems to me, one of the most important forms by which this dialectical tendency is both expressed and reinforced. The works of Joyce are another.

5. *Faith and Freedom*

It has been my purpose to show the limitations of previous approaches to the issue of Joyce and Catholicism and to suggest some of the complexity of Catholicism in the belief that this would indicate that Joyce had to give some assent to Catholicism if for no other reason than that it was incontrovertibly present as a central fact of Irish experience. At the other extreme it has to be assented to because it provides an epistemology which can set that local experience in the context of a totality. My remaining purpose is to show a few (a very few) of the marks of that assent in Joyce's work, to show, that is, the ways in which 'I will not serve' interacts with 'I am a servant'.

The Joycean Non serviam is located in a number of places, most notably perhaps in the concept of exile. This can be variously glossed and is usually considered in terms of escape, flight and denial, with the unsuccessful exile at the end of *A Portrait* being attributed to Stephen's unpreparedness. This leads to the return of *Ulysses* and the sense that this time exile will be successful. This secular glossing of exile as escape and denial sets Joyce apart from Ireland and from Catholicism with some curious consequences for his literary and other relations. M. P. Hederman, for example takes the exilic Joyce to extremes when he states that a consideration of Joyce as 'thinker' 'must be on his own terms . . . [because he] appropriated [outside] influences in a way that precludes the possibility of examining their interaction in terms of cause and effect'.[37] The effect of this is to create a Joyce who is not just deracinated and epistemologically self-sufficient, but also beyond criticism; it defers to Joyce in such a way as to disable criticism. Similarly, W. J. McCormack, for the purposes of creating a Joyce who will fit the category of European modernism, accepts the exilic Joyce and notes the 'dislocation of Yeats and Joyce from Irish chronology', a dislocation which is redressed by 'their place in European literature. To move from a discussion of Charles Lever to the work of Joyce . . . is to cross seismic lines of demarcation'.[38] This is so because, according to McCormack, 'what distinguishes the Protestant from the Catholic in cultural terms is his relation with the past, his *possession* of a history'.[39] A general answer to both Hederman and McCormack requires that we acknowledge that the human condition is, in Catholic terms, one of exile (we are all 'the poor *banished* children of Eve'). Given this perspective, the Joycean exile is not just a separation but also an experience shared with humanity. Even in exile Joyce is not self-sufficient; once this point is taken we are better placed to provide specific answers to the points raised by Hederman and McCormack.

Taking Hederman first we can place Joyce in relation to particular philosophical traditions without in any way being reductive or imposing closure on Joyce's works. Aquinas, for example, did not come naturally to Joyce's mind but rather *via* Leo XIII who gave impetus to a groundswell in favour of Thomism which had started during the course of the nineteenth century.[40] The importance of this point is that it enables us to uncover references to Aquinas in places other than the carefully controlled context of the aesthetic theory of *A Portrait*; Aquinas, that is, as part of an intellectual background which Joyce shared with others rather than as the personal property of Stephen. Thus, when Cranly questions the limits of Stephen's freedom their conversation turns first of all to property rights (*AP*, p. 250) which is rather surprising unless we remember that the issue had been recently addressed in *Rerum Novarum* which had restated Catholic views on the inviolability of private ownership and had, furthermore, quoted Aquinas on the right uses of money and property. From this we might move to the same document's quotations from Aquinas on the absolute nature of paternal authority.[41] This in its turn might cause us to consider how Joyce and Aquinas squared this concept of paternal authority with, on the one hand the mystical nature of paternity — in which both were interested, and on the other hand with their shared sense of the autonomy of the individual, an idea which Aquinas propounded and which Joyce derived from Aquinas, J. S. Mill and Benjamin Tucker.[42] My point here is not that a causal chain links Joyce's thoughts on freedom with his thoughts on property and on paternity but rather that his thinking on all these issues, *contra* Hederman, exists within an intellectual framework available to Joyce within his historical moment. The ramifications of Joyce's texts do not form a closed circuit; they exist as bridges between the texts and the world. Criticism, as a pontificial exercise, should illustrate that it is possible to make connections both between the components of the text and between the text and the world in which it is situated. The connections adumbrated above function as such a link between the text and its worldly moment and have the further advantage, for our present purposes, of showing that the roots of Joyce's concept of freedom are in Catholicism.

We can deal with McCormack's point about the dislocation of Joyce from Irish culture and history in a similar way by noting that while the progression from Lever to Joyce is strange, the progression from Lever to George Moore to Joyce is much less so. If we overlook Catholicism we must overlook the central part it has to play in the relationship between Moore and Joyce, a relationship which once again places Joyce within a history which is both Irish and Catholic. Moore can be seen as a type for Joyce; thus his *Confessions of a Young Man* prefigures *A Portrait, The Untilled Field* prefigures *Dubliners* (and precludes the need for Joyce's planned sequel *Provincials*) and Moore's record of his failure to write the 'national epic' (*U*, p. 158) *Hail and Farewell* is answered by Joyce's successful attempt in *Ulysses*. It was in *Hail and Farewell* that Moore had made a fool of himself by his attempts to argue that 'Catholicism is an intellectual desert' which, if nothing else did, would have helped to prompt Joyce to assent to the intellectual richness of Catholicism.[43] There are a number of places where Joyce can only be answering Moore directly in a kind of covert debate about Catholicism. Thus in *A Portrait* when Cranly asks if Stephen will become a Protestant the reply is:

I said that I had lost the faith . . . but not that I had lost self-respect. What kind of liberation would that be to forsake an absurdity which is logical and coherent and to embrace one which is illogical and incoherent? (*AP*, p. 248.)

This is both a response to Moore's public declaration of Protestantism in 1903 (his letter to the *Irish Times* is quoted in *H & F*, p. 670) and an adaptation of Moore's question about how 'something that seemed utterly absurd [Newman's description of the balance of sin against human suffering] could be said to be logical' (*H&F*, p. 391). Finally in regard to Moore we must also consider the word 'liberation' in Stephen's comments to Cranly. As I have noted the gap between 'I will not serve' and 'I am a servant' cannot be comprehended by a secular criticism which must fail to take account of faith. The challenge which Joyce really takes up from Moore is thus how to achieve freedom while assenting to the power of those dogmas which, according to Moore, 'draw a circle round the mind' and stifle the creative will (*H&F*, p. 384). Joyce's work refutes Moore's comments on Catholicism not by displaying a belief in dogma but by assenting to Catholic doctrine in a way that reveals Joyce's faith in Catholicism as a mode of consciousness and as an epistemology of human (especially Irish) experience. Faith and freedom then are the extreme forms of assent and denial but neither is possible to Joyce because for him they exist in a dialectical relationship, a relationship what is more in which all the controlling terms are Catholic.

This is evident if we turn to that moment which is usually taken as the source of the Joycean Non serviam, the Christmas dinner in *A Portrait*. Here we have what is regarded as the moment in which the young Stephen sees the distinction between the priestridden and the free. The first thing to be said is that Joyce has tipped the scales against the Catholic Church by placing it in the position of Parnell's betrayer. This is historically inaccurate[44] but I would suggest deliberately so in order to have clear lines of argument, at least initially. What Joyce really knew about the historical record is suggested by Simon Dedalus' question 'Were we to desert him at the bidding of the English people?' (*AP*, p. 33) which question can only arise from a knowledge that it was in England that the anti-Parnellite movement began. Regardless of these historical niceties this scene is taken as a first instance for Stephen of the repressiveness of the Irish Church and his question to himself, 'Who was right then?' (*AP* , p. 37) usually receives the answer: the anti-clerical faction. This answer is not as straightforward as it might appear, however.

The scene begins just after an unspecified 'they' have just come home although we assume that it refers to Simon Dedalus, John Casey and Stephen Dedalus having come in from a walk. Simon's first words to Dante Riordan are affable: 'You didn't stir out at all, Mrs Riordan?' but receive a curiously hostile answer: 'Dante frowned and said shortly: —No.' (*AP*, p. 28). The interchange is only comprehensible if we accept that Simon's question is in fact provocative. What he is really asking this religiose woman is 'Have you been to Mass today?'. Christmas is, in cultural terms, probably the most important Holy Day of Obligation in the calender (although ranking behind Easter, Pentecost and Epiphany in religious terms)[45] so Dante's answer is surprising to the reader but, it seems, not to Simon. If Dante has not been to Mass (thereby committing a mortal sin) there is a strong probability that the Dedalus family, including Simon and also John Casey, have been since this is a special Christmas for Stephen. Simon certainly appears to be referring to a recent event when he says 'That was a good answer our friend made to the canon' and both he and Casey, we must assume, have been in church recently enough to have been offended by politics from the pulpit. Furthermore, if we accept that Dante has not been to Mass then we must ask, to whom is Simon's sung couplet ('O, come all you Roman Catholics/That never went to Mass.') addressed? The obvious target is John Casey who has just defended himself against Dante's charge of being a renegade Catholic. In the standard reading this is taken to be hypocritical and makes the couplet a joke between friends. However, Casey's defence of himself:

> I am a catholic as my father was and his father before him and his father before him again when we gave up our lives rather than sell our faith. (*AP*, p. 36)

has in its implicit equation of Irish experience and Catholicism an air of greater dignity than anything the increasingly hysterical and bigotted Dante has to say. All of this serves to introduce an air of ambivalence into the argument which increases the complexity of Stephen's questions. If the pro-Parnell, anti-clerical faction are seen by Stephen as practicing catholics, and if Dante who is anti-Parnellite and pro-clerical is seen by Stephen not practicing the issue becomes for him and for the reader very much more complex. Is Dante, the 'spoiled nun . . . [who] had come out of the convent . . . when her brother got the money from the savages. . .' (*AP*, p. 36), really concerned about religion and politics or are we meant to take a point about repression from the details here?

Either way Stephen is presented with a very much more ambivalent set of data than is usually assumed. In this reading those who deny God and Catholicism nevertheless assent to them (however hypocritically); while Dante, who is supposed to assent appears to deny. Stephen is not, therefore, faced with a simple choice between politics and religion, but has, like Connolly, to confront their symbiosis in Irish experience. The path that Stephen will follow from this point is not as straightforward as is usually assumed but this ambivalence in the Christmas dinner scene serves to ground his later ambition 'to forge . . . the uncreated conscience of my race' (*AP*, p. 257) in the circumstances of his own family background. Without the ambivalence of this scene the members of his family would be divided into the vigorously political and the fervently religious and would thus be separate from the more usual experience of Joyce's Dubliners for whom the mixture of politics and religion results in precisely that confused quietism which necessitates the creation of a conscience.

Stephen's later ambition is, of course, grounded in the social realities of *Dubliners*. The keyword attached to these stories is 'paralysis' about which Joyce is more precise in *Stephen Hero* when he refers to 'hemiplegia of the will'.[46] What Joyce attends to in *Dubliners*, despite his exposition of the grimness of Dublin's social reality, is the moral condition of the citizens. The image of the Trinity they present is an imperfect one; their wills are paralysed, their understanding is imperfect and, as 'Ivy Day in the Committee Room' shows, their memory is inexact. Consequently, they can be neither faithful nor free. Their social condition may be understood in doctrinal terms: their moral condition is imperfect and their wills, their abilities as human agents, remain frozen. They form an attrite rather than a contrite community, ruled by fear rather than love. The necessity of discussing this in theological terms stems from the precision of 'hemiplegia of the will', in which one of the components of the human reflection of the Trinity is affected by a physical pathology, and moves towards the forging of the uncreated conscience. This latter term is also precise because it refers not to the creation of a moral sense but to the reshaping of an already given knowledge.

For two obvious reasons Stephen at the end of *A Portrait* is unable to fulfil the Joycean project. Firstly he is trying to move towards denial of and separation from both Ireland and Catholicism. Because of this he is unable to forge a conscience because it involves, as Robert Boyle has pointed out, a knowing with,[47] a shared knowledge. The necessary pattern that is thus established is that Stephen must retreat from denial and separation towards assent and community. For him to do so Joyce has to show the reactivated will which involves a recasting of the Trinity in the form of Stephen, Bloom and Molly. This, of course, has been said before but we need to set it back in the context of Catholicism rather than metaphor to understand both how radical it is and how much it assents to Catholic doctrine.

Leo XIII had, in *Divinum Illud* (1897), restated the centrality of the mystery of the Trinity to Catholicism. In doing so he pronounced upon the necessary indivisibility of the Trinity and upon how certain qualities could nonetheless, be appropriated, as Aquinas put it, to each person of the Trinity: thus power to the Father, wisdom to the Son and love to the Holy Ghost who was also to be acknowledged as the Incarnating principle.[48] Each of these qualities can be aligned with its human equivalent: power with will, wisdom with understanding and, therefore, love and the incarnating principle with memory. To appropriate wisdom and understanding to Stephen is reasonably straightforward; these are the qualities he must gain but his epistemology must be *with* others rather than just of others, it must be an epistemology of communion and assent if the Joycean project of conscience is to succeed. Molly's role as the Holy Ghost can also be understood — her soliloquy is after all in large part a memory of love and, closing *Ulysses* with the word of assent, leads directly to the decentred and Pentecostal language of *Finnegans Wake*. Joyce's radicalism here (predating Catholic orthodoxy by, shall we say, a century) is to insist on a feminine principle as part of the Trinity rather than as merely the vessel for the power of the Trinity. (The untouched Gerty McDowell rather than Molly is Joyce's satire on Irish hyperdulia.) What Joyce does with Bloom is most radical for in Bloom he recasts the power of the Father as a passive rather than an active quality, changing it from the ability to create to the ability to withstand. In doing this he equates Bloom with the contemporary Church which, lacking temporal power on its own account had to withstand the pressures of history rather than shape them. He also equates Bloom with the God, not of creation but of the period after creation. God having created humanity with free will, i.e. separate from his own, has then to withstand and assent to the activity of that creation regardless of whether it tends towards assent or denial. Bloom is thus a scapegoat. The increased freedom and vitality in *Ulysses* as compared to *Dubliners* is achieved by rendering Bloom as a God whose power is passive, whose ability to act is secondary to the will of his creation.

What Joyce saw in Catholicism was a totality, one which if it had to live up to its name, could not allow for the existence of others outside itself. This led to the decentred structure of the Church which provided Joyce with a model of how Ireland, an obviously peripheral country, could function as a centre. The refusal of the Catholic Church to allow for otherness also meant that it had to subsume contradictions through an integrating dialectic. Given this total integration the exercise of human will, whether towards assent or denial, becomes paramount. For this reason the Catholic epistemology is redirected from God towards humanity. This is not at all the same as saying that Catholicism in Joyce is a set of metaphors for the human condition; it is instead a real knowledge of the experience and consciousness of (Irish) humanity in which the dialectical materials of Catholicism are 'transaccidentated'.[49] If Joyce were simply producing metaphors from Catholicism he would be removing its substance, instead of which he keeps the question of substance in abeyance, and concentrates on the accidental (material and historical) forms of the dialectic to produce a Catholic reading of the world of his social, political and religious experience. In *Finnegans Wake* this results in a new form of communion in the figure of Hosty ('no slouch of a name') whose first appearance is as Vico's revolting plebian (*FW*, pp. 40–1)[50] but who re-appears to sing 'The Ballad of Persse O'Reilly' (the *Wake* in miniature, *FW*, pp. 44–7) and to impersonate Joyce (*FW*, p. 48) thus subsuming both the artist and the rabblement in a communal figure.

This materialisation of the Catholic epistemology is Joyce's response to a particular historical moment, usually referred to as the moment of modernism. And here we must return to our beginning because modernism is a concept which is grounded in the responses of a secular criticism to what it perceived as the fragmentation of its world and the arrival of new modes of consciousness. Joyce is understood by this criticism and its successors as a modernist. As Raymond Williams says:

> Joyce's originality . . . is a necesary innovation if this way of seeing — fragmentary, miscellaneous, isolated — is to be actualised on the senses in a new structure of language.[51]

To conjoin Joyce and Catholicism is to challenge this received category of modernism because, it seems to me, Joyce was not just aware of fragmentation and isolation, he was also aware of the integration and collectivity offered by the Catholic Church. When T. S. Eliot refers to Joyce using myth to bring order to the chaos of the contemporary world[52] Eliot is overlooking the fact of Catholicism. This use of myth is true of Eliot's own work in which he had to establish what Said has called affiliative relations as a kind of 'conpensatory order' for an order which had failed and passed away.[53] The movement from filiation to affiliation is central to Said's reading of modernism and it sums up the idea of modernism as the attempt to re-invest values in myths which had lost their power in order to make sense of the world. Said refers to Joyce in this connection but this whole sense of Joyce as modernist overlooks the fact that Catholicism still allowed for the possibility of filiation since it was not an order which had failed. Rather it was an order which answered to the affective and experiential needs for integration and community and which did so both in the form of a Church possessing a universal grandeur and in the form of a local Church which had moulded itself to the shape of Irish experience.

Whatever Joyce's own beliefs (and these have *not* been under question) his attitude to Catholicism must be seen as filiative even if this (especially if this?) necessitates a reassessment of Joyce as literary modernist, or even a reassessment of literary modernism. We cannot ignore the fact of Catholicism as a still functioning part of Joyce's native experience and consciousness which provided him with an epistemology by which he could comprehend the world as an integrity and negotiate between the opposites of freedom and faith, negation and affirmation, isolation and community, and denial and assent.

FRANCIS STUART AND RELIGION: SHARING THE LEPER'S LAIR

ANNE McCARTNEY

> And finally I prayed, though not as bid:
> 'Lord, make me clean!'
> But: 'Come and share with me my leper lair,
> That's if you dare.'
> And so he did.[1]

Throughout Francis Stuart's long literary career, religion has played an important part in his novels, both as a major theme and as the kernel of his aesthetic theory. In his autobiographical novel, *Black List, Section H*,[2] Stuart chronicles his own spiritual quest which led him from his Presbyterian origins, through his conversion to Catholicism on his first marriage, and his obsession with the lives of the mystics, to his own unorthodox brand of religion — a religion which incorporates all the vagaries of experience which go to make up Stuart's view of reality. It is this form of religion, rather than any orthodox theology, which permeates Stuart's work, providing it with its ability to shock, and also ultimately its authority, as any attempt to evaluate Stuart's contribution to literature must necessarily include an understanding of his religious views.

Although Stuart's views on religion have evolved by means of experience and reflection, the underlying dissatisfaction with orthodox religion is apparent in even the earliest novels. *Pigeon Irish*,[3] the first of Stuart's novels to receive critical acclaim, contains within it the embryo of his mature religious outlook. The unity of the physical and the spiritual, which Stuart believes to be the essence of religion, is embodied in his use of the pigeons as metaphor; while the free flight of his intuitive religion is contrasted with the deadening restrictiveness of the established Church in the image of the pigeons flying from the monastic ruins of Glendalough.[4] The narrator of the novel, Frank Allen, who takes a stand against the onslaught of the materialistic and scientific forces threatening to sweep over an Ireland which is the last bastion of spirituality, eventually becomes an archetype of the figure of the outcast so central to Stuart's religious view. Again, an early expression of Stuart's religious beliefs is shown in the nature of Frank's condition, that of 'martyrdom, an inner stripping bare',[5] his refusal to compromise his values despite his defeat and degradation, and the strength and spiritual insight he discovers through his ordeal, all of which point to the redemptive nature of suffering and sacrifice. However, despite this early sowing of the seeds of Francis Stuart's religious viewpoint, and the fact that its shoots are evident in all his pre-war fiction, the plant failed to take root and flourish until fed and nourished by his experiences during the War.

Whether or not Stuart's decision to live and lecture in wartime Germany was the result of a conscious or an unconscious desire for ignominy and rejection is open to question. Writing several decades after the event, Stuart would certainly have us believe that the decision was a conscious one:

> In agreeing, H was turning from the busy street to slink with thieves and petty criminals down dim alleys, leaving the lawful company to which he'd belonged to become, in its eyes, a traitor.[6]

What is beyond dispute however, is the effect the isolation and rejection Stuart experienced as a result of this decision, and his subsequent imprisonment by the French, has had in the development of his work. As Stuart points out, 'it was essential for me as a writer, and perhaps even as a person, to go through what I did go through',[7] and certainly as a result the notion of redemption through suffering, which is hinted at or intuited in the earlier novels, achieves the power and intensity of a felt experience.

In Stuart's first postwar novel, *The Pillar of Cloud,*[8] the protagonist, Dominic Malone, an Irish poet living in Germany just after the war, undergoes much the same initiation into isolation and suffering as Frank Allen in *Pigeon Irish,* but in the later novel the writing has a more convincing edge, due no doubt, as Olivia Manning noted in her review, to its being 'written with a poetic force that comes out of the very core of suffering'.[9] *Redemption,*[10] which deals retrospectively with the end of the war and the Russian invasion of Berlin, although set in Ireland, still retains the intensity of suffering captured in *The Pillar of Cloud,* despite the distance, both spatially and temporally, between the physical suffering of the violence and destruction of the War, and the action of the novel. The main reason for this intensity is that the suffering Stuart is concerned with is not primarily physical suffering, but the inner turmoil experienced by the outcast and humiliated.

Although the hero of *Redemption*, Ezra Arrigho, has returned to the peace and security of a quiet Irish village, he is still haunted by the nightmare of war, and is as a result unable to tolerate the complacent shallowness of the people who surround him. Upsetting this small community with blasphemy and violent fits of despairing anger, Ezra explodes the cosy, protective world which they inhabit, stripping it of its naivety and exposing its mediocrity. It is only when each of the characters has suffered the torment of 'an inner stripping bare', a recognition of themselves as they really are, and can reach out to others for support, that this sharing of a common suffering delivers each of them out of his own torment. it is the inner mental anguish, rather than any external factors, which proves to be the common bond out of which a new sense of fraternity and peace arises, and it is this 'inner anguish' which holds the key to Stuart's religious and aesthetic theories.

However, the force of *The Pillar of Cloud* and *Redemption* arises not merely from the poetic exposition of this basically Christian doctrine of salvation through suffering, but also from the intensity with which it is presented and worked through. A note in Stuart's wartime diary, written at the time when the work which later became *Redemption* was in progress,[11] helps to throw some light on this artistic commitment.

All that is to be done and is worth doing can, for me, only be done well through struggle and work. One's heart and soul must go into it. This is of course above all so with my work. . . This energy comes from communion with the Truth, which we call God.[12]

But for a more thorough understanding of this idea we must turn to one of Stuart's more recent works.

In an essay published on his eighty-fifth birthday, *The Abandoned Snail Shell,*[13] Stuart expounds his philosophy concerning the nature of reality, and the relationship of his religious beliefs and his work to this reality. Stuart first of all questions the commonly held perception of reality as an external, given world, which is distinct and separate from the human consciousness which perceives it. Exploring the realm of scientific knowledge, which is considered to concern itself closely with the 'real' world, Stuart maintains that the observing consciousness of the scientist is a limiting factor of our knowledge of reality. Scientific discoveries are brought about, not by any fundamental change in an external world, but by an expansion of the consciousness of the scientists involved. What scientists fifty or a hundred years ago would have deemed impossible or unthinkable, their contemporaries today take for granted. Stuart finds support for this theory from Max Planck who initiated the quantum theory of physics.

When the pioneer in science sends forth the groping fingers of his thoughts he must have a vivid intuitive imagination, for new ideas are not generated by deduction, but by an artistically-created imagination. . .[14]

What emerges from this hypothesis is the ultimate subjectivity of all models of reality, limited as they are by their creator's consciousness, but Stuart goes on to attempt to extract 'reality' from the grips of the solipsistic trap in which, on first consideration, he has placed it.

By his contention that 'the consciousness of man . . . is the apical reality of the universe',[15] Stuart seems to be placing a question mark over any certain knowledge of reality, since it is shaped and formed by an individual consciousness in which the imagination plays a major role, as Paul Ricoeur has pointed out:

The mediating role of imagination is forever at work in lived reality. There is no lived reality, no human or social reality which is not already represented in some sense.[16]

It is Stuart's belief however, that 'certain intense experiences, particularly pain', produce a 'marked growth of consciousness'[17] in which an intuitive insight into the heart of reality is attained. 'Reality' therefore for Stuart is a form of psychic energy and it is that which forms the link between his sense of religion and his writing.

This definition of 'reality' as something we catch glimpses of at times when our consciousness is at its most intense, when confronted with birth or death for instance, breaks down the distinction between fact and fiction. For Stuart, 'whatever is imagined intensely enough becomes reality',[18] and in the same way he believes that 'the imaginative writer can invent his facts'.[19] The truth of reality becomes instead the intensity with which it exists, 'the validity with which it is charged'.[20] Like Heidegger, Stuart believes in the cosmic power of poetic language,

. . . some burning impulse impels the novelist to write every sentence he does. It may only be 'X walks down the street', but if you read on, or read before, you'll know that it is a crucial sentence[21]

and this power is ultimately connected to his religious beliefs.

The New Testament holds an important place in Stuart's religion, in that for him, the stories related there hold 'the priceless buried pearl'[22] of truth. For Stuart, Jesus was 'the prototype of the artist'[23] who used parable and metaphor to hide what he wished to convey, because 'directly stated it is unthinkable'.[24] Concentrating on the human element of Jesus, and the sense of failure he must necessarily have felt in order to make the agony of Gethsemane possible, Stuart explores the difficulty of 'reconciling this short earthly life of suffering and humiliation . . . with the concept of the supreme spirit'.[25] Stuart sees the life of Jesus, his earthly failure, crucifixion, and resurrection as a metaphor, not only for the Christian message of salvation through suffering, but also for his view of reality.

Reality, as Stuart envisages it, is a 'seamless garment',[26] the folds of which contain all oppositions, suffering and joy, success and failure, but most of all matter and spirit. In the figure of Jesus, Stuart finds a personification of this all-embracing reality, but more than that, in the Resurrection, he finds an authority for his contention that despite appearances, there is a merging of the physical and the spiritual in everyday existence. In keeping with the Catholic doctrine of Incarnation Stuart argues that following the Resurrection, Christ entered the consciousness of the disciples as 'the indwelling spirit of the risen crucified one',[27] giving rise to the idea of 'a divine presence in the consciousness'.[28] This interpretation not only combines matter and spirit; it also gives credence to Stuart's concept of psychic reality in that it gives a direction and authority to an otherwise seemingly subjective intuition.

When seen in the light of this theory, the sense of religion in *The Pillar of Cloud* and *Redemption* stems not only from the content, but from the force of their artistic execution. The sense of suffering is so strongly and intensely portrayed, it has 'the impact of reality',[29] and given Stuart's notion of reality, this suffering is linked, in an invisible chain, with the suffering of Jesus, Stuart's own suffering, and that of all who have, through pain, humiliation and isolation, reached an awareness of the commonality of all existence. In his exploration of the relationship between religion and art, Daniel Murphy confirms that one aspect of this relationship is the symbolic representation of the phenomenon of immanence:

> . . . the artist is especially empowered, by virtue of the symbolic resources of aesthetic form, . . to comprehend the paradox of immanence, i.e. the reality of God's presence in creation and the need to attest to his presence through its manifestation in the finite, the conditioned and the temporal. The symbols of art, being themselves rooted in space and time, both mediate and affirm the reality of God's immanent presence in time.[30]

In attesting to the sense of joy and fraternity which is achieved through suffering, and by using language as a system of translucent hints rather than transparent designators, in much the way Heidegger developed in *Poetry, Language, Thought*,[31] religion is not merely confined to being the subject matter of Stuart's novels, but is as well an active 'presence' within the novels. In these earlier novels therefore religion is the primary concern, but in Stuart's more recent fiction there has been a subtle shift of emphasis.

In the more recent novels, religion is treated as an integral part of existence, and is thus not magnified and isolated from all other experiences. In *Black List, Section H,* religion is seen as just one strand among the many which constitute the psyche, others in this case being a concern for literature, an obsessive sexual appetite and a love of the race-course. In keeping with Stuart's view of reality, all these strands and more are held together in the novel and interwoven to the point of merging:

> all over Paris, in the sanctum of hotel and private rooms, attics, parked cars, the Bois, in any corner where it was possible, the miracle would be performed according to its various rites and accompanied with all kinds of private incantations.[32]

This fusion allows Stuart to deconstruct the notion that sex, religion and sport are somehow contained in separate watertight compartments, distinct from each other and from everyday existence. Religion therefore is seen to be an integral part of Stuart's psychic reality, not something beyond it, and the religious sense is not restricted to the sacred but is revealed in the most mundane experience when perceived in 'the pure ray shed by the loss of all man-measured value',[33] the pure ray which is cast when the consciousness is at its most intense. For Stuart therefore the religious revelation is not some transcendent vision, but an expansion of the consciousness which highlights the miraculousness of the mundane. *Black List, Section H* emphasises the inward direction of the revelation in that it is an intuitive grasp of something already in the consciousness, such as that which occurs to H in the middle of a Berlin blitz:

> Looking up at the night sky above the park and gazing into the black depths in the pale shoal that ran across it, they glimpsed depths that weren't completely strange to them, and they were conscious of contemplating reflections of abysses in themselves.[34]

In keeping with his belief in a divine presence in the consciousness, Stuart's religion is concerned with an immanent spirituality, and consequently with the religious element of everyday experiences.

One story in the New Testament which Stuart repeatedly refers to and which has become a touchstone for him, is the description of the disciples coming in from fishing on Lake Galilee and finding Christ grilling fish over a wood fire on the beach. In this passage Stuart detects the 'limpid notes of the psyche's song',[35] in that its mystery is contained in its naturalness, in the image of the resurrected Christ performing a simple human act. It is this juxtaposition of the sacred and the profane which Stuart attempts to achieve in his work. In *Memorial*[36] Stuart uses inversion to break down the sacred/profane distinction, the sacred being made profane, and the profane sacred. In the novel the narrator's fascination with his car and the value he placed on it sanctifies this otherwise profane object, as does its eventual conversion into a funeral hearse. For the most part though this inversion is achieved through Stuart's style and technique, in that all that could be profane, the sexual element and the violence, is dignified and sanctified, and all that is normally thought of as sacred is humanised. The effect of this is to shock the reader into questioning the basis of the compartmentalisation of human experiences.

In *Faillandia*,[37] Stuart successfully fuses the sexual and the spiritual by means of a ritual which the two sisters in the novel, Pieta and Kathy, perform following Kathy's wedding ceremony, a ritual which is at one and the same time religious and erotic. Reciting from the Songs of Solomon, Pieta acts as handmaiden to her sister and disrobes her in preparation for the consummation of the union. The biblical feel of the language allows Stuart to introduce eroticism in a way which makes it acceptable and indeed mystical, such that the intensity of the sexual act takes the form of a spiritual ecstasy:

> He was this time more fully aware of her, as a dove in the cleft of the rock, but also as the cleft itself leading through the impenetrable rock — back to the beginning, where in the orgasms he was one with her, one flesh, as it was when creation was still whole, undifferentiated into man and beast, male and female.[38]

It is not Stuart's intention though, to emphasize the spiritual over the physical, but to introduce to the reader's consciousness a situation in which sexual lust and spiritual purity are compatible within a single experience. In this way Stuart hopes to disrupt the complacency of moral preconceptions and give the reader some sense of the complete union of his reality, in which Stuart believes all forms of existence, whether animal or human are one.

> . . . the nerve cells of body and brain once were like bunches of grapes ripening with the others on the common vine stock in a sun that was a star in a great star-cluster. We all belonged together, not yet blighted by isolation.[39]

In placing religion within everyday experiences, Stuart attempts to expose the danger of a mode of thinking which allows it to become the sole property of the Church:

. . . the kind of religiosity in which many of these people seemed to find all they need in the way of an image of God . . . had a mechanical tick. Set to a parochial clock, they went tick-tock, piously recording the do's and don'ts for each day of the week.[40]

The problem with this form of religious outlook is that it restricts the consciousness, in that it leads to a passive acceptance of moral and religious views from an authority whose main concern is power and control rather than truth:

. . . a tribe of witch-doctors in black exerting what they call their God-given authority, encouraging superstition and observances instead of true religion which if it happened to catch on might make them redundant.[41]

For Stuart, true religion comes through an exploration of the consciousness to its deepest levels, an exploration which is assisted by 'certain intense experiences, particularly pain',[42] which expand the consciousness to a degree which changes perception, so that a more illuminating light is cast over certain aspects of experience:

. . . it is the addition of the last few degrees in the expansion of the already almost fully stretched consciousness, that makes it possible to pass a hitherto uncrossable threshold, to think the unthinkable.[43]

The 'unthinkable' for Stuart is the glimpse of reality which occurs once the conscious mind is freed from all restrictive moral and social taboos, and it is the 'unthinkable' which Stuart attempts to evoke in his novels.

Before the 'unthinkable' is achieved, commonly accepted moral and social norms must be undermined, and Stuart does this time and time again in his novels, sometimes by direct shock tactics, but more often by enticing the reader rhetorically to accept what would normally be considered unacceptable. As a result of this the reader's mind becomes more open to a wider form of morality, one in which no distinction is drawn between animal and human passion, for example, or between lust and piety. Restrictive moral codes limit the consciousness in the same way as a passive acceptance of religious dogma, in that they diminish the 'wild wonder'[44] of the untamed world. Stuart believes that passion, like pain, is a necessary prerequisite to achieving a religious outlook, since 'incapable of true, self-forgetting passion, there's no compassion possible'.[45]

In his novels therefore Stuart attempts to break down and undermine normal patterns of thought, and disrupt the comfortable complacency of society. It is for this reason that he believes novelists and poets are the true disciples of Christ, since by refusing to conform to society's view, the writer, like Christ, becomes an outcast. The writer's task is to 'see life through the pure eye of the losers',[45] and in order to be able to do this Stuart believes that the writer must experience life 'in the leper's lair'. It is because of this binding together of art and life that religion plays such a major role in both for Stuart. In seeking the life of the outcast, Stuart's life reflects that of Jesus, and in a small way therefore Stuart considers he has experienced the same sense of suffering as Jesus, and at times, too, has gone beyond this to the peace which is the basis of the Christian message.

Stuart does not underestimate the difficulties involved in the path he has taken,

> Of the men and women who have experienced extremes of inner or mental suffering, there are few records to tell of those who were destroyed by it through insanity, suicide or by escape into criminality.[47]

Nor does he over-emphasize the salvation at the end of the line:

> . . . he may hear a few words. I won't say any astounding vision that may make him optimistic, but something that is not the pure despair he thought was the inevitable end of the crucifixion.[48]

It is this sense of extreme suffering and understated hope which permeates Stuart's recent work and gives it a unique sense of honesty and also its religious fervour. It is also to some extent responsible for its relative lack of popular success since it does not comply with the complete despair of the pessimist, nor does it offer a popular conception of optimism. It is Stuart's belief however that even a small number of readers is sufficient for his purpose:

> . . . if only a handful of readers respond with understanding and delight then a counter-current is set flowing.[49]

In keeping with the example of Jesus, Stuart believes that the writer should not expect acceptance in his lifetime, but should be satisfied to plant the seed of his vision of reality and await its eventual growth:

> . . . imaginative passion is a slow, underground, eroding process and it spreads from mind to mind and heart to heart, until one day . . . unforseen events are suddenly inevitable.[50]

Francis Stuart does not seek instant conversion to his views but a gradual acceptance, and perhaps the steady growth of his literary reputation in recent years is an indication that this is precisely what has happened. Certainly among the literary community of Ireland Stuart has at last gained much acclaim and respect, but it is perhaps a mark of his uniqueness, and a testimony to the strength of his convictions concerning the nature of existence, and the writer's role in society, that although many writers sense the truth of Stuart's theories, very few, if any, would actually go so far as to share his leper's lair.

RECEIVED RELIGION AND SECULAR VISION: MACNEICE AND KAVANAGH

ALAN PEACOCK

(i) *Louis MacNeice: The Horatian Expedient*

Louis MacNeice was never a flag-bearer for any wave of technical innovation in poetry; in his ideas he avoided extremes; and his subject-matter is often everyday, urban and based on observations and impressions which are not obviously outside the scope of anyone's intelligent response to modern life. So, at any rate, ran a very durable notion of his poetic personality: 'very much the poet as an urban man, speaking to urban men'.[1] MacNeice's freedom from conspicuous obscurity and his disinclination to parade his intellect and learning have always ensured a certain readability and popularity; but they have also carried with them the danger that his technique and thought will be underestimated, that his work will be seen as admirable within its limits, full of lively observation, alert to the glamour of the moment — but failing ultimately to engage at a deeper level of significance.

The counter-case has been pursued in the last decade or so, notably in Terence Brown's *Louis MacNeice: Sceptical Vision* (a title properly assertive of the particular kind of philosophical seriousness in MacNeice's work), and in William T. McKinnon's study which is also concerned with MacNeice's philosophical content.[2] It is in fact paradoxical that this Northern Irish, highly educated intellectual with a deep knowledge of the Classical past, a fraught sense of time and transience, and whose work constantly canvasses the possibility of a unifying vision of the experienced particulars of life, should have gained a reputation as the affable chronicler of the English urban scene. Much of this is a matter of literary-historical accident. MacNeice's bracketing with Auden, Spender and Day Lewis, for instance, as a socially aware Thirties Poet, though just from a limited perspective,[3] essentially undersold his range and personality as a poet. His Anglo-Irish background in particular was a blind-spot for much criticism, even though 'having been brought up in the North of Ireland' is the first thing mentioned by MacNeice in an account of his poetic conditioning.[4] It is of course a basic consideration for any assessment of his work; and, for the purpose of the present topic, it is of obvious relevance to note that from his early years as a Church of Ireland rector's son in Carrickfergus he had close contact with Christian practice, liturgy and belief within the particular Ulster context. The phraseology of the Bible was imprinted at an early age on his memory ('My father was a clergyman, and from a very early age I was fascinated by the cadences and imagery of the Bible.'),[5] to surface over the years as an expressive resource in his poetry; and he retained, as an agnostic in adult life, a nostalgic awareness of the ability of a committed Christian like his father to make institutional religion the corner-stone of a rich life.[6] But though institutional Christianity was an important part of his early environment, it was essentially one part of a whole complex of social, cultural and territorial allegiances which he came to question or reject.

Cutting across all this however and providing a special perspective on all such considerations is another dimension in MacNeice's intellectual make-up which has perhaps been underestimated even more than his Irishness, namely his education and career in the Classics. MacNeice spent his student years at Oxford and then his years as a university lecturer in Birmingham and London as a specialist in ancient literature and culture. The Classics form the basis of his intellectual training; and they provide a perspective on modern culture, ideology and belief which is second-nature to him, but which is alien to much of his readership.

It is notable how in his book *Modern Poetry* (1938), where he is essentially championing the work of contemporaries such as Auden, he does this not from a limited, partisan, glibly modern point of view, but from the position that the poetry of that period, with its humanistic focus, is in line with perennially valid criteria. The model invoked on pages two and five is Fifth Century Athens, and the rationale is set out squarely on page one: 'the Greek poet of the fifth century B.C. wrote his poems as a member of a city-state, a member who took as much part as most people in the activities of the community and who shared with that community a certain morality, a certain number of social and aesthetic preferences, a nucleus of religious belief'.[7] Three things are notable here: in the first place, the recognition of consensual religion as a healthy element in society; secondly, the firm placing of this within a range of elements conducing to the balanced society in which the poet can ideally flourish; and thirdly, the effortlessly broad cultural and historical perspective within which MacNeice makes this formulation. Within the time-scales that MacNeice, day-by-day, was thinking in for his Classical interests and responsibilities, great movements of sensibility and thought like Romanticism in the literary field, or Christianity in the religious one, were comparatively late-arrived systems of value and belief among those available to him in the formulation of a personal *credo*. Ancient philosophy, history and literature are immediate to him in an unusual way, natural constituents of his everyday outlook.

In 'Memoranda to Horace', written towards the end of his life, MacNeice notes the special sense of intimate communication he can feel with his temporally remote addressee (and simultaneously how distant he can feel from his own 'far-near' or 'erstwhile' country of Ireland):

> Returned from my far-near country, my erstwhile,
> I wonder how much we are defined by negatives,
> Who have no more seen the Bandusian
> Spring than have you the unreadable Atlantic,
>
> You to whom seraph and gargoyle were meaningless
> And I to whom Roman roads are a tedium
> Preferring the boreens of a country
> Rome never bothered her ponderous head about.
>
> So what have we, Flaccus, in common? If I never
> Boasted a Maecenas, you never summarised
> Life from Rockefeller Centre
> And if you never moved in a Christian framework
>
> I never moved in a pagan. . .[8]

What they do have in common, and what can be communicated between the pre-Christian and Christian era over an historical gap 'reducible only by language' is a sense of a need to find a workable moral and philosophical perspective on historical circumstance:

> It is noisy today as it was when Brutus
> Fell on his sword, yet through wars and rumours
> Of wars I would pitch on the offchance
> My voice to reach you. Yours had already
>
> Crossed the same gap to the north and future,
> Offering no consolation, simply
> Telling me how you had gathered
> Your day, a choice it is mine to emulate.

The simple philosophy to 'seize the day' remains true across two millenia. MacNeice, it may be noted, renders the Horatian maxim (*carpe diem*) literally in terms of 'gathering' the day, indicating how he is taking his cue directly from Horace rather than adopting a transmitted formula (at about the same time he also translated the poem, *Odes* 1, 11, from which it is taken: *CP* 550). Importantly, though, it is not the strikingness of the maxim which is at issue, but the weight it accrues in the context of Horace's life and writings. Hence the saturation of *Memoranda to Horace* with echoes of his work.[9] The advice comes from an individual with high poetic aspirations, claiming (in *Odes* 3, 1 whose phraseology MacNeice echoes) that his poems would live as long as Rome and its hallowed institutions. In the light of history of course, the grand claim seems piquantly limited:

> Fame you no longer presumed on than pontifex
> And silent Vestal should continue daily
> Climbing the Capitol.

Horace's programme to produce 'Aeolian measures' proving 'more lasting than bronze' (in MacNeice's echoing of the familiar phrases) has been realised triumphantly — and this in spite of ordinary human failings and compromises: 'Yes, Augustus had to arrive in a sealed train / And you had to praise him and even think you meant it. . .' There is insight as well as human sympathy here; and when MacNeice, therefore, launches his voice 'on the offchance' to reach the Roman poet, the un-rhetorical casualness of the phrase makes it seem more than conventional poetic apostrophe: the notion of Horace's surviving consciousness is fleetingly entertained against rational conviction.

If MacNeice is a 'religious' poet, he is one in the same agnostic, undoctrinaire, questioning way that Horace is. Horace combined a sense of the phenomenal world and everyday sensual pleasure with a simultaneous sense of melancholy and transience; this plus the need to register such antinomies in poetry of a philosophical cast which nevertheless respects common human experience, knowledgeably sieving systems of philosophy and belief with human need as the guideline. MacNeice is similarly 'religious' in the sense that his poetry shows a continuing concern to achieve a sense of wholeness of response to life which, within our culture, has historically been derived from religious belief and observance (for the Roman intellectual of Horace's day, philosophy performed this function).

The Epicureanism which Horace professes (more technically and passionately expounded by Lucretius), when he advises to 'gather the day' is of course based on a materialist premise whereby the whole world is composed of atoms and void randomly aggregated to form people, things, phenomena; they can, and will, dis-assemble, ensuring extinction and oblivion for the individual. Hence life and its human pleasures should be embraced while, fleetingly, it is possible. In enrolling himself behind Horace therefore ('Telling me how you had gathered / Your day, a choice it is mine to emulate.') the modern agnostic is recognising the logic of such a philosophical programme.

He does so however with the sceptical, reflective resignation of a Horace rather than with the doctrinaire zeal of a Lucretius. Hence the nostalgic hankering after transcendence of physical worlds, contrary to philosophical conviction, in 'Memoranda to Horace'. Similarly, MacNeice's professed unbelief in the existence of God simultaneously involves, as Terence Brown puts it, 'a serious awareness of the dereliction such loss must occasion'.[10] The vacuum is articulated in 'Autumn Journal':

> Whom shall we pray to?
> Shall we give like decadent Athens the benefit of the doubt
> To the Unknown God or smugly pantheistic
> Assume that God is everywhere and round about?
> But if we assume such a God, then who the devil
> Are these with empty stomachs or empty smiles? (*CP* 137)

Decadent Athens provides one model and Romantic pantheism another — but the everyday world of experience is the preferred point of reference. The humanity here acquires a moral force in its questioning and in its recognition of spiritual need. The philosophic scepticism of such a passage is of a different order of seriousness than, say, the more casually undogmatic, almost condescending sentiments of 'Whit Monday' with its 'perhaps there is something in them' attitude to 'familiar words of myth' ('The Lord's my shepherd') (*CP* 201). When in fact MacNeice comments on specifically Christian contexts, the results tend to be like this — poetry of reasoned observation; nothing is seriously at issue. 'Place of a Skull', a poem about the crucifixion, further illustrates MacNeice's position in this area — that of dispassionate commentator rather than seeker after illumination:

> Earth water stars and flesh — the seamless coat
> Which is the world, he left; who from to-day
> Had no more need to wear it. The remote
> Metropolis yawned, the parchment flapped away. (*CP* 237)

The seamless coat of Christian tradition must represent a perfect myth of creation, an account of the world which answers all the questions; but when the Roman soldier who wins it at dice puts it on the result is disappointment: 'Why the first time I wore / That dead man's coat it frayed I cannot say.' The myth is seen to be historically limited. In MacNeice's dual perspective the crucifixion is simultaneously a central event in the rise of Christianity and an insignificant happening in a corner of the Roman world.

Still less, for someone with this broad sense of historical context, is twentieth century Christianity a source of anything approaching religious experience. In 'Carrickfergus' (1937) his socio-religious birthright is reviewed.

> The Scotch Quarter was a line of residential houses
> But the Irish Quarter was a slum for the blind and halt. (*CP* 69)

Differences in socio-religious status are clearly encapsulated: the disadvantaged Irish (Catholics) and the Scotch (Protestants) are pigeon-holed in their specialised Ulster nomenclature. The lower-case 'anglican' observer however is mentally removed: a socially and historically aware commentator:

> I was the rector's son, born to the anglican order,
> Banned forever from the candles of the Irish poor;
> The Chichesters knelt in marble at the end of a transept
> With ruffs about their necks, their portion sure.

As was suggested earlier, MacNeice's attitude to Christian belief can include an acknowledgement of the in some ways enviable spiritual satisfaction available to the believer; but this is not an option available to him. It is in secular terms that any unifying vision must be sought. The terms of the debate, therefore, will be philosophical, though the effective medium will be poetry. Hence the relevance of Horace's example.

More than any modern poet, Horace seems to provide a model for MacNeice's practice in reconciling a lyric response to the world of experience and phenomena in all its plurality with the perennial questions of ultimate reality or coherence. Moreover, key aspects of MacNeice's technique can be rescued from undue trivialisation by comparison with Horace's practice. The conversational idiom, for instance, in which MacNeice writes so much of his poetry and which reaches a notable apex of development in 'Autumn Journal' is not a matter of casualness or relaxedness, but a hard-won formal manner which artfully affects conversational ease and informality — the technique of Horatian *sermo* in fact, developed by Horace to deal persuasively and unpretentiously with moral and philosophical issues, particularly in the *Satires* and *Epistles*.

Possibly, as much as anything else, it is the regular use of a conversational style which has been responsible over the years for an underestimation of MacNeice as a poet of deep metaphysical preoccupations. A poet of MacNeice's Classical background would be instinctively aware of the fact that there is no contradiction between informality of manner and seriousness of purpose. Terence Brown has written of MacNeice's style that:

Such writing with its sturdy prosaicisms is reminiscent of the tradition of Hardy in English poetry; in its flattened language it has similarities to Movement verse, while it reveals something of the Ulsterman's traditional blunt honesty.

He goes on however:

Its creation of a sense of fundamental philosophic unease, however, is its most important characteristic setting it apart from all of these.[11]

Exactly, but not from Horace; and it is interesting to note, as Brown remarks, that MacNeice in later life was puzzled at the failure among critics to register the metaphysical implications of his poetry, and how years earlier MacNeice had noted of Horace: 'People misunderstand Horace because . . . they demand of him the directness and simplicity of a purely lyrical poet, whereas Horace is a contemplative poet. . .'[12] The words might be applied directly to the reception of MacNeice's own work.

The way things happen is easy to see. 'Ode' (1934) opens with a stanza that seems to confirm the notion of MacNeice as descriptive poet, as gifted reporter, as the projector of a determinedly 'modern' sensibility:

To-night is so coarse with chocolate
  The wind blowing from Bournville
That I hanker after the Atlantic
  With a frivolous nostalgia
Like that which film-fans feel
  For their celluloid abstractions
The nifty hero and the deathless blonde . . . (*CP* 54)

Of course the chocolate smell would, and does, waft from the Bournville factory over the area of South Birmingham where MacNeice took up residence; and the other details here are notably contemporary. In a technique however seen regularly in Horace's *Odes*, an arresting descriptive opening only prefaces stanzas of taut philosophical speculation:

If God is boundless as the sea or sky
The eye bounds both of them and Him,

We always have the horizon
Not to swim to but to see:
God is seen with shape and limit
More purple towards the rim,
This segment of His infinite extension
Is all the God of Him for me.

MacNeice in this poem is discoursing seriously on philosophical questions. The classical ideal, notably appropriated by Horace, of the 'golden mean' is specifically advocated, as is the Horatian aspiration to a 'sufficient sample'; and for his son he wishes, with a sane sense of moderation and decorum worthy of Horace, 'let his Absolute / Like any four-walled house be put up decently'. It should be noted too how the much-quoted endorsement of the 'blessedness of fact' is conjoined with Epicurus' atom-dance in a richly modulated discursive rhetoric which, at this juncture, is given a special resonance also by its echoing of Yeats's 'A Prayer for My Daughter':

Let him accumulate, corroborate while he may
The blessedness of fact
Which lives in the dancing atom and the breathing trees. . .

Such passages realize in practice very precisely MacNeice's critical view in *Modern Poetry* that the artist 'must move in a concrete world', avoiding the example of philosophers who 'have drawn too sweeping a distinction between the actual and the ideal' making the ideal world 'a substitute for the actual or, at best . . . something to be abstracted from the real world by, it may be, the artist, the aesthete, the philosopher, or the mystic'.[13] MacNeice, since his Oxford days studying 'Greats', had been sceptical of academic philosophy as a route to comprehensive truths or absolutes, preferring Aristotle to the Idealist Plato; but here is the notion that the poet too may compromise his specialised angle of vision if he fails to remain true to particulars, if he involves himself in an 'escape from the actual to some transcendent reality'.[14]

It is in this light that the plethoric descriptive elements in a poem such as 'Train to Dublin' (1934) should be regarded:

All over the world people are toasting the King,
Red lozenges of light as each one lifts his glass,
But I will not give you any idol or idea, creed or king,
I give you the incidental things which pass
Outward through space exactly as each was. (*CP* 28)

This strict philosophical prescription governs the rich itemization of the details of the Irish countryside in the following stanzas:

> I give you the smell of Norman stone, the sqelch
> Of bog beneath your boots, the red bog-grass,
> The vivid chequer of the Antrim hills, the trough of dark
> Golden water for the cart-horses, the brass
> Belt of serene sun upon the lough.

There is more than pure description involved here, as MacNeice, with a characteristic sceptical caution, finally makes clear:

> I would like to give you more but I cannot hold
> This stuff within my hands and the train goes on;
> I know that there are further syntheses to which,
> As you have perhaps, people at last attain
> And find that they are rich and breathing gold.

The moment of synthesis or vision has been glimpsed, but the discursive philosophical censor has intervened. It is clear however that a susceptibility to 'the drunkenness of things being various' as they impinge on the senses is a key aspect of MacNeice's make-up as a religio-philosophical poet. The linkage is made analytically explicit in the retrospective 'Dedicatory Poem to *Collected Poems, 1925–1948*, To Heidi':

> At one time I was content if things would image
> Themselves in their own dazzle, if the answers
> Came quick and smooth. . . (*CP* xvii)

But 'Those April answers' have 'withered off their Question' and 'now I am not content, the leaves are turning / And the gilt flaking from each private image'. The 'half-blind questions' may 'still lack their answers', but there is no doubt that the *sui generis* resources of poetry are the medium of the enquiry: 'Which was the right turning? / Rhythm and image and still at best half answers. . .'

Like the Horace of the *Odes* at about the same age, MacNeice ('Acting younger than I am and thinking older') adopts a somewhat middle-aged tone, working the familiar Horatian theme of a symbolic relation between the cycle of the seasons in nature and the 'seasons' of a man's life (cf. the above quotations with the references to April, things withering and leaves turning);[15] and the faculty of achieving insight by means of the poetic image is explicitly related to youthful inspiration. The middle-aged poet lays his 'ear to the ground', but receives no response from the earth:

> Though I know that the Word, like a bulb, is there, is present
> And there the subterranean wheels keep turning
> To make the world gush green when, we being older,
> Others will be in their prime to drench a volume
> In the full leaf of insight and bloom of image.

The reference to the 'Word' as the ultimate focus of MacNeice's intuitive poetic quest indicates a 'religious' element in the type of vision to which youth has some measure of privileged access.

It is in this connection, therefore, that we should perhaps look at a poem such as 'Snow':

> The room was suddenly rich and the great bay-window was
> Spawning snow and pink roses against it
> Soundlessly collateral and incompatible:
> World is suddener than we fancy it.
>
> World is crazier and more of it than we think,
> Incorrigibly plural. I peel and portion
> A tangerine and spit the pips and feel
> The drunkenness of things being various.
>
> And the fire flames with a bubbling sound for world
> Is more spiteful and gay than one supposes —
> On the tongue on the eyes on the ears in the palms of one's hands —
> There is more than glass between the snow and the huge roses.
> (*CP* 30)

Notoriously, the whole of Western philosophy has been ransacked in exegetical attempts to elucidate the play of thought in this poem.[16] The poem however asserts nothing of a ratiocinatory nature. Everything is effected in terms of poetic suggestion. The stress on sense-data, the vibrant response to the phenomenal world, may be as much related to the 'Word' revealing itself in the natural world to the fresh intuition of the young poet enjoying 'the full leaf of insight' as to any particular philosophical notion such as 'the one and the many'. Clearly the poem is written by someone au fait with certain key philosophical concepts; but the philosophical suggestiveness is marshalled in support of a non-philosophical vision, rather than the other way round; just as the religious implications of the 'Word' in the poem 'To Heidi' are used to give spiritual depth to the consideration of episodes of essentially secular vision. What is important is the suddenness, the dizzy intensity and, in the last analysis, arbitrariness of the experience in 'Snow'. MacNeice himself notes how the poem 'has often puzzled people though it means exactly what it says; the images here are not voices off, they are bang centre stage, for this is the direct record of a direct experience, the realisation of a very obvious fact, that one thing is different from another — a fact which everyone knows but few people perhaps have had it brought home to them in this particular way, i.e. through the *sudden violent perception* [my stress] of snow and roses juxtaposed'.[17] MacNeice's language here underlines, in spite of his characteristic appeal to common experience, the special kind of hyperaesthesia which is behind the poem.

The kind of vision at issue, then, is sudden, surprising and strangely transfiguring. There is no direct appeal to anything beyond phenomena, but there is an unusually intense response to them: an unpredictable access of 'insight' and 'bloom of image' ('To Hedli') Because however the poet is determined to remain true to phenomena (avoiding the retreat to philosophical abstraction which we saw MacNeice criticising earlier), the danger of being seen as an essentially descriptive poet persists. Horace, significantly, has suffered precisely the same sort of misunderstanding. His great 'Soracte' ode for instance (*Odes* 1, 9) where a visual evocation of a prospect of snow-clad Mount Soracte leads, by symbolic association, to thoughts of death, transience — and then Epicurean counter-attitudes, has not escaped carping topographical analysis (Where is the poet positioned? What might he realistically see?).[18]

There is a deep coincidence of vision between the two poets; and their method, their descriptive sharpness and fidelity to experience, incurs necessary risks: a rigorously sceptical lack of philosophical insistence may be misread in shallow or trite terms. Not that Horace has a patent on the kind of theme and experience we have been discussing — Rilke is an obvious modern instance of similar preoccupations. It is just that, for someone of MacNeice's educational background, Horace is a natural and expedient exemplar — a second-nature focus for imitation and allusion; a paradoxically immediate influence.

In 'The Sunlight on the Garden' (1937) we have a classic instance of the early vision that the later MacNeice nostalgically harked back to in 'To Hedli'. The sense of transience in the first stanza ('We cannot cage the minute /Within its nets of gold') is expanded in stanza two:

> Our freedom as free lances
> Advances towards its end;
> The earth compels, upon it
> Sonnets and birds descend;
> And soon, my friend,
> We shall have no time for dances. (*CP* 84)

In a typically deft MacNeician touch, the tired phrase 'free-lances', with its accretion of modern journalistic and commercial overtones, is refurbished, chivalrically, by the simple omission of the hyphen. Then, to clinch this heightening tone, the final line quietly and resonantly recalls Horace's injunction to his friend in the

Soracte Ode (mentioned above) to count each day as gain in the face of transience and not to neglect love and 'dances' while yet young ('nec dulcis amores / sperne puer neque tu choreas': 'Nor in your youth spurn sweet loves or dances'). One word ('dances': set at the end of a stance in each case) can deepen the tone of the poem in this allusive way, generalising the sentiments while avoiding abstraction; and hence the poem can modulate through the famous, expansive Shakespearean reference and into the final appeal to experience and phenomena, reiterated from the first stanza:

> The earth compels,
> We are dying, Egypt, dying
> And not expecting pardon,
> Hardened in heart anew,
> But glad to have sat under
> Thunder and rain with you,
> And grateful too
> For sunlight on the garden.

The disquietude involved in the dialectic leading to the final celebration of things-as-they-are is ultimately metaphysical, the resolution akin to religious vision (in so far as this is possible within a materialist view of the world).

Ultimately (to take a final glance at a key twentieth century exemplar of this kind of theme), as Rilke asserts in the ninth of the *Duino Elegies*,[19] the teleologically deprived modern poetic sensibility can 'praise this world to the Angel' only by telling him '*things*'. 'Shunning Destiny' we 'long for Destiny', 'because being here is much, and because all this / that's here, so fleeting, seems to require us and strangely / concerns us. Us the most fleeting of all.' Transcendence is impossible and yet 'we keep pressing on':

> But into the other relation,
> what, alas! do we carry across? Not the beholding we've here
> slowly acquired, and no here occurrence. Not one.

The dilemma is precisely MacNeice's; and interestingly enough Rilke's view at this point is deepened by a conscious or unconscious echoing of Horace's plangent statement on the fleetingness ('Eheu fugaces') of human existence in *Odes* 2, 14 which contains the stanza:

> linquenda tellus et domus et placens
> uxor, neque harum quas colis arborum
> te praeter invisas cupressos
> ulla brevem dominum sequetur. . .

Farewell to lands, home, dear and affectionate
Wife then. Of all those trees that you tended well
Not one, a true friend, save the hated
Cypress shall follow its short-lived master.[20]

Rilke is able finally to embrace death and affirm in a visionary cancelling of rational perspectives:

Look, I am living. On what? Neither childhood nor future / are growing less. . . . Supernumerous existence / wells up in my heart.

MacNeice perhaps never reaches this intensity of affirmation, but much of his lyric poetry aspires to the same category of vision.

(ii) Patrick Kavanagh: Mock-Heroic Manoeuvres

Patrick Kavanagh is in many ways the antithesis of MacNeice: largely self-educated, of small-farmer stock, rough in his habits, anti-academic and socially abrasive. But MacNeice and he have suffered from a similar kind of reductive critical type-casting — that of the poet-reporter in the one case, and that of the 'peasant-poet' in the other. In spite of their profound respective influences on important developments in modern Irish poetry in English, their literary-critical standing has lagged strangely behind their now manifest literary-historical importance. Practitioners, however, such as Heaney and Longley have no hesitation in proclaiming their respective debts, with Longley recently boldly asserting the 'greatness' of both Kavanagh and MacNeice in the same breath.[21]

Both writers make extensive use of a conversational style which gives an impression of seemingly casual, colloquial artlessness; and as with MacNeice it is no doubt the case that Kavanagh's hard won accomplishment in this demanding mode has sometimes been mistaken for a limited ingenuousness. Horace's 'art which conceals art' is again an apposite consideration. Direct influence is not of course being argued in this connection; but in his maturest work Kavanagh notably seeks to treat the deepest issues in an apparently casual and even inconsequential manner, and with a relaxed humour reminiscent of Horace's technique. The best comparison may be with Auden's late achievement in *About the House* where, no doubt in this case with a conscious Horatian indebtedness, we have a kind of philosophical and autobiographical stock-taking done in determinedly domestic terms, with an Horatian stress on friendship and the ironic deployment of an urbane and superbly competent verbal dextrousness. Kavanagh's admiration of Auden's comprehensive talents is a useful clue to the development of his own work.

In his final period, Kavanagh saw himself as graduating to a lyric mode which is limited in scope and unassuming in manner, but which puts even such an achievement as 'The Great Hunger' in diminishing perspective. He did this moreover while living a life reminiscent of a down-at-heel Beckettian character, lounging about St Stephen's Green or on the banks of the Grand Canal during his convalescence after a remarkable recovery from lung cancer in 1955 — a complete subscription in other words to the ordinary, the local and the quotidian in life-style and in the outward themes of his poetry. Reading the sporting press on the sunny side of the Grand Canal, Kavanagh was able to affirm the phenomenal world in a kind of 're-birth'. Most importantly, though, he was able to deploy a formal technique which registered this access of generalised 'love' arising out of the particular.

In his Author's Note to the 1964 *Collected Poems*[22] Kavanagh remarks:

> *The Great Hunger* is concerned with the woes of the poor. A true poet is selfish and implacable. A poet merely states the position and does not care whether his words change anything or not. *The Great Hunger* is tragedy and Tragedy is underdeveloped Comedy, not fully born. Had I stuck to the tragic thing in *The Great Hunger* I would have found many powerful friends.
>
> But I lost my messianic compulsion. I sat on the bank of the Grand Canal in the summer of 1955 and let the water lap idly on the shores of my mind. My purpose in life was to have no purpose.

He is using 'comedy' of course in a special sense. As he notes in his 1958 course of lectures at University College, Dublin:

> . . . in the real comedies, *King Lear, Hamlet, Macbeth, Richard the Third,* etc. he [Shakespeare] is a riot of excitement, outrageous in his abandonment. This is the comic spirit, the generous-hearted thing.[23]

In the same place, again appositely for the late sonnets, we find:

> I am very fond of the sonnet form and not merely because it has been the most popular vehicle for the expression of love but for its strict rules, which like other rules, Shakespeare broke so wonderfully . . .

The notion is of an unforced, relaxed, expansively life-embracing mode which in its lack of posturing and openness carries a special kind of moral integrity: one which 'forces the mind to moral activity but is not itself forced.'

MacNeice, sitting in E. R. Dodds's study,[24] was alive to a microcosmic significance in a vase of roses set by a window. Kavanagh shows a similar susceptibility in 'The Hospital' as he recovers from his illness:

> A year ago I fell in love with the functional ward
> Of a chest hospital: square cubicals in a row
> Plain concrete, wash basins — an art lover's woe,
> Not counting how the fellow in the next bed snored.
> But nothing whatever is by love debarred,
> The common and banal her heat can know.
> The corridor led to a stairway and below
> Was the inexhaustible adventure of a gravelled yard.
>
> This is what love does to things: the Rialto Bridge,
> The main gate that was bent by a heavy lorry,
> The seat at the back of a shed that was a suntrap.
> Naming these things is the love-act and its pledge;
> For we must record love's mystery without claptrap,
> Snatch out of time the passionate transitory.[25]

Within a drastically limited *mise-en-scène*, large notions of love and acceptance are articulated — and simultaneously defused of any suggestion of portentousness by humour and ironic juxtaposition. The poem insistently plays off elevated and 'low' details against one another in a mock-heroic technique which charges the ordinary with momentous significance, but which postulates nothing beyond the itemized phenomena and the experience itself. The witty exaggeration ('the inexhaustible adventure of a gravelled yard') at one level eliminates bathos by its own willingness ironically to undermine grandiloquence, but the elevation of concept is what ultimately wins through. Similarly, the final ringing assertion of a general, emcompassing love, wrested from ordinary experience, gains weight from the fact that other kinds of love have already been playfully alluded to — in the comic juxtaposition of human love and inanimate love-object in the opening lines and in the bolder physical suggestion of 'her heat can know'. The 'naming of things' is the ultimate 'love-act' as the poem now deftly relinquishes its ironic flirtation with the terminology of eros for its final impassioned, visionary declaration. The last line might have come from MacNeice or Rilke.

Francis Stuart has referred to 'The Hospital' in the following terms:

> Clumsy, unworkable grammar, no literary graces, not 'about' anything, not illustrating a previously conceived idea, but to those to whom it speaks, new and wonderful![26]

This undoubtedly communicates part of the feel of the poem, though it does not fully bring out its formal complexity, of which casual conversational grammar is one part. The mock-heroic structure of the poem, the casual cast given to the strict sonnet form, the crucial element of 'comedy' (rightly stressed in Kavanagh's prose writings) — all these add up to a highly developed technique climaxing years of development.

Francis Stuart goes on to say that,

> Like Blake's lyrics in his *Songs of Innocence*, the best of Kavanagh's poetry cannot be analyzed or explained. Kavanagh gives himself spontaneously and directly, without literary artifice between himself and the reader.

The stress on the element of vision here is apt and necessary, though perhaps Kavanagh's work is more capable than is suggested of analysis, as in the mock-heroic structuring of 'The Hospital' which allows the visionary element to be tempered and humanized by comic imagination.

The micro-cosmic angle of vision, the appeal to experienced phenomena, the directness and easiness of tone which seems to involve no striving after effect ('My purpose in life was to have no purpose.') matches exactly the prose statements quoted earlier: it is a knowing synthesis of vision and technique. It is specifically as a poet and through the medium of poetry that, as with MacNeice's 'Snow', Kavanagh projects his vision — a *sui generis*, ultimately unparaphrasable poetic process. As with MacNeice again, religious or philosophical exegesis is possible to some extent, though misplaced. Kavanagh is not expounding *agape*, but presenting a transfiguring vision of the ordinary realities of life. No doubt Kavanagh, as a practising Catholic, would if put to it ascribe the experience ultimately to a divine source; but that would be as irrelevant as if MacNeice were to offer a philosophical analysis of 'Snow'. The vision is implicit in the form of the poem itself.

No matter how convinced an individual may be in his religious persuasion, his actual deepest experiences of a religious kind may occur not in terms of orthodox religious observance or contemplation, but perhaps unconventionally and surprisingly out of contact with, say, the phenomena of the natural world. By the same token, as we have seen with MacNeice, an agnostic or atheistic poet may have experiences of this same order. With Kavanagh, it may be the case that, as Michael O'Loughlin puts it, 'in his religious, political, and social beliefs, he always remained a Monaghan small farmer'[27] — the utter antithesis of MacNeice's position. As poets however, in their avoidance of metaphysical bombast and their commitment to the deeper resonances of the ordinary and the quotidian in human experience, the two poets show notable points of comparison.

Kavanagh's celebration of the local, the banal and the ostensibly inconsequential therefore is more than just a response to literary-historical circumstance. Darcy O'Brien speculates how:

> after Yeats and Joyce, immediately after them, perhaps self-limitation was the best course for an Irish writer, since the history of the human race, the nature of the unseen world, the possibilities of linguistic experiment, and what Kavanagh liked to call contemptuously 'the Irish thing' all had been adequately covered. What was left? Daily life. Mud, stones, flowers, food, drink, faces, joy, sickness, hope, despair, spite, resentment, family, love, hate, and the occasional intimation of – something.[28]

The sense of this 'something' is important: without it, we have a minor, reactive talent; with it, we have the potential for the serene ironies of the late sonnets. The drastic limitation of subject-matter within the mock-heroic manoeuvrings of these poems is a development of a consistent tendency in Kavanagh to treat the large by way of the small, the universal by way of the local – or the 'parochial' in his well-known, assertive reversal of the usual pejorative connotations of that term.

The micro-cosmic cast of Kavanagh's sensibility, his striving to glimpse the transcendental in the ordinary and the everyday, is evident in his earliest work, though without the crucial element of comedy, and diffused often in the post-Romantic diction of that period. Within the conventional celebration of beauty, tranquillity and ecstasy in a poem such as 'Ploughman' (1930), Kavanagh finds 'a star-lovely art / In a dark sod.' (*CP* 2) The art-metaphor of the first stanza ('I . . . paint the meadow brown / With my plough.') is developed here from the picturesque into the cosmic: for surely 'star-lovely' is not a case of decorative epithet-mongering, but a correlation of the dark sod with the dark expanse of space in the way that the atom mirrors the universe in structure. The same idea is found in 'To The Man After The Harrow' (*CP* 10):

> Now leave the check-reins slack,
> The seed is flying far today –
> The seed like stars against the black
> Eternity of April clay.

The uncertainties, however, of the early work are well enough known: the vague exoticism of 'The Intangible':

> Spendours of Greek,
> Egypt's cloud-woven glory

> Speak no more, speak
> Speak no more
> A thread-worn story. (*CP* 1)

the anthropomorphism of 'To a Late Poplar' (*CP* 2): 'Not yet half-drest / O tardy bride!'; the over-heated sacramental imagery of 'Worship' (*CP* 16) and so forth. Beauty, Wisdom, Truth and a conventionally mystical vision are the rhetorically-hunted quarry of many of the early poems; and the presence of obvious influences is a factor of variable value. A.E.'s example is no doubt behind the mystical vagueness of 'The Intangible'; though the Blakean intensity of 'Blind Dog' works well enough:

> I follow the blind dog
> Over the twisted trail,
> Bled by the wild-rose thorns
> Where he lashes his comet tail.
>
> I follow the blind dog,
> Crying to my star: O star
> Of a passionate pagan's desire,
> Lead me to the truths that are. (*CP* 14)

It is within the context of this general striving after intensity of vision that the importance of a poem such as 'Inniskeen Road: July Evening' becomes apparent with its watchful, analytical placing of the poetic sensibility within a particular landscape and community. Any vision will have to arise out of this dual perspective on the poet as at once removed and privileged and, simultaneously, a rueful, sad-sack figure in his isolation:

> I have what every poet hates in spite
> Of all the solemn talk of contemplation.
> Oh, Alexander Selkirk knew the plight
> Of being king and government and nation. (*CP* 19)

The same perspective is behind the ironic disparities in 'Shancoduff' (1937):

> My hills hoard the bright shillings of March
> While the sun searches in every pocket.
> They are my Alps and I have climbed the Matterhorn
> With a sheaf of hay for three perishing calves
> In the field under the Big Forth of Rocksavage. (*CP* 13)

As the final stanza stresses, it is a poet who owns 'them hungry hills', and his ruefully mock-heroic, transforming vision is not shared by his neighbours. Place, as has often been noted, is important in Kavanagh, but essentially it is the angle of vision which counts — as the utter arbitrariness and, by conventional standards, inconsequence of the locale and details celebrated in 'Hospital' ultimately make clear.

In his essay 'From Monaghan to The Grand Canal' (1959) Kavanagh correlates his 'rediscovery' of his roots in his 'grove on the banks of the Grand Canal' with his early experience of the 'same emotion'[29] in Monaghan. His sense of roots however is now emphatically schooled away from the merely social or topographical:

> Roots in the soil meant that you knew about people living close to nature, struggling for survival on the small farm, and you had a practical knowledge of animal breeding.
>
> But of course roots in the soil have nothing to do with these things. What are our roots? What is our material?
>
> Real roots lie in our capacity for love and its abandon. The material itself has no special value; it is what our imagination and our love does to it.

It is this confident discovery, plus the conviction that 'laughter is the most poetic thing in life'[30] that differentiates the late sonnets from the early lyrics — a new perspective which is already exemplified in 'Epic' (1951).

In this poem, after the explicitly mock-heroic signalling of the title, the local is grandiloquently inflated:

> I have lived in important places, times
> When great events were decided, who owned
> That half a rood of rock, a no-man's land
> Surrounded by our pitchfork-armed claims. (*CP* 238)

Whatever Kavanagh's kinship however with the local farmers, whose Homeric disputes exert more claim on his attention than 'the Munich bother', it is with nothing less than Homer's ghost as mouthpiece that the true creative purview is resoundingly articulated:

> He said: I made the Iliad from such
> A local row. Gods make their own importance.

This is a quite different mock-heroic note from the depreciatory techniques of the Dublin satires of the forties.[31] It is the forerunner of the expansive, assertive humour ('the right kind of loving laughter')[32] which is to be developed in the more intensely personal vision of 'The Hospital' and, definitively, in 'Lines Written on a Seat on The Grand Canal, Dublin, "Erected to The Memory of Mrs Dermot O'Brien" '. 'After a lifetime of experience, as Rilke pointed out, we find just a few lines.' ('From Monaghan to The Grand Canal'):[33]

O commemorate me where there is water,
Canal water preferably, so stilly
Greeny at the heart of summer. Brother
Commemorate me thus beautifully.
Where by a lock Niagarously roars
The falls for those who sit in the tremendous silence
of mid-July. (*CP* 295)

The 'Niagarous falls' is nothing more than the overflow over the lock gates by Kavanagh's favoured spot beside Baggot Street Bridge. This modest corner of suburban Dublin is transformed into an ideal locale by the poet's celebratory imagination:

No one will speak in prose
Who finds his way to these Parnassian islands.
A swan goes by head low with many apologies,
Fantastic light looks through the eyes of bridges –
And look! a barge comes bringing from Athy
And other far-flung towns mythologies.
O commemorate me with no hero-courageous
Tomb – just a canal-bank seat for the passer-by.

The 'tremendous silence' of July, the Parnassian perspective, the 'far-flung towns' and 'mythologies' of the canal's reach, all these aggrandising touches build towards the final epic disclaimer, where the Homeric compound in 'hero-courageous' gives way to the modest aspirations of the final line. In a telling collocation, the pomp of 'tomb' with its emphatic placing at the beginning of the line is dissipated in the subsequent relaxed, colloquial assertion of the local and the ordinary. The playing off against each other in this way of great and small, fabulous and local, formal and informal is integral to the poem's bracing, joyful mixture of simplicity and largeness of vision – a formula deftly reinforced by the bold use of unlikely half-rhymes within the formal patterning of the sonnet. Kavanagh is handling his medium with the kind of relaxed imperiousness which we saw him praising in Shakespeare.

Kavanagh's later sonnets are, by common consent, visionary, mystical or religious in their tenor. I have tried to argue that the articulation of this vision calls upon deep and no doubt by now largely instinctive resources of art. In particular, the mock-heroic cast of these poems is important in the expression of Kavanagh's tendency towards a micro-cosmic view of the world – his ability to intuit the universal in the local and particular. Moreover, the mock-heroic mode also carries with it an endemic sense of humour and comedy – hence accommodating what, as we have seen, Kavanagh saw as being an important part of a mature poetic vision. The controlling idiom however remains conversational, 'For we must record love's mystery without claptrap', and the overall impression remains one of artless directness and informality. Kavanagh's control of this unassuming colloquial decorum is central to the achievement of these poems, and as with MacNeice there is an irony in the fact that his very mastery in this demanding technical area might be too successful and blind the reader to the full measure of the poetry.

"A MYTHOLOGY WITH WHICH I AM PERFECTLY FAMILIAR": SAMUEL BECKETT AND THE ABSENCE OF GOD.

LANCE ST JOHN BUTLER

Religion is a raw place in Samuel Beckett's mind. When approached or touched it generates pain, laughter, blasphemy, scatological association. Only slowly, through the withering fire of these defences, do we come to perceive its importance to him and to notice that, in some less obvious corners of his work, it has an altogether gentler status.

The reader of Beckett, consequently, swings somewhat alarmingly from the comic and dismissive treatment of Christianity (Moran's questions, in *Molloy*, include 'What was God doing with himself before the creation?' and 'How much longer are we to hang about waiting for the antichrist?'[1] to an anguished desire for the 'divine prospect' of 'never having been'.[2] Or he lurches from Mr Spiro's magazine, *Crux* (in which, as he explains to Watt, he runs competitions 'of a devout twist': 'Rearrange the fifteen letters of the Holy Family to form a question and answer. Winning entry: Has J. Jurms a po? Yes'[3]) to the gentle and beautiful echoes of Dante that are scattered through his work from the earliest fiction to the latest texts. About religion Beckett is unambiguously ambiguous.

There has been some doubt cast on the date of Beckett's birth, but he himself seems to favour April 13 1906, that is to say the Good Friday of that year, which is exactly as much of an omen as he chooses it to be.[4] He was brought up in the strict Protestantism that seems to thrive in Ireland alongside a general Catholicism and a distressed Anglicanism. There is a photograph, now well-known and reproduced in Deirdre Bair's biography,[5] which shows Beckett, perhaps aged two, kneeling in front of his mother in an attitude of infantine prayer. Without a doubt he received a thorough grounding in the Bible as a child and added to it, as Irishmen must, a close knowledge of the astonishing detail of Catholic doctrine and belief. This double heritage, Christianity in two of its strongest forms, constitutes the 'mythology' with which he has declared himself *perfectly familiar*. Beckett's double attitude to this double heritage is already apparent in the early collection of stories, *More Pricks than Kicks* of 1934.

In the story 'Yellow',[6] for instance, we find this description of the hero, Belacqua Shuah, apparently a self-portrait of Beckett himself: Belacqua is 'a dirty low-down Low Church Protestant high-brow'. This is given in the context of a 'funny story':

> First of all an angel of the Lord came to his assistance with a funny story . . . about the parson who was invited to take a small part in an amateur production. All he had to do was to snatch at his heart when the revolver went off, cry 'By God! I'm shot!' and drop dead. The parson said certainly, he would be most happy, if they would have no objection to his drawing the line at 'By God'. . . He would replace it . . . by 'Mercy!' or 'Upon my word!'. . . 'oh my I'm shot!'; how would that be?
>
> But the production was so amateur that the revolver went off indeed and the man of God was transfixed.
>
> 'Oh' he cried 'oh. . .! BY CHRIST! I AM SHOT!'
>
> It was a mercy that Belacqua was a dirty low-down Low Church Protestant high-brow and able to laugh at this sottish jest. Laugh! How he did laugh, to be sure. Till he cried.[7]

This story ('funny'? or a 'sottish jest'?) is apparently anticlerical. The parson swears when he is really hurt and his earlier reluctance to blaspheme is thus rendered questionable, even hypocritical. But what quite, then, are we to make of the 'angel of the Lord' and the phrase 'It was a mercy'? Why *these* expressions among all others, with their explicitly religious references? And, more seriously, why does Belacqua cry? it is of course, the merest cliché to speak of laughing till one cries, just as something's being a mercy is no more than a common English idiom, but there is more to tears, in Beckett, than that.

The fact is that religion for him is simultaneously laughable and heartrending, or, if you will, comic and tragic. The ludicrous idea, even in a fourth-rate piece of theatre, of somebody responding to a bullet in the chest with the expression 'Upon my word!' shows how trivial and yet bizarre other such ejaculations are on such an occasion. 'Mercy!' has a dated and hopelessly inadequate ring to it, but then, as we extend the list to a more serious proposal (the original line, 'By God!') it seems less absurd and then, at the extreme point at which the parson, in true fear, is provoked to call out 'By Christ!' we are in the presence of a cry that is in some degree heartrending: the man *in extremis* calls upon the crucified saviour; it *is* hilarious, of course, but it is also tragic; there is nothing funny about crucifixion, nothing really funny about death, even under ludicrous circumstances. Seeing this, Belacqua cries; as we are made to realise more clearly by the structure and punctuation of the last sentences, he really and truly weeps.

In the first story of *More Pricks Than Kicks*, 'Dante and the Lobster', the tragic element in religion is superbly manifested through the Dantean pun on *'pietà'* (to mean either 'pity' or 'piety')[8] which is connected with the hanging of McCabe the Malahide murderer and with the boiling alive of a lobster. This, and some later stories, offer an almost explicitly Christian meditation on mercy but, in the same volume, in the story 'A Wet Night', the Polar Bear ('a big old brilliant lecher') has this, among other things, to say of Christ to a Jesuit friend:

> He is the first great self-contained playboy. The cryptic abasement before the woman taken red-handed is as great a piece of megalomaniacal impertinence as his interference in the affairs of his boy-friend Lazarus.[9]

There we have the mixture — Christ called upon in a funny story at the moment of death and Christ gratuitously insulted as a homosexual; stories about pity told with a ruthless comic gusto. Belacqua himself only has a 'small stock of pity' but it is at least 'devoted entirely to the living . . . the nameless multitude of the current quick . . . assigned without discrimination to all the undead, without works'.[10] The semi-comic theological thrust of those last two words 'without works' is quite typical of the mixture: it is a joke but it is serious; it is a laugh at the expense of the traditional debate between faith and works but we suspect that there is also authorial approval of Belacqua's pity for humanity and this acts as an insistence that man is, ipso facto, not guilty. The ambiguity could perhaps be summed up in a line from the poem, 'Calvary by Night', recited at the party in 'A Wet Night'.[11] The vague *symboliste* imagery of this poem reveals a positive attitude to the crucifixion, but the ambiguity, here the negative slipped in among the positives, cannot fail to appear:

> kingfisher abated
> drowned for me
> lamb of insustenance mine

The supererogatory prefix to 'sustenance' gives away the game.

This ambiguity is not a chance fact about this early collection of stories. Throughout his writing Beckett works both sides of his ambivalence hard. First let us look at the comic or negative side.

In *Watt* (written 1945) Mr Spiro reads Watt the following letter which he has received as editor of *Crux*:

Lourdes
Basses-Pyrénées
France
Sir,

A rat, or other small animal, eats of a consecrated wafer.

1. Does he ingest the Real Body, or does he not?
2. If he does not, what has become of it?
3. If he does, what is to be done with him?

Yours faithfully
Martin Ignatius Mackenzie
(Author of The Chartered Accountant's Saturday Night.)

Here Mr Spiro is in his element; he, the author of *A Spiritual Syringe for the Costive in Devotion*, is able to answer the enquiry at length, 'for he was a man of leisure.' Of all the lengthy answer, however, Watt 'heard nothing'.[12]

Later in *Watt* the hero and his friend Sam befriend the long black rats that they meet on walks in the grounds of what appears to be their asylum:

We would sit down in the midst of them, and give them to eat, out of our hands, of a nice fat frog or a baby thrush. Or seizing suddenly a plump young rat, resting in our bosom after its repast, we would feed it to its mother, or its father, or its brother, or its sister, or to some less fortunate relative.

It was on these occasions, we agreed, after an exchange of views, that we came nearest to God.[13]

It would appear that religion leads Beckett to think of rats, and vice versa, and that God is a monstrous tyrant.

In *Mercier and Camier* (written in 1946) Mercier is unable to open his umbrella as the rain starts to come down 'in buckets'. he swears and then

With both hands Mercier raised the umbrella high above his head and dashed it to the ground. He used another nasty expression. And to crown it all, lifting to the sky his convulsed and streaming face, he said, As for thee; fuck thee.

Camier asks him

Is it our little omniomni you are trying to abuse?. . . You should know better. It's he on the contrary fucks thee. Omniomni, the all-unfuckable.[14]

'Omniomni' is, we must suppose from the context, the omnipotent, omniscient God of classic theology. I would say 'omnipresent', too, but for the tenth 'concept' on which light 'floods' for Mercier and Camier in the fifth chapter of the novel:

10. Contrary to a prevalent opinion, there are places in nature from which God would appear to be absent.[15]

Among other concepts in this list we find a definition of 'soul' as 'another four letter word' and, equally typically of this association of the religious and the obscene, the next chapter opens with a pub discussion of 'the interest taken by Jesuits in mundane matters' in which an article on artificial insemination is cited 'the conclusion of which appeared to be that sin arose whenever the sperm was of non-marital origin'.[16] This tendency to reduce God, the divine, and religion generally to the level of the obscene and the ludicrous persists all through what might be termed Early and Middle Beckett, that is, pre-war Beckett (between his first published poem, *Whoroscope* of 1929 and *Watt*) and the immediate post-war Beckett up to about 1960.

Thus in *Molloy* (1951) the narrator observes:

What I liked in anthropology was its inexhaustible faculty of negatiam, its relentless definition of man, as though he were no better than God, in terms of what he is not.[17]

A more immediate and shocking reduction is achieved in the discussion of Molloy's weakest points. At 'the seaside' these got worse only slowly:

So that I would have hesitated to exclaim, with my finger up my arse-hole for example, Jesus-Christ, it's much worse than yesterday, I can hardly believe it is the same hole.[18]

We are, I think, prevented from taking this 'Jesus-Christ' as merely an Irish expletive first by its gratuitousness and secondly by the context of multiple references of this kind. In this mood, one of his basic moods it would seem, Beckett automatically associates the obscene and scatological with the holy. In the second half of *Molloy*, of course, it is Moran who provides the vehicle for blasphemous comedy:

I remembered with annoyance the lager I had just absorbed. Would I be granted the body of Christ after a pint of Wallenstein? And if I said nothing? . . . But God would know, sooner or later. Perhaps he would pardon me. But would the eucharist produce the same effect, taken on top of beer, however light?[19]

In the end Moran decides he will visit Father Ambrose and ask for a private communion:

I came to ask you a favour, I said. Granted, he said. We observed each other. It's this, I said. Sunday for me without the Body and Blood is like

— He raised his hand. Above all no profane comparisons, he said. Perhaps he was thinking of the kiss without a moustache or beef without mustard. . . I'll go and get my kit, he said. He called that his kit. . . He came back with a kind of portable pyx, opened it and dispatched me without an instant's hesitation. I rose and thanked him warmly. Pah! he said, it's nothing.[20]

Here the tone is strangely hard to catch; the intelligence and perceptiveness of Moran, who can follow Father Ambrose's train of thought like a trained cynic and who knows exactly the degree of sin that he is committing, are at odds with his credulous need for communion and his desire to get a consecrated wafer into his stomach, even sinfully, as if it were some kind of spiritual Alka-Seltzer. Perhaps, amongst the comedy of this, we can perceive the Beckettian dichotomy: he returns, for all his inability to believe, again and again to the details of faith. When, nearing the end of his narrative, Moran says of himself that 'Certain questions of a theological nature preoccupied me strangely' we might wonder if these words do not apply in some degree to Beckett himself, or at least to the narrator behind the narrators of the trilogy. The 'questions' do indeed include such curiosities as 'Did Mary conceive through the ear, as Augustine and Adobard assert?' included no doubt in part for the assonance of the last five words, but they also include a clue to Beckett's constant association of the holy with the profane: 'What is one to think of the Irish oath sworn by the natives with the right hand on the relics of the saints and the left on the virile member?' Furthermore, an element of the seriously-ludicrous or ludicrously-serious lies to hand in such questions as 'Is one to approve of the Italian cobbler Lovat who, having cut off his testicles, crucified himself' or 'What if the mass for the dead were read over the living?' This last question, particularly, goes to the heart of much that torments Beckett; *Endgame, Krapp's Last Tape, Come and Go, That Time, Breath* and many other pieces could be seen as requiems for life.[21]

In *Endgame*, first performed in 1957, Hamm suddenly announces, at the end of one of his inconclusive narratives, 'Let us pray to God'. Clov, who has just entered, immediately announces something that will not now surprise us: 'There's a rat in the kitchen!' God, rats, rats, God. Hamm, once he has been reassured that the rat 'can't get away' proceeds with his prayer, Clov, Nagg and Nell joining in. When none of them achieves any immediate response to their supplications Hamm bursts out 'The bastard! He doesn't exist!' At this point we may be reminded of G. K. Chesterton's comment on Hardy, that he combined a disbelief in the existence of God with a hatred of him for not existing.

Here, perhaps, is a convenient point at which to switch to the other side of Beckett's view of religion. As early as *More Pricks Than Kicks*, as we have seen, a partially-positive view of Christ, especially in the poem 'Calvary By Night', coexists with the obscene debunking of religion. This more positive side persists into what may be called Later Beckett, that is the Beckett of *How It is* (1961) and later texts,[22] in a way that the comic-scatological side does not. After *Molloy* in the prose and *Endgame* in the plays the old compulsion to blaspheme, to reach for the chamber-pot when religion is mentioned, seems to wane. But, as we shall see, the highly tentative and heavily-qualified positive aspect of Beckett's handling of religion does not alter greatly.

Thus, although the tone is again extremely hard to catch, there is at least some reason to take this statement, from *More Pricks Than Kicks*, without too large a pinch of salt:

> It was one of those spring evenings when it is a matter of some difficulty to keep God out of one's meditations.[23]

Whether we take this to imply that Belacqua is trying to keep God out for religious or, as it were, for anti-religious reasons, it is not an entirely frivolous or ironic sentence, in context. Nor is the later comment, by the narrator of these stories, that 'God at least was good, as He usually is if we only know how to take him'.[24] But one might, in any case, point to the pity in 'Dante and the Lobster' as at least a version of Christian sympathy.

In *Murphy*, of 1938, we do not find many references to religion either way, but in the case of the heroine, Celia, one of his most gently-treated characters, we have at least the possibility that her name is significant. She is, for the partially-enamoured Murphy, Heaven itself, in part. She is intensely physical, indeed a prostitute, but she has a kindness, a heavenly pity perhaps, not often to be found in Beckett.

And in *Watt*, too, there is a heaven of sorts offered in the shape of the enigmatic Mr Knott:

> But to Mr Knott, and with Mr Knott and from Mr Knott, were a coming and a being and a going exempt from languour, exempt from fever, for Mr Knott was a harbour, Mr Knott was a haven . . .[25]

Mr Knott is Watt's 'destination' and before he reaches it he hears a 'mixed choir' singing a 'threne' of which the last lines are 'And everyone is gone/ home to oblivion'.[26] The mystical implications of this, Mr Knott (obviously the quintessence of the negative) as the heaven-haven of 'oblivion', must wait until later. Of more immediate relevance to our purpose would be the twenty-five page 'short statement' made by Watt's predecessor in Mr Knott's house, Arsène, before he leaves to make room for Watt.

This speech of Arsène's bears careful examination. It hints that Watt, and all like him, are perhaps types of Christ.

> The man arrives! The dark ways all behind; all within, the long dark ways, in his head, in his side, in his hands and feet. . .
>
> The long blue days for his head, for his side, and the little paths for his feet. . .
>
> How I feel it all again, after so long, here, and here, and in my hands, and in my eyes, like a face raised, a face offered, all trust and innocence and candour, all the old fear and soil and weakness offered, to be sponged away and forgiven![27]

It is clear enough that this is a crucifixion scene (the full text reveals something like an early Italian paining with blue distances, roots and flowers) and that Arsène, Watt and all Mr Knott's servants share with Christ, at least, the agony of the Cross. This in the book where the absurd Mr Spiro ('My friends call me Dum . . .D-U-M. anagram of Mud') edits the ludicrous *Crux*.

Perhaps, like Hardy, Beckett has a deep sympathy for the suffering (and possibly misguided or even betrayed) Christ. Perhaps, paradoxically, these atheists see Christ as indeed the Son of Man, the archetype of a suffering humanity. Certainly Watt takes on something of a Christ-like appearance. Sam offers us this parenthesis concerning him:

> His resemblance, at that moment, to the Christ believed by Bosch, then hanging in Trafalgar Square, was so striking, that I remarked it.[28]

Sam goes on to claim that he, too, bears this resemblance. A few pages later Sam 'annoints' Watt's face and hands.

Another Christ-figure appears in *Calmative*, written in 1945–46, one of the novellas collected in *No's Knife*. The narrator enters a town 'by what they call the Shepherd's Gate' and sees 'the first bats like flying crucifixions'. He realises that it is Sunday. He meets a 'young boy holding a goat' who is not afraid of him but who is 'barefoot and in rags'.[29] The boy offers the narrator a sweet and their hands brush together. The narrator then speaks to him, as nicely as he knows how, being out of practice, but feels shame at having spoken and comments 'If I had had a penny in my pocket I would have given it to him, for him to forgive me'. The next event in the story involves a visit to a rare establishment in the Beckett canon, a cathedral. After making this visit the narrator comments

I wasn't returning empty-handed, not quite, I was taking back with me the virtual certainity that I was still of this world, of that world too; in a way.

In Beckett this is *déjà beaucoup*. But the narrator goes further:

I would have done better to spend the night in the cathedral, on the mat before the altar, I would have continued on my way at first light, or they would have found me stretched out in the rigour of death, the genuine bodily article, under the blue eyes, fount of so much hope.[30]

And there is yet more. The narrator encounters a man who offers to exchange a 'phial' for a kiss. This kiss is given and received and only then does Beckett's persistent agony in the face of hope reassert itself: the kiss occurs, the narrator looks away, 'It was then I noticed we were sitting opposite a horse-butchers.' Subsequently, nonetheless, there are non-ironic references to 'blue and white, colours of the virgin', a book 'of common prayer perhaps' and even a character in a story who 'gleamed an instant and was gone' like the symbolic hope of renewed faith in Arnold's 'Dover Beach'.[31]

In one of the companion pieces to *The Calmative*, the novella *The End*, there is an interesting bridging of the divide between the two sorts of religious reference we have so far found in Beckett. A public speaker, a left-wing demagogue presumably, addressing the passers-by from the roof of a car, catches sight of the down-and-out who is the narrator and starts to use him as evidence of the wickedness of charity; as the narrator starts to leave the scene the orator calls after him, 'Do you hear me; you crucified bastard!'[32] Here the identification of suffering man with suffering Christ is somehow heightened rather than lessened by the addition of the insult.

In *Molloy*, in spite of its rich crop of obscene or ludicrous references to Christian religion, there are some strangely positive ones, too. Molloy, for instance, sees *donkeys* drawing a barge towards him on a tow-path. The barge is carrying a cargo of *nails* and *timber*, on its way, he supposes, to some *carpenter*. The boatman has a *long white beard* while the sky, at sunset presumably, burns with *sulphur* and phosporus. Molloy gets down into the ditch and lies at full stretch 'with outspread arms' waiting, perhaps, for a crucifier to come along and apply the nails and timber to him at th behest of the boatman. Molloy awakes, in the morning, under the gaze of a *shepherd* who he thinks might take him, like the substitute for Isaac, for a '*black sheep entangled in the brambles*.' Molloy wishes that he smelt like a *sheep* or a *goat* . . . but the *shepherd* goes away without a word to him.[33]

Thus when later Molloy comments '(God forgive me') that the

thought of his mother's image mingling with that of the women with whom he has had sex is 'literally unendurable, like being crucified' we are entirely disinclined to laugh.[34] Nor are we in the comic mode or mood when we read, a little later still, that when Molloy's legs become even worse than before his progress is reduced to 'a veritable calvary, with no limit to its stations and no hope of crucifixion'.[35]

With all this in mind it is not, I think, absurdly optimistic to read at least some religious hope into the ending of the first half of *Molloy*:

> The day came when the forest ended and I saw the light, the light of the plain. . . I opened my eyes and saw I had arrived. . . I heard a voice telling me not to fret, that help was coming. Literally. . . Don't fret, Molloy, we're coming. . . It must have been spring, a morning in spring. . . I did not fret. . .[36]

This is, at least, not sarcastic, nor is it taken away in the next breath, at least not entirely; this section of the novel ends:

> I longed to go back into the forest. Oh not a real longing. Molloy could stay, where he happened to be.

There is something positive that has been offered to him, he is not quite empty-handed.

Whereas the sarcastic-ironic-obscene-blasphemous element largely drops out of Beckett's work after about 1960 this more positive (ambigiously positive) element persits, as I have said. Although in *Krapp's Last Tape* of 1958 mention of a Vespers hymn is followed by 'Went to sleep and fell off the pew', in the companion-piece *Embers* of 1959 there is a plethora of hints about Christ's death and to the effect that Henry is another of the Beckettian Christ-figures.[37] Some of the material in *Embers* is ludicrous in quality, too ('I have a panhysterectomy at nine' cried Holloway) but the tone of, for instance, Henry's repeated calls of 'Christ!' is, I think, entirely serious.

In the novels, although we enter the desperate world of *The Unnamable* (1953) and *How It Is* (1961) there are still moments of non-comic religious reference offered. In *The Unnamable*, for instance, the narrator says of the simultaneous voices he hears that

> One would take it for a single voice, a single mouth, if one did not know that God alone can fill the rose of the winds, without moving from his place.[38]

This is, of course, not unambiguous and the tone has various shades of meaning within it but the prevalent note struck by the central metaphor is, at least, neither blasphemous nor ludicrous.

Passing, at last, into the realm of Later Beckett we find only the very slightest touches of the old sarcasm towards religion. In *The Lost Ones* (1972, originally published in French in 1971) there is a certain amount of Swiftian satire on the search ofr meaning. The 'cylinder' in which the text is set is full of 'lost bodies'.

> From Time immemorial rumour has it or better still the notion is abroad that there exists a way out. Those who no longer believe so are not immune from believing so again. . .[39]

If this is not enough to suggest a parallel with religious faith, Beckett drops in significant words. He talks of 'two opinions', the 'old belief', 'conversion', 'persuasions', 'either sect', and 'credence'. This smacks of the high-heeled and low-heeled inhabitants of Lilliput but there is pity in his tone, a kind of icy compassion, a controlled madness of shared pain.

In *Not I* of 1973, although the mouth has a 'good laugh' at the idea of a 'merciful . . . God' she also repeats 'God is love', without full irony, several times, and ends her monologue, if it is the end, with

> . . . God is love . . . tender mercies . . . new every morning . . . back in the field . . . April morning . . . face in the grass . . . nothing but the larks . . . pick it up –

Here, if nothing else does, the 'April morning' guarantees a certain level of seriousness – the April morning of Good Friday when Samuel Beckett was born; then there is the face, like that of the crucified Molloy, pressed into the grass. . .

In *Footfalls* of 1975 there is no laughing matter. But there is this to be digested, to be fitted into the purgatorial pattern: M[May] paces up and down, as she has learnt to pace in a 'little church'. She tells a story about a girl identical to herself [Amy] whose mother asks her: 'Did you observe anything strange at Evensong?' Amy answers: 'I observed nothing of any kind. . . I saw nothing . . . I was not there.' Her mother replies, utterly prayer-like, 'But I heard you respond. . . I heard you say Amen. . . The love of God, and the fellowship of the Holy Ghost, be with us all now; and for ever more. Amen'. . .[41] This reply is not religious, it is a story about a quotation of a quotation, but it is designed to touch something, somewhere that is not absolutely alien from religion; it is not, at least, fully ironic.

In *All Strange Away* of 1976, among the imagined 'murmurs' we find 'Mother, mother, Mother in heaven, Mother of God, God in heaven, combinations with Christ and Jesus'.[42]

In *Ill Seen Ill Said* of 1982 (French original, 1981), a strange and gloomy evocation of an old woman, isolated in her 'zone of stones', besides odd lambs ('there had to be lambs') and the suggestion of 'A shroud of radiant haze. Where to melt into paradise' Beckett returns yet again, however elusively, to the April day and the crucifixion. He is describing the lack of curtains in the old woman's abode and observes all that is left:

> Alone on the one hand the rods alone. A little bent. And alone on the other most alone the nail. Unimpaired. All set to serve again. Like unto its glorious ancestors. At the place of the skull. One April afternoon. Deposition done.[43]

The complex tone here is worth analysing. The nail can 'serve again', humbly. It is, biblically, 'like unto' its predecessors ('Can there be any sorrow like unto his sorrow?' asks Isaiah prophetically of the crucified Christ). The predecessors, however, are 'glorious' ancestors which provokes us to ask what exactly was *glorious* about the nails that attached Christ to the cross. To the meditating believer they are the symbols of salvation, spurs to self-mortification, instruments of God's purpose. But that does not deny, indeed that depends for its meaning upon, a more human vision of them as instrumants of torture. The place of the skull is Golgotha, as specified by the Evangelist. The April afternoon is the 3 pm of Good Friday usually assigned to the crucifixion. The deposition is the Deposition, the *Pietà*, the taking down from the cross, the nails' dismissal, the narrator's last word on the subject.

Also in 1982 Beckett's television film *Nacht und Träume* was produced in Germany. In it we see a dreamer and his dream, and the dream, surprisingly, is one of solace. A hand, 'from dark beyond and above' the dreamer's head, is placed on the dream-image of that head; it wipes its brow, it holds the dreamer's dreamt hand; it offers him a cup which it puts gently to his lips; the dream is repeated with identical actions. Here may be a clue to all the motifs from Christianity that Beckett uses: we need solace, we have a passionate desire for comfort, and the comfort is there, but it is only a dream.

The picture we have built up of Beckett's *use* of religion ('Christianity is a mythology with which I am perfectly familiar, so naturally I *use* it')[44] can now be seen to be ambiguous in the way a spinning coin is ambiguous — it may equally well come down heads or tails. But in the end, what matter? Whether Beckett blasphemes or meditates, whether he treats religion comically or tragically, it has the same meaning, it is a raw, sore place where salvation, hope and comfort are on offer in a way that, if true, would overwhelm Beckett's world with a heartbreaking joy. Christianity seems to offer exactly what is needed, it is tailor-made ('Look at the world – and look at my TROUSERS!') for solving the insoluble enigmas of existence but ('Christ! What a planet!') the one thing needful is just the one thing unavailable. And at the heart of Christianity stands the perfect symbol for all this, the crucifixion wherein man has found, in the dreadful image of one of his fellows being tortured to death, a reason for, of all things, hope.

So, when one looks, even selectively, at a wide range of Beckett's work, matters seem a little more complex, even, than is allowed for by Hersh Zeifman in his essay 'Religious Imagery in the Plays of Samuel Beckett'.[45] Beckett's drama, he says

> Far from offering hope of religious consolation . . . is a *kyrie eleison* of suffering and despair, in which anguished cries of spiritual emptiness alternate with a bitterly outraged and frequently outrageous indictment of the extent of divine malevolence. Instead of providing support for a Christian interpretation, the presence of biblical imagery in the plays serves rather to undermine such an interpretation through ironic counterpoint. For the thrust of Beckett's religious reference suggests that man is the victim of a heartless metaphysical ruse. . .[46]

This seems to me to catch only half the truth about Beckett's work as a whole. The obscene-blasphemous-ludicrous elements can certainly be read as 'anguished – outraged – outrageous' but the further point about the heartless metaphysical ruse, although it can be supported from some of the plays in particular, does not sufficiently account for all the available evidence. There simply is too much *sympathy* scattered through Beckett, too many allusions to Christ that are not blasphemies or 'anguished cries', too many moments of the vision of hope for this to be the whole story.

The Unnnamable, for instance, takes a different approach from that which Zeifman finds in the plays:

> What have I done to God, what have they done to God, what has God done to us, nothing, and we've done nothing to him, you can't do anything to him, he can't do anything to us, we're innocent, he's innocent, it's nobody's fault, this state of affairs. . .[47]

And isn't *innocence* precisely one of the strongest impressions created by reading Beckett? Again like Hardy he blames nobody, there are few villains in his work and those that there are seem in the end more sinned against than sinning. The derelicts who dominate the narratives are childlike, humble, uncomprehending. The maniacs who people his stages (Pozzo, Hamm, Krapp) are desperate, theatrical, terrified, hollow. For all of them the best thing would be never to have been born. As in *The Lost Ones* 'all is not yet quite for the best' — the best of all possible worlds will be the *end* of this last gasp of existence.[48] And as in *Ill Seen Ill Said*, where the old woman is vanishing, the narrator looks at her chair and comments: 'It will end by being no more. By never having been. Divine prospect'.[49] Or as in *Endgame* where the thrust of the play is towards having done with life, towards the abolition of engendering, towards the extermination of potential procreators. The only good is the void.

God as *God*, as a positive element within the universe is a devastating hope fitted to man's needs but who, alas, is absent. If he existed, too, he would be as innocent as his creatures and for him, too, figment as he is, Beckett has sympathy. God as the void, the other God who, for other reasons, doesn't exist either, is another matter. Towards him we may yearn as towards the never-having-been-born:

> The paradise that the Beckettian protagonist seeks is the void that, for Beckett (as also for Sartre), lies at the core of consciousness, outside of time and space — therein resides the essential self.[50]

A positive Christian interpretation is certainly unwarranted but there is far too much evidence of sympathy, innocence and a yearning for the absolute negative for us to go to the opposite howling extreme. Perhaps the best description of Beckett's position might be this sentence from *The Unnamable*:

> One alone turned towards the all-impotent all-nescient, that haunts him, then others.[51]

Beckett's is the voice, the consciousness that is haunted by its double — void yearning for void. The 'others' are all the innocent ones, the whole of the great chain of being, from top to bottom. It is Beckett who wrote in 1937: 'And more and more my own language appears to me like a veil that must be torn apart to get at the things (or the Nothingness) behind it'.[52] And it is in *Watt* that we find a whole range of negativistic prayers and meditations, from:

> This mind ignoring. These emptied hands.
> This emptied heart. To him I brought. To
> the temple. To the teacher. To the source. Of nought.[53]

to:

> Then the gnashing ends, or it goes on, and one is in the pit, in the hollow, the longing for longing gone, the horror of horror, and one is in the

hollow, at the foot of all the hills at last, the ways down, the ways up, and free, free at last, for an instant free at last, nothing at last.[54]

Beckett is at least clear as to what is behind the veil.

Later, in *Molloy*, the narrator recites the 'pretty-quietist Pater' ('Our Father who art no more in heaven than on earth or in hell. . .)[55] and much later again Beckett is still circling the same idea when the narrator of *Worstward Ho*, of 1983, suggests eyes staring 'Into the hell of all. Out from the hell of all' in contrast with the void, the 'Unmoreable unlessable unworseable evermost almost void.'[56]

This analysis could be greatly extended ('Enough — Ample, said the lady'). Nothing much has been said of *Waiting for Godot* or *Murphy* or *How It Is*, little of *Endgame* and *All That Fall*, not to speak of the poems. But none of these is free from the haunting obsession with religion or from the pattern of Beckett's use of it: desperate comedy, calmer tragedy, hopeless hope, innocence, sympathy, the yearning for the void.

These themes have been developed usefully by critics who have explored their relations with cognate religious writers and with philosophers.[57] Pascal, Schopenhauer, Kierkegaard and Heidegger, John Climacus and Spinoza have been pressed into service and with considerable effect.

But what it all comes to, when one has spun one's own 'wordy-gurdy' out into webs of interpretation is that Beckett, without being a *Buddhist* is buddhist (if the lower case is admissible). At least we might ask in what other religion we find the following constellation of ideas:

1 Nothing exists
2 So nothing *exists*
3 In spite of which — compassion for all
4 Including the gods and all caught in the toils of illusion
5 In default of never having been we must minimise existence — learn to feel the longing for longing gone.

As handled by Beckett the Christian religion fits in very well as an illustration of 3 and 4 and is a very useful mythology for exploring both these and expressing what things would be like if, as Christian optimism asserts, 1, 2 and 5 were wrong. But the religion that works on the basis of all five at once is Buddhism.

Writing of the painter Henri Hayden Beckett says that his works show the beauty of an artist:

> Qui a su, toute sa vie et comme peu d'autres,
> résister aux deux grandes tentations, celle du réel
> et celle du mensonge.[58]

Reality and lies are temptations, illusions to be resisted. This leaves us with the equation Truth = Void. It should not surprise us that, also talking of Hayden, Beckett chose to quote the Buddha:

> Gautama disait qu'on se trompe en affirmant que le moi existe, mais qu'en affirmant qu'il n'existe pas on ne se trompe pas moins.[59]

Or, as he puts it in *Ill Seen Ill Said*,

Absence supreme good and yet.[60]

PILGRIMS' PROGRESS: ON THE POETRY OF DESMOND EGAN AND OTHERS

PATRICK RAFROIDI

Reading Desmond Egan's recent poem 'Echo's Bones' (For Sam beckett on his eightieth birthday), I began meditating on the last lines:

later an embrace and you step out firmly into streets gone eighty years old
God bless now Desmond

– and you Sam our navigator our valiant necessary wanderer to the edges of this interpreted world God bless.

It was not so much the use of the Irish form of farewell by such a famous agnostic that struck me, though – some of my Trinity friends visiting Beckett in Paris had already quoted the fact, – but the thought that Desmond Egan's repetition of the formula was one of the rare instances of the naming of his creator (albeit without a capital C) in the works of that catholic poet. From the standpoint I am taking – a very different one from classifying people according to what foot they dig with – is there any such thing in Ireland, anyway, as a 'catholic' poet in the sense that Hopkins in England or Claudel in France were? Is there any 'catholic' literature at all? I remember Camille Bourniquel quoting an Irish cleric on Georges Bernanos's *Diary of a Country Priest* (or was it a novel by Mauriac?):

why do we almost always find in your novelists that call themselves catholics these sweating agonies, these doubts, these stomach-troubles, this diffidence when confronting an atheist, this morbid uncertainty? . . there is pride and joy in being able to say you are a member of the Church of Rome!

Catholic literature can only spring, perhaps, out of a quarrel with oneself *and* one's God and Irish writers have tended to quarrel only – rhetorically – with others: the Church (vide, for instance, Austin Clarke) or 'the other side' or to take their faith for granted.

Only lately have there been a few signs of change, and this among friendly renegades and orthodox followers alike.

In the recent fiction of Brian Moore — in *Catholics, Cold Heaven, The Robe* — the desolation of faith comes to play a more and more important part.

In *Station Island,* Seamus Heaney goes beyond the Maundy Thursday imagery of 'Summer Home' or the Good Friday metaphor of 'Westering'.[1]

Even young priests with a gift for poetry are seen occasionally to abandon their songs of praise in order to express a doubt as to the adequacy of their view of the kingdom to the situation of the valley of tears.

This is true of the Dominican Paul Murray in 'Prime':

> What requiem shall the Choir sing?
> Other than the need to overcome despair,
> Somehow to give order to this thing
> What use our ritual? What prayer
> Can breathe back breath, restore those lying
> In the conscience of our city? At night, gunpowder
> Flames above the asphalt. Only the sirens sing.[2]

or of the Augustinian Padraig J. Daly in 'Novitiate':

> Christmas was the start of our disillusion:
> Advent was full of light and promises and stars.
> At Christmas we expected the world to explode
> So full was all the earth of expectation,
> And justice to pour down like rain out of the skies.
> We found ourselves that afternoon by the french windows
> Looking down on the city,
> Excluded from familiar warmth
> Like Joseph seeking room in Bethlehem.[3]

Such questioning is not to be found in Desmond Egan's collections which, previous to his *Collected Poems* of 1984,[4] include *Midland* (1973), *Leaves* (1975), *Siege!* (1976), *Woodcutter* (1978), *Athlone?* (1980), *Snapdragon* (1983), *Seeing Double* (1983) and to which he added *Poems for Peace* in 1986. But this does not mean that his mind — like that of most of his countrymen — is not pregnant with the religion in which he was bred in his Athlone childhood and adolescence, and perhaps longer (judging from the number of his clerical friends), and in which he still believes.

There are religious allusions all right, although not so numerous after all. There is (p. 53) the crocus seen 'fevering through its soggy *chasuble*'; we are taken (p. 129) 'Near St Brigid's Well'; there is Gregorian chant at Ezra Pound's Funeral ('Late But! One for Ezra'), and the optimistic 'In paradisum deducant te angeli' is quoted in the original Latin:

. . . too late too late for a gesture it doesn't matter any more but it does to me
who join with the priest in the Gregorian chant at your funeral
In paradisum
deducant te angeli
rest troubled Hercules! your best labours shine like new words
the remainder as with anyone else doesn't count; (pp. 136–7)

nuns and convent schools appear on page 155, a Corpus Christi procession in 'Mrs Ned' (p. 156), the Sacred Heart in Francis Ledwige's cottage (p. 210), and the theme of crucifixion is present in both *Midland*, the first volume (p. 51) and in the last:

> just to go for a walk out the road
> just that. . .
>
> just to join the harmony. . .
> just that!
>
> but Sweet Christ that
> is more than most of mankind can afford
> with the globe still plaited in its own
> crown of thorns
>
> too many starving eyes
> too many ancient children
> squatting among flies
> too many dog jails too many generals
> too many under torture by the impotent
> screaming into the air we breathe
>
> too many dreams stuck in money jams
> too many butter mountains of selfishness
> too many poor drowning in the streets
> too many shantytowns on the outskirts of life. . .
>
> too little peace.[5]

I have quoted this poem at some length not only because it is that rare achievement: a piece with good intentions that do not condemn it to the hell of literature with which the place is supposedly paved, but because it shows how inadequate the 'reference' approach is to define the obviously 'religious' quality to be found here — and, in slightly different guise, before, in the works of Desmond Egan.

I use the word 'religious' instead of 'catholic' on purpose.

Liturgical and other references are, after all, only evidence of a certain cultural background and may be used with only a slight connection with the subject treated. This is what happens, I think, with 'Requiem' (p. 77), a very fine pagan poem of only four lines:

music you loved has filled like autumn with sadness
and places we used to be I can hardly bear
flowers are less than flowers days are of-darkness
something fell like a leaf when you went away.

On the other hand, although the catholic references may be absent there, some other poems undoubtedly bear witness to a view of the universe which is altogether spiritualist and — at first, at least — God-centred, and I mean the Christian or even the Catholic God, as seen, for instance, in 'For John Berryman' (p. 49–50) where some sort of wholeness seems to follow Berryman's return to belief and practice with, finally, a suggestion in this complex poem, of ultimate grace and forgiveness:

. . . all his kingdom buckling down together
smaller and falling smaller
all his americas
into the river-tarmac
(*Are there tears in his eyes*?)
Are there tears in my eyes?)
one last breath
pluming — like Gabriel's message — out of his lips
to flower
                    to ripple away
chopping into the thought-knurls
slowly sinking, sinking deeper
Ha ha alas so long Berryman
Christ — who knew the fall the jerk —
save us all

Rightly or wrongly, I find Desmond Egan's collections after *Midland* just as christian but far less 'catholic', at any rate in the traditional (and largely outmoded) sense of the term. *Leaves* already provides a turning point from relative security to fragility, doubt and near despair. *Seige*! displays evident indignation at what is becoming of Catholic Ireland, and not only on account of capitalists, army, police and politicians but also through priests who are a long way from Father Prendergast of 1798.

In the later poems, the virtues praised — directly or obliquely — by the poet — love, liberty, peace, humaneness, — are certainly not at odds with the thinking of some catholic theologians of the post-Council era, but, reading for instance, 'For Father Romano on his 45th birthday', I shudder to think of what the Holy Inquisition's judgement would have been concerning his 'désacramentalisation' of the eucharist and the 'laïcisation' of prayer, to use two fashionable terms of current French criticism:

> in you Romano I salute the few
> who hand out like bread to others
> their ordinary life
> and build up block by block
> anonymous in the loneliest villages
> their chapel to the spirit
>
> who bear witness in remote market places
> wearing white against the sun
> who make their flesh and blood an angelus
> pealing across huts and plots[6]

The state of the world and the necessity of adapting religion to it do not seem, however, to shake Desmond Egan's faith. For him 'the resurrection continues'. One may wonder, all the same, whether the pilgrim's progress of that remarkable poet has not led him nearer to the humanism of his beloved Samuel Beckett than to the orthodoxy of 'the scarlet-coated bishops of the Courts of Rome'.

RELIGION?

DESMOND EGAN

If you are a believer it will affect your sense of form, it will influence the very sentence you write, its rhythm, structure, energy . . . as much as its content. And how could it not? Your native place determines your accent, the way you walk.

After a few pages, a reader can sense the personality and make a fair guess at the philosophy of an author, including his or her approach to religion. Certainly the hints are there, if one has an ear.

Poor humans! blessed and cursed with *consequentiality* we wander about our life leaving fingerprints on everything we touch, pursued by our destiny as relentlessly as any Greek hero.

. . . .

The Gospel embodies an attitude towards living, not a theology. Creative writing follows the same approach in its treatment of religious themes, and for much the same reason. A sense of the mysterious workings of grace will always defy direct formulation: one must speak softly in the holy place.

. . . .

By 'religious' I do not mean, therefore, tendentious or moralising writing — the opposite, in fact. I mean writing that achieves completness: the work of an integrated person, nourished by a sense of place, by a shared wisdom, by a whole and coherent point of view. W. B. Yeats spent most of his life sailing valiantly towards this Byzantium which he never reached. That is why, due to no fault of his, Yeats is not one of the supreme writers — and why Patrick Kavanagh, due to no special virtue, is.

Until Ireland regains some kind of wholeness, no major poet is likely to emerge. How many people nowadays read Austin Clarke?

. . . .

One corollary of a religious sense: a keener realisation of personal limitation and, consequently, an unwillingness to take this world and its values wholly seriously. Imaginativeness is a religious response, just as much as modesty. So is humour; so too, irony. Does this tell us something about Samuel Beckett?

. . . .

The religious impulse will also reveal itself as a search for wholeness, a concern about one's roots, a longing for psychological and cultural individuality. Such preoccupations, never far away in modern writing, are the most obvious expression of the religious instinct in this turbulent century.

A century otherwise obsessed, in its thinking and writing, with the perception of chaos. Understandably so, in view of the wars, the genocide, the bombs, the concentration camps, the torture and the mistery which have so characterised modern times; but as an asethetic an intuition of meaninglessness offers a very shaky base for any full perception of the human condition. Herein lies the greatest weakness of twentieth century writing: its lack of a sense of value. Not on chaos alone doth man live. *In* perhaps, but not *on*. If chaos and anxiety, an obsession with the abyss . . . lead to the rejection of any objective truth towards which the spirit might orient itself, then the chance to express anything of permanent value about human life may be lost.

The frivolity and shallowness which plagues contemporary writing in general also afflicts Irish writing, most of it. Future generations may yet identify ours as an age of sand and, finding most modern Irish writing – poetry not least – unnourishing, consign it to the basement if not the trash heap.

. . . .

Kavanagh: the most integrated Irish poet of our time. He alone has had the toughness and courage to achieve his own voice completely. Whole as the Homer of *Iliad*; as Chaucer; as Cervantes; as Shakespeare; as Dostoievsky. A man who happens to write because he *has* to – the very opposite of 'a man of letters':

> Art is never art. What is called art is merely life.
>
> (*Kavanagh's Weekly*, vol. 1, no. 6)

An intimation of 'God's breath in common statement' comes naturally to Kavanagh, lending a mystical profundity to his poetry. His example suggests that there is no such thing as religious poetry – only true poetry, which is merely life.

. . . .

And Samuel Beckett: must we accept the common perception of him as 'Ireland's best-known atheist' and one whose work lacks a religious dimension? I wonder. His commitment to truth, to facing the pathos of living without flinching from it and without any comforting fictions or *dei ex machina*, without props and without deceptions . . . amounts to an *absolute*. It seems, to a believer, something the equivalent of a religious vision:

I can't go on. I must go on. I go on.

— why, otherwise, *must* he go on? Godot may not show up but Beckett's characters (ageing, most of them) wait nevertheless and are not derided for so doing. Does Beckett ridicule Lucky, Pozzo, Belacqua, Molloy, Murphy, Watt and company? Or are we not more aware of his sympathy for even the most deluded of these? Failure, humiliation, death may lie in store inexorably, do, but as in *The Iliad* where the vision is as bleak and tragic, nothing precious is mocked-at and bitterness stems from the only source we could tolerate: compassion. In Beckett's case it is further leavened by a wild humour — the language of acceptance.

The man himself, modest, courteous and not without a twinkle in his eye, hardly ties-in with the image of gloomy pessimist. I tried to suggest all this — and indeed something of my own perception of religion — in a small tribute I wrote for *The Irish Times* on the occasion of his eigthtieth birthday:

FOR SAM BECKETT ON HIS 80th BIRTHDAY

what have we to do with this hotel
its glass and boutiques and revolving chrome
and black waiter looking for a tip?

where we are sitting again at doubles of coffee
conferring like exiles between the years
your voice as gently 'Dublin as Yeats's
like my father's into age

austere and kindly — a monk on his day out
ready to consider any topic for a change
even writers! Joyce and that death mask —
Auden's verse about which we share doubts —
meeting Patrick Kavanagh in Paris —
the fifteen minutes you sat *post-prandium*

when neither you nor Pound uttered a word —
the Paris exhibition? one shrug
puts them further off than Ireland
(and who could imagine you anyway
stalking peering with a catalogue?)
Company with your own father's 'loved trusted face'
calling to you out of the Forty Foot waves . . .

'Marijuana in Ballymahon — there's a poem for you!'

and you still surprise me now as you
lean across the marble top with ravelled face
and blue eyes that make us responsible
to quote from Watt those lines
'of the empty heart
of the empty hands
of the dark mind stumbling
through barren lands . . .'

and my mind knots again in loneliness
and we are no longer in a coffee bar but somewhere
in the outer space of your words
that almost intolerable silence where
we must try to hang onto some kind of dignity
out in the blinding dark you never shirked

later an embrace and you step out firmly
into streets gone eighty years old
God bless now Desmond

— and you Sam our navigator our valiant necessary
wanderer to the edges of this interpreted world

god bless

. . . .

MIS AND DUBH RUIS: A PARABLE OF PSYCHIC TRANSFORMATION

NUALA NÍ DHOMHNAILL

What with feminist theologians like Mary Daly howling with Hag energy, let me tell a little tale of West Kerry.

Mis was the daughter of Dáire Donn who came in to Ventry at the head of the forces of the Eastern World, and who was promptly dispatched to eternity by Fionn Mac Cumhail and the Fianna in the Battle of Ventry which some say lasted a year and a day. When Mis found her father's body lying decapitated on the sand, she sucked at the wounds, drank their blood and then fled in total insanity into the wilds where she grew fur and killer claws with which she attacked and tore to pieces anyone she met. The intensity of her madness was such that she could run like the wind and no living thing was safe from her. She ate the meat and drank the blood of anything she caught so that the whole barony of Clainne Mhuiris was turned into a wilderness bereft of people, as the king had decreed that no one should kill her. Now the king, a smart man, thought that half a kingdom was better than no kingdom at all and he thereby promised same, and Mis's hand in marriage, to anyone who brought her down, alive, mind you he said, mindful as ever of her former status. The best warriors went against her, all done up in armour and had no luck. She made mincemeat of them. Soon there weren't many warriors left. The king was getting worried.

'If its alright with you', said Dubh Ruis, the harper, 'I'll have a go'.

'You!', laughed the king, 'what with?'

'With my harp'.

The king fell about the place laughing, but when Dubh Ruis said he would need a handful of each of gold and silver to accomplish the task he let him have them. So Dubh Ruis took the gold and the silver and went up the side of Slieve Mis, to where he thought he might find her, and spreading his cloak out beneath him, he laid out the gold and silver all around the edges. Then he laid down on his back, placed the harp above him, opened up his trousers, exposed himself and started to play his harp. Suddenly there she was, perched on a tree above him. She hops down beside him.*

'Aren't you a human?', she asks.

'Yes', sez he.

'What is this?', putting her hand on the harp.

'A harp', sez he.

'Hmmmm', sez she, 'I remember the harp. My father had one of them. Play it for me.'

'I will', sez he, 'only no harm to me or mine.'

'Done', sez she, 'I'll not harm you.'

Then she sees the gold and silver.

'What are these?'

'Gold and silver.'

'I seem to remember them. My father used to have gold long ago, ochón ó.'

Then she glanced at his nakedness and his comely manliness and said 'What are these?' to his balls, and he told her.

'And what is this', said she, to the other thing she saw.

'A gaming stick', sez he.

' 'Sfunny', sez she, 'I don't remember that. I don't think my father had one of them. A gaming stick, is it now?', sez she again, 'And what is the game?'

'Sit down here beside me', sez he 'and I'll play the game of the stick with you.'

So she did and they did and . . .

'Ha-ba-ba', sez she, 'that's a good game. Do it again.'

'I will', sez he, 'but I'll play the harp for you a while first.'

'Throw away that bloody harp', she said, 'and play the game instead.'

'I must eat something', he said, 'I'm starving.'

'I'll catch you a deer', she said.

'Do that,' sez he, 'I've got bread here with me.'

'Where is it?' she asked.

'Here.'

'Ha-ha', she said, 'I remember bread. My father used to have it,' she said, and then, 'Don't leave me.'

'I won't leave you.'

The upshot of it all is that he cooks the deer that she delivers unto him and she remembers that cooked meat is better than raw. Then he boils up the deer fat and bathes her in it and rubs her down until

* As my friend Máirín Ní Dhonnchú, an Old Irish scholar, keeps pointing out to me, these last two lines are not in the original, but I can't help it — I can just picture her, holding on to a branch with her long claws, like a harpie.

a lot of the fur comes away from her. He makes her a bed of moss, covers her with the deer skin and lies down beside her and next day builds a hut around her. She doesn't wake until afternoon, and thinking him gone, makes a lament which he overhears and which contains the immortal lines; —

'It is not the gold that I miss, nor the sweet harp, nor the balls but the gaming stick of Dubh Ruis Mac Raghnaill.'

This idyll lsted for two months and every day he bathed and scrubbed her down until all the fur fell away and her memory and reason returned to her and Dubh Ruis dressed her in splendid apparel and brought her home with him and she returned to her former beauty and she was the same age that she had been before she went mad on the mountain. Dubh Ruis married her and she gave him four children and was accounted one of the most beautiful and accomplished women of Munster in her time. . . .

This is my favourite version of a theme which has been called central to Irish Literature since time immemorial, the ideal of a loathly hag or 'cailleach', a 'puella senilis' signifying the tribal land or sometimes even the whole island and who when united with the rightful king in the conjugal act is transformed into her rightful form of 'spéirbhean', woman of great beauty or goddess. Such a tradition lies at the heart of the 'aisling' genre, of Merriman's *Midnight Court* and was even recycled with great aplomb by W. B. Yeats, encapsulating neatly the emotional nexus of turn-of-the-century Nationalism:

'Did you see an old woman go down the road?'
'No, but I saw a young girl, and she had the walk of a queen.'

To a visitor from another planet, or even from another island on this planet, it must seem quite inconceivable that a whole generation of otherwise seemingly rational beings would shed blood and be prepared to lay down their own lives for what is after all at one level just an image in a poem or a play. But they did. And they do, and will continue to do so while the underlying mythic drama is kept from conscious evaluation but instead has to be literally acted out.

So what is the meaning of the tremendous emotional appeal of the basic image? The tradition itself is immeasurably old, and would seem to reach back to pre-Celtic strata of Mother-Goddess worshippers. It is tempting to date it back to at least Newgrange itself, as the mid-winter penetration of that enormous womb by a ray of sunlight is no accident, but rather an architectural marvel by which the central sacred image of the religion of the time, the penetration of the Earth-Mother by the Sky-God, the sacred marriage or 'Hieros gamos' can take place physically before our very eyes. This very powerful image was naturally usurped by the invading Celts and pressed into play for their own political purposes. The Uí Néill dynasty made their own of it with a superb sleight of hand in the story of how their eponymous ancestor, Niall Naoingiallach, unlike his over-fastidious brothers, not only kissed an ugly hag at a well, in return for a drink of water, but actually slept with her. Whereupon she was transformed into the spéirbhean, and announced that this was no mere water that she was giving him, but the drink of Sovereignty and with it the right to rule to him and his. A related branch of the Celtic invaders, the Eastern Eoghantacht, adapted the basic mytheme to even more blatant political effect, taking up the story of Lughaidh Laighde and his brothers at the well. One of the brothers, consents to peck the 'Cailleach' on the cheek and when she is later revealed in all her resplendent splendour as the Goddess of Sovereignty ('Is mise an Fhlaitheas', she says) he is rewarded with the promise of kingship to one of his descendents. Lughaidh, of course, being the hero, does everything right, and not only kisses the Cailleach but sleeps with her, and so his heirs are propheisied as kings for several generations after him with the one exception as repayment to his brother for the kiss. A formidable reworking of a an ancient concept. Newspeak, how are you. The rewriting of history did not begin in the Stalinist era, and discrepancies in the lists of kings throw light on a few interesting 'non-persons', among them, a certain Dubh Ruis, of the Éireann, associated with Móir Mumhan, who flourished in the ninth century, and who may be, aptly enough, the hero of our tale.

Rightly or wrongly, I take the main mytheme of our story, the transformation theme, to have had cultic significance. The fact that the particular version of the theme in our story is of late enough origin and shows signs of having been elaborated considerably in a purely literary or paraliterary manner as a damn good story, does not particularly matter. The basic material is undoubtably very ancient. it has been suggested by some that the madwoman tales with their attendent motif of leaping or flying are older than the Suibhne Geilt story and that the Suibhne legend may have been patterned largely after them. In one form or another our story must have formed part of a liturgy. The very least we can say about it is that it is a sacred script. This may not be quite as farfetched as it sounds because if all other documentation was lost now, and all that was left of Christianity to decipher were a few snippets of literary classics, how could we ever piece together the ethos that was the major religion of the West, never mind try to reconstruct in detail the ceremony of the Mass? Living religions are enacted totally and passionately, not described objectively.

Many have described the 'Cailleach' as being the mot potent image working subliminally on the collective psyche of this island. Why it should be the Negative Mother Archetype rather than any other form of the Goddess which describes the underlying psychic reality of this island I would barely hazard a guess. Some say it is the result of the curse of Macha; a miasma or mother-curse. Others blame the climate. I have even heard it suggested that the Tooth-Mother is always overridingly prominent on the Western seaboards of continents, due to the cultic use of the magic mushroom psylosybe which grows naturally in this biozone. The toothed monsters on the totem-poles of the Amerindians of the North West Pacific coast have been cited as an instance of this. Elsewhere I have seen it mooted that it is due to a very strong male bias in the consciousness of the Celts, which denies the deep Feminine, and is rewarded by a negative image from the repressed psychic contents. This makes a lot of sense to me because if, as Anne Ross suggests, the head was the central icon of the Celts, being to their religious ethos what the Cross is to Christianity, then already long before the arrival of St Patrick and his cohorts, our ancestors were severely cut off from what the French feminist literary theorists call the 'language of the body'. This is not to suggest that women did not have a relatively powerful role in Celtic society, — there is enough evidence which suggests they had, — but, merely that the traits valued in women were basically the masculine ones of warlikeness, rather than the more nurturant virtues. We are in much the same dilemma today, what with women in this generation rushing pell mell to 'beat men at their own game', often at great psychological cost to themselves, without our asking ourselves is the so called 'real world' of male authority really worth entering at all in the first place. Without wishing to exonerate established Christianity from an unmistakeable patriarchal bias it may be that the death-dealing propensities of our head-hunting Celtic forebears had a role to play in perverting the basically moderately life-enhancing qualities of the message of Christ into the particularly virulent life-denying force that has come to be Irish Catholicism. The Celts were already in their time too deeply patriarchal for them to be of much use to us in any attempt to affect the inner conversion which must be made in face of the imminent destruction of this planet.

But there is a deeper stratum of consciousness still alive on this island. Unlike most of the countries of Northern Europe, the door between this world and the Otherworld was never slammed shut. Somebody always kept a foot in it, whether the poet in his chieftain's hall, or the seanchaí by his fireside.

The fact that a highly elaborate conceptual framework exists in Irish to describe and deal with the Otherworld, or 'An saol eile', is proof of that fact, — a framework that, incidently, is virtually untranslateable, due to an inbuilt bias in the English language against the validity and tangibility of this experience. Put into English this perfectly serious interest in unconscious mentation and alternative states of consciousness becomes reduced to superstition or 'Pisroguery' and fairies-at-the-bottom-of-the-garden.

Happily we live on an island in which large masses of people regularly see statues leaping about the place. Leaving the sometimes rather dubious orchestration of such phemomena out of it, the event is still significant enough in itself. In spite of the mass-media and an educational system which has vowed to destroy the imagination this is proof that we have not yet entirely capitulated to purely rationalist empiricism. (If it moves, measure it!) Also, and what is even more to my point, the moving statues are all female statues. Interestingly enough there has been no significant incidence of Jesus getting down from his Cross, a la Marcelino (a film which terrified many of us when hawked around the country in the fifties, for the benefit of what worthy cause nobody now can rightly remember). Neither has St Joseph taken to tampering with anyone with his lily, or more surprisingly, given the propensity of his vicars for the exercise, never has the ubiquitous St Patrick delivered anyone a belt of his crozier. If an image is on the move within us, it is a female image, and we project outwards what is the reality within.

I take our story, like the central truths of many different religions, to be a gift from the subconscious that cannot be rationally explained. But it can be pondered, worried over, wondered at, told over and over again, and because of its deeply symbolic significance it never loses anything in the telling. Besides the fine psychological insight that it was the vulnerable man, in all his nakedness, who overcame the hag, not any of the conquering heroes, there is another level of the story which has deep significance for the times we live in. Given that such a story had a socio-political significance for its inventors, and that it was probably enacted publically in the great pulsating amoeba which was the collective psyche of the 'tuath' or tribe, it has still a very valid lesson to give to modern, almost post-psychological man. Just briefly, once more, a rerun of the main mythic elements. A king/father dies. His daughter goes mad, becoming a hag and reverting to a wild life in the woods. She is tamed and returned to her former condition as 'spéirbhean' by a vulnerable male, who is also a musician. He marries her and becomes king, through being her consort. She gives him four children, and was considered one of the most beautiful and accomplished women of her time.

What can all of this mean for us?

As the work of most feminist theologians and literary theorists would suggest, the only way forward is somehow to break out of the dominant patriarchal ethos of the age. For all of us, inwardly, the king must die. Then as the work of Mary Daly would suggest, the 'Hag' energy erupts. The too-long repressed deep Feminine comes into its own, and as we learn to come to terms with what is dark and frightening in ourselves we can release others from the burden of carrying our resentment, in the woods, in one way or another. Then a new form of male energy asserts itself in the unconscious, and challenging the hag, and uniting with her, brings forth the conscious reality of the Goddess, as spéirbhean. Rosemary Radford Ruether ends her powerful critique *Sexism and Godtalk* with an epiphany, a powerful evocation of the Goddess as spéirbhean. This is more than I can personally do with any honesty at present. having long been acquainted with the 'Cailleach' as an inner reality I have to admit that I have not yet personally met the Spéirbhean. I'm still working on that inner Harper in all his powerful dream manifestations as Enemy, Sea-Horse or Minotaur, Bull of the Mothers. But there does seem to be a way forward, and I live in hope. If it is only with the arrival of softer Spring weather that inner transformation sometimes seems to take place, as happened I think when I wrote the poem 'Primavera.'

PRIMAVERA

D'athraigh gach aon ní nuair a ghaibh sí féin thar bráid.
Bhainfeadh sí deora áthais as na clocha glasa, deirim leat.
Na héanlaithe beaga a bhí go dtí seo faoi smál,
d'osclaíodar a scórnaigh is thosnaigh ag pípeáil
ar chuma feadóige stáin i láimh gheochaigh, amhail
is gur chuma leó sa diabhal an raibh nó nach raibh nóta acu.
Bláthanna fiaine a bhí chomh cúthail, chomh h-umhal
ag lorg bheith istigh go faicheallach ar chiumhaiseanna
na gceapach mbláth, táid anois go rábach, féach an falcaire fiain
ag baint radharc na súl díom go hobann lena réilthínní craoracha.

Bhíos-sa, leis, ag caoi go ciúin ar ghéag,
i bhfolach faoi dhuilleóig fige, éalaithe i mo dhú dara,
ag cur suas stailce, púic orm chun an tsaoil.
Thógfadh sé i bhfad níos mó ná meangadh gáire
ó aon spéirbhean chun mé a mhealladh as mo shliogán,
bhí an méid sin fógraithe thall is abhus agam roimhré.
Ach do dhein sí é, le haon searradh amháin dá taobh,
le haon sméideadh meidhreach, caithiseach, thar a gualainn
do chorraigh sí na rútaí ionnam, is d'fhág mé le miabhán
im'cheann, gan cos ná láimh fúm, ach mé corrathónach, guagach.

PRIMAVERA

Everything changed as soon as her nibs passed this way,
she'd bring tears of joy to the very stones themselves, i'm telling you.
The little birds who were up to now in disgrace
have opened their throats and started piping it out
for all the world like a tinwhistle in the hands
of a teenage boy, as if they don't care a damn
whether they have or they havn't a note in them.
The wild flowers, once so shy and servile,
begging permission to lodge on the edges of flowerbeds,
are now unrestrained, look at the pimpernel
blinding my eyes with its sudden profusion of scarlet stars.

I too was quietly weeping, far out on a limb,
gone to ground under a fig-leaf, become a grumpy old thing,
in a fit of the sulks, vexed generally with life.
I had announced beforehand, far and wide,
that it would take a lot more than a winsome smile
from a fair damsel to coax me out of my shell.
But she did it, with one shake of a milky thigh,
with a laughing, lascivious beam out over her shoulder
she wrenched up my roots, and left me addled, high and dry
footless, footloose, fanciful and fretful.

NOTES

INTRODUCTION

Robert Welch

1 Eoghan Ó Tuairisc, *Religio Poetae agus Aistí Eile* (An Clóchomhar, Baile Átha Claith, 1987), p. 11. Translation by the author.
2 *Uncollected Prose by W. B. Yeats*, Vol. II, ed. by John P. Frayne and Colton Johnson (Macmillan, London, 1975), pp. 81–2.
3 W. B. Yeats, *Essays and Introductions* (Macmillan, London, 1969), p. 518.
4 Patrick Kavanagh, *Collected Poems* (Martin Brian & O'Keeffe, London, 1972), p. 153.
5 Paul Durcan, *Going Home to Russia* (Blackstaff Press, Belfast, 1987), p. 96.
6 See Robert Welch, 'Seán O Ríordáin: An Existential Traditionalist', in *An Introduction to Celtic Christianity*, edited by James Mackey (T. & T. Clark, Edinburgh, 1989), pp. 335 ff.
7 Seán O Ríordáin, *Eireabaill Spideoige* (Sáirséal agus Dill, Baile Átha Cliath, 1952), p. 111. Translation by the author.
8 W. B. Yeats, *Collected Poems* (Macmillan, London, 1959), p. 222.
9 W. B. Yeats, *Mythologies* (Macmillan, London, 1977), p. 221.
10 Nicholas Williams (ed.), *The Poems of Giolla Brighde Mac Con Midhe* (Irish Texts Society, Dublin, 1981), p. 214. Translation by the author.
11 Samuel Beckett, *Collected Poems in English and French* (John Calder, London, 1977), p. 63.

PAGANISM AND SOCIETY IN EARLY IRELAND

Séamus MacMathúna

1 For the original Latin text, see *The Tripartite Life of Patrick*, ed. Whitley Stokes, 2 vols. (Rolls Series, Her Majesty's Stationery Office, London, 1887), Vol. 2, p. 278. Translation by Francis John Byrne, *Irish Kings and High-Kings* (B. T. Batsford Ltd., London, 1973), p. 65. See also Ludwig Bieler, *The Patrician Texts in the Book of Armagh* (Dublin Institute for Advanced Studies, Dublin, 1979). Muirchú is almost certainly referring here to the Feast of Tara. For further comment, see articles by Kim McCone referred to in note 4 below.

2 See *Thesaurus Palaeohibernicus*, eds. Whitley Stokes and John Strachan, 2 vols. (Dublin Institute for Advanced Studies, Dublin (repr. 1975)), Vol. 1, pp. 307–21.
3 David Greene, 'The religious epic', *Early Irish Poetry*, ed. James Carney (Mercier Press, Cork, 1965), p. 78.
4 See Kim McCone, 'Dán agus tallann', *Léachtaí Cholm Cille* xvi (An Sagart, Má Nuad, 1986), pp. 9–53; esp. 28 ff.; 'Dubthach maccu Lugair and a matter of life and death in the pseudo-historical prologue to the *Senchas Már*', *Peritia* 5 (Journal of the Medieval Academy of Ireland, Dublin, 1988), pp. 1–35.
5 Donnchadh Ó Corráin' 'Legend as critic', *The Writer as Witness: Literature as historical evidence*, ed. T. Dunne (Cork University Press, Cork, 1987), pp. 23–38, p. 26.
6 Proinsias MacCana, 'Conservation and innovation in Early Celtic literature', *Études Celtiques* xiii (Société d'Edition 'Les Belles Lettres', Paris, 1972), pp. 61–119, p. 86.
7 See Proinsias MacCana, Review of *History and Heroic Tale: A Symposium*, ed. T. Nyberg et al. (Universitetsforlag, Odense, 1985), *Celtica* 18 (Dublin Institute for Advanced Studies, Dublin, 1986), p. 214. See also Máire Herbert, 'The world, the text, and the critic of Early Irish Heroic narrative', *Irish Studies*, eds. D. Cairns and S. Richards, *Text and Context*, No. 3 (Department of Humanities, Staffordshire Polytechnic, Beaconside, Stafford, 1988), pp. 1–9, p. 5.
8 Whitley Stokes and John Strachan, *op. cit.*, p. 317.
9 For further comment on the etymology of *síd*, see Heinrich Wagner, *Studies in the Origins of the Celts and the Early Celtic Civilisation* (Max Niemeyer, Belfast/Tübingen, 1971), pp. 245–46.
10 Whitley Stokes and John Strachan, *op. cit.*, p. 265.
11 Whitley Stokes, 'Rennes Dindshenchas', *Revue Celtique* xvi, pp. 35–36.
12 See *Táin Bó Cúalnge from the Book of Leinster*, ed. C. O'Rahilly (Dublin Institute for Advanced Studies, Dublin, 1967), p. 247.
13 See Mircea Eliade, *Patterns in Comparative Religion* (Sheed and Ward, London/Sydney, 1958), p. 193 ff.
14 See *The Tripartite Life of Patrick*, *op. cit.*, pp. 123–323.
15 See T. F. O'Rahilly, *Early Irish History and Mythology* (Dublin Institute for Advanced Studies, Dublin, 1946), pp. 322–23.
16 See Patrick Logan, *The Holy Wells of Ireland* (Colin Smythe Ltd., Gerrards Cross, 1980).
17 J. Caesar, *De Bello Gallico* VI, p. 14. See J. J. Tierney, 'The Celtic Ethnography of Posidonius', *Proceedings of the Royal Irish Academy*, lx C5 (Royal Irish Academy, Dublin, 1900), pp. 189–275.
18 *Ab urbe condita* V 46, 3. See Tierney, *op. cit.*
19 Fergus Kelly, *A Guide to Early Irish Law* (Dublin Institute for Advanced Studies, Dublin, 1988), p. 60.
20 See *Corpus Iuris Hibernici*, ed. D. A. Binchy (Dublin Institute for Advanced Studies, Dublin, 1978), 1612.8. See also Fergus Kelly, *op. cit.*, p. 233.

21 D. A. Binchy, 'Secular Institutions', *Early Irish Society*, ed. Myles Dillon (Cultural Relations Committee, Dublin, 1954), pp. 52–65.
22 Francis John Byrne, *Irish Kings and High-Kings, op. cit.*, p. 7.
23 See Fergus Kelly, *op. cit.*, p. 9.
24 *Ibid.*, p. 9.
25 *Ibid.*, pp. 44–45.
26 See D. A. Binchy, *Celtic and Anglo-Saxon Kingship* (Clarendon Press, Oxford, 1970), p. 3 ff.
27 See *Audacht Morainn*, ed. Fergus Kelly (Dublin Institute for Advanced Studies, Dublin, 1976).
28 See Heinrich Wagner, *op. cit.*, p. 6 ff.
29 See Tomás Ó Cathasaigh, 'The Semantics of "síd" ', *Éigse* 17 (The National University of Ireland, Dublin, 1978), pp. 137–55.
30 *Immram Brain: Bran's Journey to the Land of the Women*, ed. Séamus MacMathúna (Niemeyer, Tübingen, 1985), pp. 39, 52; see also, 'Myth, metaphor and merging in Early Irish literature and society', *Irish Studies*, op. cit., pp. 29–38, esp. pp. 32–34.
31 P. De Brún *et al* (Cork University Press, Cork, 1983), pp. 1–19.
32 See Proinsias MacCana, *Celtic Mythology* (Hamlyn, London, 1970), pp. 60–61; A. and B. Rees, *Celtic Heritage* (Thames and Hudson, London, 1961), p. 112 ff.
33 E. A. Gray, 'Cath Maige Tuired: myth and structure (24-120)', *Éigse* 19, p. 4.
34 Pádraig Ó Riain, 'Celtic mythology and religion', *Geschichte und Kultur der Kelten*, ed. K. H. Schmidt (Carl Winter Universitatsverlag, 1986), p. 248.
35 Eoin MacNeill, *Celtic Ireland* (Martin Lester, Dublin, 1921), pp. 56–57.
36 Pádraig Ó Riain, *op. cit.*, p. 249.
37 *Ibid.*, p. 250.
38 Máire MacNeill, *The Festival of Lughnasa*, 2 vols. (Oxford University Press, Oxford, 1962), Vol. I, pp. 99–221.
39 See Anne Ross, *The Pagan Celts* (B. T. Batsford Ltd., London, 1986), pp. 124–25.
40 See T. F. O'Rahilly, *op. cit.*, p. 318 ff.; Proinsias MacCana, *Celtic Mythology, op. cit.*, p. 24.
41 See Proinsias MacCana, *ibid.*, p. 24; Francis John Byrne, *Irish Kings and High-Kings, op. cit.*, pp. 166–68.
42 Translation by James Carney, *Early Irish Poetry, op. cit.*, p. 21 ff.

LITERATURE AND RELIGION IN EIGHTEENTH CENTURY IRELAND: A CRITICAL SURVEY

Joseph McMinn

1 Population figures for Ireland in this period are still controversial, although there is greater agreement on religious proportions within the population. See J. L. McCracken, 'The Social Structure and Social Life, 1714–1760', in *A New History of Ireland*, Vol. IV, *Eighteenth Century Ireland 1691–1800*, edited by T. W. Moody and W. E. Vaughan (Oxford University Press, 1986), pp. 31–55.
2 See J. G. Simms, 'The Establishment of Protestant Ascendancy, 1691–1714', in Moody and Vaughan, pp. 16–19.
3 See F. G. James, *Ireland in the Empire, 1688–1770* (Harvard University Press, Cambridge, Mass., 1973), pp. 99–109, and E. M. Johnston, *Ireland in the Eighteenth Century* (Gill and Macmillan, Dublin, 1974), pp. 55–60.
4 See Brian Ó Cuív, 'Irish language and literature, 1691–1845', in Moody and Vaughan, pp. 374–419.
5 J. C. Beckett, 'Literature in English, 1691–1800', in Moody and Vaughan, pp. 425–470.
6 *Ibid.*, p. 426.
7 See L. Landa, *Swift and the Church of Ireland* (Oxford University Press, 1965), pp. 189–195.
8 See O. W. Ferguson, *Jonathan Swift and Ireland* (University of Illinois Press, Urbana, 1962), pp. 83–95.
9 *The Prose Works of Jonathan Swift*, edited by Herbert Davis, 14 Vols. (Basil Blackwell, Oxford, 1939–1968), Vol. X, p. 3.
10 Davis, Vol. X, p. 63.
11 See J. G. Simms, *Colonial Nationalism 1698–1776* (Cork University Press, 1976), p. 23f.
12 Davis, Vol. X, p. 62.
13 The *Letter* to Middleton is the sixth of the *Drapier's Letters*, although it was not published until 1735 with Swift's *Works*.
14 Davis, Vol. X, p. 105.
15 L. Landa dates this sermon between August and October 1724, towards the end of the Wood's half-pence controversy. *Doing Good* is one of only eleven surviving sermons by Swift. For an excellent discussion of these texts, see L. Landa, 'Introduction to the Sermons', in Davis, Vol. IX, pp. 97–137.
16 Davis, Vol. IX, p. 233.
17 *Ibid.*, p. 238.
18 See McCracken, *op. cit.*, pp. 34–41.
19 Davis, Vol. XII, pp. 57–58.
20 *Ibid.*, p. 112.
21 *Answer to a Paper Called a Memorial*, Davis, Vol. XII, p. 23.

22 See I. Ehrenpreis, *Dean Swift, Swift — The Man, His Works, and the Age*, Vol. 3 (Methuen, London, 1983), pp. 706–726.

23 Berkeley also wrote a leaflet, *The Irish Patriot or Queries Upon Queries*, towards the end of his life, in which he returned to the topic of a National Bank. The MS. of this leaflet was preserved by Bishop Percy of Dromore, editor of the *Reliques of English Poetry*. See *The Querist*, edited with an introduction by J. M. Hone (The Talbot Press, Dublin, 1928).

24 Hone, pp. 14–18.

25 For details of legal case, and discussion of this pamphlet's influence, see Ferguson, *op. cit.*, pp. 49–57.

26 Hone, *op. cit.*, p. 75.

27 *Ibid.*, p. 58.

28 The English edition was published simultaneously with the Dublin edition. See Hone, *op. cit.*, p. 18. Berkeley's desire to distance himself from Swift may date from his having lost a Dublin appointment in 1716 on the grounds that he was a friend of the Dean. See Ehrenpreis, *op. cit.*, p. 60.

29 Hone, *op. cit.*, pp. 93–94.

30 *Advice to the Freemen of Dublin* (1733), Davis, Vol. XIII, p. 82.

31 *An Duanaire 1600–1900: Poems of the Dispossessed*, edited by S. Ó. Tuama and T. Kinsella (Dolmen Press, Dublin, 1981), pp. 164–165.

32 *Ibid.*, pp. 156–157.

33 *Ibid.*, p. xxiii.

34 *Ibid.*, pp. 216–219.

35 *Ibid.*, pp. 228–229.

36 But see Vivian Mercier's argument for Swift's influence, in *The Irish Comic Tradition* (Oxford University Press, 1962), pp. 194–195.

37 *An Duanaire*, pp. 310–311.

38 *Ibid.*, p. 345.

39 Ó Cuív, *op. cit.*, pp. 410–411.

40 *Ibid.*, pp. 387–389.

41 Charlotte Brooke, after the death of her father, had asked for financial help from the Bishop of Dromore, one of Ireland's best-known antiquarians. See *Reliques of Irish Poetry* by Charlotte Brooke, Introduction by Leonard R. N. Ashley (Scholars' Facsimiles and Reprints, Florida, 1970), p. vi.

42 For a short profile of Henry Brooke's own literary career, see Beckett, *op. cit.*, pp. 461–462.

43 *Reliques*, p. vii.

44 *Ibid.*, pp. vii–viii.

45 See Seamus Deane's discussion of this early Celtic Revival in his *A Short History of Irish Literature* (Hutchinson, London, 1986), p. 62f.

46 'To Sir Hercules Langrishe, M.P.', in *Two Letters on Irish Questions*, with Introduction by Henry Morley (George Routledge and Sons, London, 1886).

47 *Ibid.*, p. 283.

48 This is the criticism of Burke made by Louis Cullen, who feels that most simplifications of the effects of the Penal Laws come from Burke's 'partisan perspective'. Cullen argues that there were many notable
exceptions to Burke's drastic picture of eighteenth-century Ireland, which should make us wary of taking his words too seriously. But Burke is a politician, not an historian. See 'Catholics under the Penal Laws', *Eighteenth-Century Ireland/Iris an dá chultúr*, edited by Andrew Carpenter, Vol. I, pp. 23–36.

RELIGION AND SOCIETY IN NINETEENTH CENTURY IRISH FICTION

Barbara Hayley

1 *Church Hymnal (By permission of the General Synod of the Church of Ireland)*. A.P.C.K., Dublin, 1897. Hymn 600. In *Historical Guide to Hymns Ancient and Modern*, ed. Maurice Frost (London 1962), we read: 'Most modern hymn book compilers omit [this] stanza, though why rich and poor do not qualify as part of God's creation is never explained.'
2 *Irish Priests and English Landlords*, by the author of 'Hyacinth O'Gara (R. M. Tims, Dublin, 1833), p. 75.
3 *Ibid.*, p. 7.
4 *Ibid.*, p. 55.
5 *Ibid.*, p. 113.
6 The O'Hara Family, *The Croppy: A Tale of the Irish Rebellion* (Colburn, London, 1833), Vol. I, pp. 50–51..
7 *Ibid.*, Vol. I, p. 129.
8 William Carleton, *Traits and Stories of the Irish Peasantry* (Curry and Orr, London and Dublin, 1843), Vol. I, p. 185.
9 *Ibid.*, Vol. I, p. 199.
10 William Carleton, *Valentine McClutchy: the Irish Agent* (Duffy, Dublin, 1845), p. 28.
11 *Ibid.*, P. 132.
12 Eyre Evans Crowe, *The Northerns of Ninety-eight* (Colburn, London, 1833), pp. 216–7.
13 *Ibid.*, pp. 218–9.
14 Charlotte Elizabeth [Tonna], *Derry: a Tale of the Revolution* (Nisbet, London, 1843), p. vi.
15 *Ibid.*, p. 75.
16 *Ibid.*, p. 381.
17 Eyre Evans Crowe, *The Carders* (Colburn, London, 1833), Vol. I, p. 66.
18 Eyre Evans Crowe, *The Northerns of Ninety-Eight* (Colburn, London, 1833), pp. 21–22.
19 *Ibid.*, p. 22.

20 Lady Morgan, *The O'Briens and the O'Flahertys* (Colburn, London, 1833), Vol. I, pp. 201–2.
21 *Ibid.*, Vol. IV, p. 121.
22 *Ibid.*, Vol. IV, p. 121.
23 The O'Hara Family, *Father Connell* (The Parlour Library, Duffy, Dublin, 1840), p. 27.
24 *Ibid.*, p. 63.
25 William Carleton, *Traits and Stories of the Irish Peasantry* (Curry, Dublin, 1830), Vol. II, p. 152.
26 See Barbara Hayley, *Carleton's Traits and Stories and the Nineteenth Century Anglo-Irish Tradition* (Colin Smythe, Gerrards Cross, 1983), *passim*, for his moderations.
27 Gerald Griffin, *The Collegians* (Warne, London and New York, 1887), pp. 146–7.
28 *Ibid.*, p. 170.
29 *Ibid.*, p. 170.
30 Gerald Griffin, *The Christian Physiologist and other Tales* (Duffy, Dublin, n.d.), p. 5.

THE WORD, THE LORE, AND THE SPIRIT: FOLK RELIGION AND THE SUPERNATURAL IN MODERN IRISH LITERATURE

Dáithi Ó hÓgáin

1 Dáithi Ó hÓgáin, 'The Folklore of Castle Rackrent', in *Family Chronicles*, edited by Cóilín Owens (Wolfhound Press, Dublin, 1987), pp. 62–70 and 119–120.
2 A full study in Patricia Lysaght, *The Banshee* (Glendale Press, Dublin, 1986).
3 Seán Ó Súilleabháin, *A Handbook of Irish Folklore* (Folklore of Ireland Society, Dublin, 1942).
4 See Rachel Bromwich, 'The Keen for Art O'Leary', in *Éigse 5* (1948), pp. 236–252; *Gnéithe den Chaointeoireacht*, edited by Breandán Ó Madagáin (Clóchomhar, Dublin, 1978); Seán Ó Súilleabháin, *Irish Wake Amusements* (Mercier Press, Cork, 1967), 130–145.
5 For death in Irish folk tradition, see Ó Súilleabháin (1942), pp. 215–250, E. Estyn Evans, *Irish Folk Ways* (Routledge and Kegan Paul, London, 1957), pp. 289–294.
6 *Traits and Stories of the Irish Peasantry* (Wakeman, Dublin, 1833), Vol. 2, pp. 402–404. By 'Beal-derg' Carleton must have meant Balldearg Ó Dónaill, a warrior who features as the hero of the legend in west Ulster variants – see Dáithí Ó hÓgáin, *The Hero in Irish Folk History* (Gill and Macmillan, Dublin, 1985), pp. 134–141 and 149 and 335.
7 Discussion and references in Ó hÓgáin (1985), pp. 146–149 and 336.

8 'Wuil anam inh?' = *'Bhfuil an t-am ann!* 'Ha niel. Gho dhee collow areesht' = *Chan fhuil. Gabhaidí a chodladh aríst.* I am grateful to Dr. Séamas Ó Catháin for the elucidation of this variant west Ulster form *gabhaidí* for *gabhaigí*.

9 Quoted by Synge in Introduction to *The Well of the Saints*.

10 One clear example of Christian ideas influencing fairy lore is the mediaeval European identification of the fairies with some of the fallen angels. This identification passed also into Irish folklore, but was not allowed to distort the general drift of the tradition. For it, see Rheidar Th. Christansen, 'Some Notes on the Fairies and the Fairy Faith' in *Béaloideas 39–41* (1971–1973), pp. 95–111.

11 *The Aran Islands* (Maunsel, Dublin, 1906), p. 52.

12 Ó Súilleabháin (1967), pp. 138–145. See also the comments of the seventeenth century priest-historian Seathrún Céitinn — *Trí Bior-Ghaoithe an Bháis* edited by Osborn Bergin (Hodges Figgis, Dublin, 1931), pp. 183–193. For other death-motifs in the play, see Séan Ó Súilleabháin, 'Synge's Use of Folklore' in *J. M. Synge, Centenary Papers 1971*, edited by Maurice Harmon (Dolmen Press, Dublin, 1972), pp. 25–26.

13 Ó Súilleabháin (1972), p. 21. See also *Béaloideas 21* (1952), pp. 12–133; Ó hÓgáin (1985), pp. 21–23.

14 Synge claimed that he had been told that the young man killed his father — *The Aran Islands*, p. 89. For the folk tradition of this event, see Tomás Ó Máille, *An Ghaoth Aniar* (Comhlucht Oideachais na hÉireann, Dublin, 1920), pp. 93–98; Ó Súilleabháin (1972), pp. 2–22 and 31.

15 For a study of the idiom, see Alan J. Bliss, 'The Language of Synge' in Harmon, *op. cit.*, pp. 35–62.

16 'Twenty-Three Tons of Accumulated Folk-Lore', in *The Irish Times*, 18 April 1939.

17 From the poem 'Shancoduff', written in 1934 — see *Collected Poems* (Martin Brian and O'Keeffe, London, 1972), p. 30.

18 *Páipéir Bhána agus Páipéir Bhreaca* (Clóchomhar, Dublin, 1969), p. 9.

19 In the collection *Cois Caoláire* (Sáirséal agus Dill, 1953). Folklore in the work of Ó Cadhain is dealt with in an unpublished M. A. Thesis by Geároid Denvir in the Department of Irish Folklore, University College, Dublin.

20 Ó Súilleabháin (1942), pp. 213–214. These ideas are fully discussed in an unpublished M.A. thesis by Anne O'Connor, 'The Death and Burial of Unbaptised Children in Irish Folk Tradition' (1981), in the Department of Irish Folklore, University College, Dublin.

21 *The Types of the Folktale* (Academia Scientiarum Fennica, Helsinki, 1973). With the same numbering system, Irish versions of international tale-types are listed in Ó Súilleabháin and Christiansen, *The Types of the Irish Folktale* (Academia Scientiarum Fennica, Helsinki, 1967).

22 For example, holding the Bible vertically to avoid swearing directly

on Holy Writ, see Dáithi Ó hÓgáin, *Duanaire Osraìoch* (Clóchomhar, Dublin, 1980), p. 76. See also Carleton's 'An Essay on Irish Swearing', in *Traits and Stories of the Irish Peasantry.*

23 This folktale is studied by Eilís Ní Dhuibhne in *Béaloideas 48–49* (1980–1981), pp. 868–134. For other occurences of folktales with religious motifs in Griffin's work, see Ó Súilleabháin and Christiansen (1967), types 613, 753.

24 In *Traits and Stories of the Irish Peasantry*, Vol. 2.

25 Lists in Ó Súilleabháin and Christiansen (1967).

26 See Stith Thompson *The Folktale* (University of California Press, Berkeley, 1946), pp. 146–152. For an analysis of attitudes expressed in such stories, see Pádráig Ó Héalai, 'Moral Values in Irish Religious Tales', in *Béaloideas 42–44* (1974–1976), pp. 176–212.

27 In *Traits and Stories of the Irish Peasantry*, Vol. 2. For further remarks on Carleton and folklore, see Brian Earls, 'The Carleton Canon – Additions and Subtractions' in *Studia Hibernica 21* (1981), pp. 92–125.

28 A full description of Ó Laoire's sources in Liam Mac Mathúna's edition *Séadna* (Carbad, Dublin, 1987), pp. ix–xlviii.

29 Sources and discussion in Birgit Bramsbäck, *Folklore and W. B. Yeats* (Almqvist and Wiksell, Uppsala, 1984), p. 15–27.

30 Motif E732.1 in Stith Thompson, *Motif-Index of Folk-Literature* (Rosenkilde and Bagger, Copenhagen, 1955–1958).

31 In the collection entitled *Barney Brady's Goose; The Hedge School; The Three Wishes; and other Irish Tales.*

32 Thompson (1955–1958). The motif of charmed dancing occurs also in the international folktale which is given the type-number 592 by Aarne and Thompson.

33 Edward Schroder, *Die Tanzer von Kölbigk* (Kohlhammer, Stuttgart, 1896); Michael Chesnutt, 'The Colbeck Legend' in *Folklore Studies in the Twentieth Century*, edited by Venetia J. Newall (Brewer, Suffolk, 1980), pp. 158–166.

34 Dáithi Ó hÓgáin, *An File* (Oifig an tSoláthair, Dublin, 1982), pp. 405–408, Ó hÓgáin (1985), pp. 209–210, 246.

35 Ó Súilleabháin (1942), pp. 247–248.

36 Ó hÓgáin, (1982), p. 90.

37 Ó Súilleabháin (1942), p. 41. Unpublished essay by Geraldine Lynch, 'The March Cock' (1976), in Department of Irish Folklore, University College, Dublin.

38 Cited from A. Norman Jeffares and A. S. Knowland, *A Commentary on the Collected Plays of W. B. Yeats* (Macmillan, London, 1975), p. 155.

39 *Ibid.*, p. 153.

40 Lists in Ó Súilleabháin and Christiansen (1967).

41 For this, see Thomas F. O'Rahilly, *Dánfhocail* (Talbot Press, Dublin, 1921), pp. 36–37 & 83–86.

42 Several references to Aristotle in Mss-Catalogue at Department

of Irish Folklore, University College, Dublin. For his portrayal in international folk legend, see Alton C. Morris, 'The Aristotle of Fact and Legend' in *Folklore International*, edited by K. Wilgus and Carol Sommer (Folklore Associates, Pennsylvania, 1967), pp. 151–159.

43 For the folklore of leprechauns, see Diarmaid Ó Giolláin in *Béaloideas* 52 (1984), p. 75–150.

44 The fullest description of these is in a twelfth century text — *Lebor Gábala Erenn*, edited by R. A. Stewart MacAlister, Vol. 4 (Irish Texts Society, Dublin, 1941), pp. 97–211. Stephens could have got his information on them from a variety of published sources.

45 *See* Ó Súilleabháin (1942), pp. 455 & 463–4.

46 The Aran Islands, pp. 42–46. Other versions listed in Ó Súilleabháin and Christiansen (1967), as Type 1350. A study of this folktale, by Eilís Ní Dhuibhne, will appear in a forthcoming issue of *Béaloideas*.

47 See *Beáloideas 21* (1952), pp. 21–23: Ó hÓgáin (1985), pp. 23–24 & 208–209.

48 In the poem 'The Rebel'.

49 Ó hÓgáin (1982), pp. 15–17, 151 & 414. see also Dáithí Ó hÓgáin, 'Gach File is Fáidh' in *Comhar*, 7–8/1980.

50 Ó hÓgáin (1982), pp. 307–321.

51 For discussion of these legends, see Dáithí Ó hÓgáin, 'Eoghan Rua — an File mar Laoch' in *Feasta* 1–2/1980.

52 Patrick S. Dinneen and Tadhg O'Donoghue, *Dánta Aodhagáin Uí Rathaille* (Irish Texts Society, London, 1911), p. 116. Yeats's poem was published in *Last Poems* (1936).

53 Thompson (1955–1958), Motifs D565.5 and D735; Francis John Byrne, *Irish Kings and High-Kings* (Batsford, London, 1973), pp. 74–75; Alwyn Rees and Brinley Rees, *Celtic Heritage* (Thames and Hudson, London, 1973), pp. 74–76. For many examples of the personification of Ireland as a woman, see Brian O'Rourke, 'The Long Walk of a Queen' in *Chiba Review, 6* (1984) and 7 (1985).

54 John O'Daly, *The Poets and Poetry of Munster* (O'Daly, Dublin, 1850), pp. 132–137.

55 For the relationships between Gaelic poet-lore and hero-lore, see Ó hÓgáin (1985), pp. 216–236. A full discussion of Yeats's use of such sources in Mary Helen Thuente, *W. B. Yeats and Irish Folklore* (Gill and Macmillan, Dublin, 1980), pp. 195–238.

56 Ó hÓgáin (1982), pp. 5–32, 254–264; Ó hÓgáin (1985), pp. 257–269.

57 Birgit Bramsbäck, *James Stephens* (Hodges Figgis, Dublin, 1959), p. 37.

58 In Chapter 13. See also the reference in Chapter 16 to 'knowledge posted between his tongue and his thought'.

59 Ó hÓgáin (1982), pp. 33–79. See also Dáithí Ó hÓgáin 'The Visionary Voice', in *Irish Universiry Review*, Spring 1979, pp. 49–56.

60 Episode 12 (Cyclops) — on pp. 672–673 of Vol. 2 of the edition by Hans Walter Gabler (Garland Publishing, New York, 1984). Joyce was being critical of the accounts of these poets given by Douglas Hyde ('The Sweet Little Branch') and Daniel Corkery (D.O.C.).

61 In the collection *A Munster Twilight* (Talbot Press, Dublin, 1916).
62 Sources and discussion of composing in the dark in Ó hÓgáin (1982), pp. 107–113. For convocations of poets, see Pádraig Ó Fiannachta, *An Barántas* (An Sagart, Maynooth, 1978); Dáithí Ó hÓgáin, 'Na Cúirteanna Éigse — Fianaise an Bhéaloidis' in *Comhar* 2–3/1980.
63 *The Green Fool*, Chapter 25.
64 From the poem 'In the Same Mood' — on p. 33 of *Collected Poems*. In a religious vein, Gaelic poets often identified the reputed supernatural sources of their art with God — see Ó hÓgáin (1979) pp. 44–61; and specifically Ó hÓgáin (1982), pp. 7, 32 &48.
65 From the poem 'The Great Hunger' (1942), part 13 — see *Collected Poems*, p. 52.
66 Ó hÓgáin (1982), pp. 281–363. Kavanagh's poem is on pp. 141–142 of *Collected Poems*. See Kavanagh's interesting reference in Chapter 3 of *The Green Fool* to the power of the old poets to put nicknames on people, which 'never came unstuck for seven generations'.
67 Note to 'The Christmas Mummers' — on p. 114 of *Collected Poems*.
68 Charles Plummer, *Vitae Sanctorum Hiberniae* (Clarendon Press, Oxford, 1910), Vol. 1, pp. cxxxv & clxxiii–clxxiv; Ó hÓgáin (1985), p. 43–46.
69 Joseph Szovérffy in *Éigse 8* (1956), pp. 112–113. Clarke got his version, and its title, from Douglas Hyde, *Legends of Saints and Sinners* (Gresham, London, n.d.), pp. 22–25. His poem is in the collection *Flight to Africa* (Dolmen Press, Dublin, 1963).
70 The poem 'Song of the Books' in *Flight to Africa*.
71 Edited in Standish Hayes O'Grady, *Silva Gadelica* (Williams and Norgate, London, 1892), Vol. 1, pp. 276–289. For the text's connections with folklore, see Alan Bruford, *Gaelic Folktales and Mediaeval Romances* (Folklore of Ireland Society, Dublin, 1969), pp. 13, 153–154 & 202–203. Clarke's poem is in the collection *The Cattledrive in Connaught* (1925) — see Austin Clarke, *Collected Poems* (Dolmen Press, Dublin, 1974), pp. 126–127.

GHOSTS IN ANGLO-IRISH LITERATURE

Peter Denman

1 *The Demon Lover and Other Stories* (Jonathan Cape, London, 1952), pp. 216–224.
2 The *Cambridge Bibliography of English Literature* calls the attribution to Maginn 'implausible'; whoever the author, the opening chapters set in and around Dublin offer scenes of lively pseudo-historical interest to the reader of Anglo-Irish fiction.
3 *Collected Works*, edited by T. O. Mabott (The Belknap Press of Harvard University Press, Cambridge, Massachusetts, 1978), 3 vols, II.
4 *The Fantastic Tales of Fitzjames O'Brien* edited by Michael Hayes (John Calder, London, 1977).

5 *Yeats and the Occult*, edited by George Mills Harper (Macmillan, London, 1976); Mary Catherine Flannery, *Yeats and Magic: The Earlier Works* (Colin Smythe, Gerrards Cross, Buckinghamshire, 1977).
6 'Epic', Patrick Kavanagh, *Collected Poems* (MacGibbon and Kee, London, 1964), p. 136; 'What Then?', W. B. Yeats, *Collected Poems* (Macmillan, London, 1956), pp. 347–348; 'Station Island', Seamus Heaney, *Station Island* (Faber and Faber London, 1984), pp. 61–94; 'Butcher's Dozen', Thomas Kinsella, *Fifteen Dead* (Dolmen Press, Dublin, 1979), pp. 18–20.

SHAW AND CREATIVE EVOLUTION

A. M. Gibbs

1 A bibliography of Shaw's writings on religious and philosophical topics, and of commentaries, is provided by Charles A. Carpenter: 'Shaw and Religion/Philosophy: A Working Bibliography', in Charles A. Berst, (editor), *Shaw and Religion*, The Annual of Shaw Studies, Vol. I (Pennsylvania State University Press, University Park and London, 1981) pp. 225–46.
2 Edward McNulty, 'George Bernard Shaw as a Boy', *The Candid Friend*, 6 July 1901, p. 384. Shaw chose a religious subject for his first attempt at playwriting, at the age of 21. The fragmentary work, *Passion Play*, originally called 'The Household of Joseph' which remained unpublished during his lifetime, contains some adumbrations of Shaw's later religious thought. See Charles A. Berst, *Shaw and Religion*, pp. 12–21 for a perceptive discussion of the work.
3 *Bernard Shaw Collected Letters 1874–1897*, edited by Dan H. Laurence (Max Reinhardt, London, 1965), p. 551.
4 *The Bodley Head Bernard Shaw: Collected Plays with their Prefaces*, edited by Dan H. Laurence, 7 vols (Max Reinhardt, London, 1970–74) Vol. v, p. 338. Hereafter referred to as, *Collected Plays*.
5 Shaw gave this information to a Professor of English at the Universiry of Pennsylvania, Thomas Demetrius O'Bolger. O'Bolger was preparing a biographical work on Shaw which was never completed. Typescripts of Shaw's replies to questionnaires sent to him by O'Bolger are held in the Houghton Library, Harvard University (b MS Eng. 1046.9).
6 Shaw was born at 3 Upper Synge St. When he was about ten years old the family moved to 1 Hatch St. to join Mrs Shaw's musical associate, George Vandeleur Lee. Lee and Shaw's Rabelaisian uncle, Walter Gurly, were amongst those who exposed him early to sceptical ideas concerning orthodox religion. The character of discussions about religion in the household is suggested by Shaw's comment to O'Bolger: 'When my father, Lee and Uncle Walter got into an argument on religion or anything else, it was such an argument as no other

child in Ireland, probably, would have been allowed to listen to'. (*Bernard Shaw: Collected Letters 1911–1925*, edited by Dan H. Laurence (Max Reinhardt, London, 1985), p. 368).

7 Recalled by Shaw in 'What Irish Protestants Think' (Speech delivered to the Irish Protestant Committee, Memorial Hall Faringdon, London, 6 Dec 1912) in Warren S. Smith, editor, *The Religious Speeches of Bernard Shaw* (Pennsylvania State University Press, University Park and London, 1963) p. 50.

8 Bernard Shaw, Preface to *Immaturity* (Constable, London, 1930), p. xxi.

9 Bernard Shaw, Letter to Sir Oliver Lodge 14 June 1924; *Collected Letters 1911–1925*, p. 878.

10 Hayden Church, 'My Spoof at a Seance: Bernard Shaw Against the Spiritualists – And Why', *Sunday Dispatch*, 13 Jan 1929; *Collected Letters 1911–1925*, p. 879.

11 Bernard Shaw, *Sixteen Self Sketches* (Constable, London, 1949), p. 45.

12 Julian B. Kaye, *Bernard Shaw and the Nineteenth-Century Tradition* (University of Oklahoma Press, Norman, 1958) p. 49.

13 See *Essays and Letters by Percy Bysshe Shelley*, edited by Ernest Rhys (Walter Scott, London, 1905), p. 87. The influence of Shelley's conception on Shaw is pointed out by Charles A. Berst in *Shaw and Religion*, p. 20.

14 In the preface to *Back to Methuselah* Shaw describes *The World as Will and Idea* as 'the metaphysical complement to Lamarck's natural history, as it demonstrates that the driving force behind Evolution is the will to live.' (*Collected Plays*, V, p. 282).

15 For a discussion of Comte's influence (most conspicuous in the final speech of Father Keegan in *John Bull's Other Island*) see Julian B. Kaye, *op. cit.*, pp. 44–48, 50–54, and A. M. Gibbs, *The Art and Mind of Shaw: Essays in Criticism* (Macmillan, London, 1983), p. 150. Alan P. Barr in his *Victorian Stage Pulpiteer: Bernard Shaw's Crusade* (University of Georgia Press, Athens, 1973), p. 23, draws attention to parallels between the religious writings of Mill and Shaw.

16 Thomas Carlyle, *Sartor Resartus* (Oxford University Press, London, New York, Toronto, 1902), p. 165.

17 Theodosius Dobzhansky, Francisco J. Abyala, G. Ledyard Stebbings, James W. Valentine, *Evolution* (W. H. Freeman, San Francisco, 1977) p. 8.

19 Charles Darwin, *On the Origin of Species*, introduction by Sir Julian Huxley (Mentor, New York, 1958), p. 74.

20 Samuel Butler, *Luck or Cunning, as the Main Means of Organic Modification*? (A. C. Fifield, London, 1920), p. 18.

21 This is the main thesis of *Life and Habit*.

22 Samuel Butler, *Evolution, Old & New; or the Theories of Buffon, Dr Erasmus Darwin, and Lamarck, as Compared with that of Charles Darwin*, 3rd edition. (Jonathan Cape, London, 1921), p. 53.

23 Samuel Butler, *Life and Habit*, 3rd edition. (Jonathan Cape, London, 1916), p. 307.
24 *Evolution, Old & New*, p. 59.
25 *Collected Plays*, V, p. 294.
26 *Collected Plays*, V, 698.
27 *Luck or Cunning?*, p. 266.
28 *Ibid.*, p. 267. Cf. Shaw: 'there is behind the universe an intelligent and driving force of which we ourselves are a part — a divine spark'. (*Religious Speeches*, p. 17).
29 *Collected Plays*, V, pp. 299, 303.
30 'The general doctrine of evolution shows how, out of a perfectly amorphous form of life, something which we picture as a little speck of protaplasm, in a wonderful way by constant effort and striving evolved higher and higher forms of life, until gradually you have a thing so comparatively wonderful as men and women. That evolutionary process to me is God: this wonderful will of the universe'. ('The Religion of the British Empire', 22 Nov 1906, *Religious Speeches*, p. 6).
31 *Ibid.*
32 *Collected Plays*, IV, p. 530.
33 Collected Plays, II, p. 680.
34 'Modern Religion I', 21 Mar 1912, *Religious Speeches*, p. 49.
35 *Collected Plays*, II, p. 664.
36 *Ibid.*, p. 523.
37 *Ibid.*, p. 514.
38 *Ibid.*
39 *Ibid.*, pp. 764–65.
40 *Ibid.*, p. 776. The question as to whether the Yahoo should be exterminated is the subject of a grand debate amongst the Houyhnhnms in Chapter IX of *Gulliver's Travels*. The Houyhnhnms also practise selective breeding of their own species.
41 *Collected Plays*, II. p. 656.
42 *The Art and Mind of Shaw*, pp. 122–39.
43 *Collected Plays*, II, p. 726.
44 *Collected Plays*, V, p. 159.
45 *Ibid.*
46 *Ibid.*, p. 160.
47 *Ibid.*
48 *Collected Plays*, V, p. 41.
49 Shaw described his experiences at the Front in a three-part article, 'Joy Riding at the Front', *Daily Chronicle*, 5, 7 and 8 March 1917.
50 The importance of the war as a formative influence in the writing of *Back to Methuselah* is emphasised in J. L. Wisenthal's excellent discussion of the play in his *The Marriage of Contraries: Bernard Shaw's Middle Plays* (Harvard University Press, Cambridge, Mass., 1974) pp. 193–217.
51 *Collected Plays*, V, p. 348.

52 *Ibid.*, p. 363.
53 See *Gullivers Travels*, edited by Paul Turner (Oxford University Press, London, 1971) pp. 127–29. Our of 'love of his country' Gulliver tells the King of the marvellous destructive powers of gunpowder and cannons.
54 Edmund Wilson, *The Triple Thinkers* (Penguin, Harmondsworth, 1962), p. 212.
55 *Collected Plays*, V, p. 491.
56 *Ibid.*, p. 576.
57 See Lawrence Langner, *GBS and the Lunatic* (Hutchinson, London, 1964) p. 49. Langner records that Shaw described the Elderly Gentleman as 'an old duffer'.
58 *Collected Plays*, V, p. 551.
59 *Ibid.*, p. 567.
60 *Ibid.*, p. 574.
61 *Ibid.*, p. 612.
62 *Ibid.*, p. 630.
63 But for a different and interesting argument about the end of the play see the interpretation offered by Valli Rao in her '*Back to Methuselah*: A Blakean Interpretation,' in *Shaw and Religion*, p. 176.
64 Bernard Shaw, *The Adventures of the Black Girl in Her Search for God* (Constable, London, 1932), p. 53.
65 *Ibid.*, p. 55.
66 *Ibid.*, pp. 39, 41.
67 *Ibid.*, pp. 38–9.

CATHOLICISM IN THE CULTURE OF THE NEW IRELAND: CANON SHEEHAN AND DANIEL CORKERY

Ruth Fleischmann

1 W. B. Yeats, 'The Need for Audacity of Thought', *The Dial*, February 1926 in W. B. Yeats, *Uncollected Works*, edited by John P. Frayne (Macmillan, London, 1970), vol. 2, p. 461. Here is the text of the 'Cherry Tree' carol as Yeats gives it:

> Then up spake Mary
> So meek and so mild;
> Oh, gather me cherries Joseph
> For I am with child.
>
> Then up spake Joseph,
> With his words so unkind
> Let them gather cherries
> That brought thee with child.
>
> Then up spake the little child,
> In his Mother's womb;
> Bow down you sweet cherry tree,
> And give my Mother some.

Then the top spray of the cherry tree,
Bowed down to her knee;
And now you see Joseph
There are cherries for me.

2 Even to Protestant writers who came from poor families, like James Stephens and Seán O'Casey, the discovery of the other tradition represented an extension of their own world. James Stephens wrote: The Dublin I was born to was poor and Protestant and athletic. While very young I extended my range and entered a Dublin that was poor and Catholic and Gaelic – a very wonderworld. Then as a young writer I further extended to a Dublin that was poor and artistic and political. Then I made a Dublin for myself, my Dublin. Quoted in A. Norman Jeffares, *Anglo-Irish Literature*, (Macmillan, London, 1982), p. 175.

3 Douglas Hyde, unpublished manuscript of 194 pages in the National Library of Ireland, quoted in Gareth W. Dunleavy, *Douglas Hyde* (Bucknell University Press, irish Writers Series, Lewisburg/London 1974), p. 32.

4 Nicholas P. Canning, *The Elizabethan Conquest of Ireland: A Pattern Established 1565–76*. (Hassocks, Sussex, 1976), pp. 124–5.

5 Ibid., p. 121.

6 This aspect of Protestantism was feared by the Portuguese colonial authorities, who refused to allow Protestant missionaries into the territories they held on the following grounds: To tell a person he is able to interpret the Bible freely is to insinuate in him an undue autonomy and turn him into a rebel. . . A Protestant native is already disposed towards – not to say an active agent in – the revolt against civilising peoples.' Quoted in Thomas Hodgkin, *Nationalism in Colonial Africa* (Muller, London 1956), p. 98.

7 Douglas Hyde, *The Need for De-Anglicising Ireland* in: Charles Gavan Duffy, George Sigerson and Douglas Hyde, *The Revival of Irish Literature* (T. F. Unwin, London 1894, rpt. Lemma Publishing Co., New York 1973), pp. 118, 119, 129.

8 D. P. Moran, *The Philosophy of Irish Ireland* (James Duffy and Co. Dublin 1905), pp. 2, 9, 3.

9 Daniel Corkery, *Synge and Anglo-Irish Literature*, (University Press, Cork, 1931), p. 243.

10 Canon Patrick A. Sheehan, *Geoffrey Austin, Student*, (M. H. Gill and Son, Dublin 1895, rpt. Dublin n.d. 1952) Phoenix, p. 154.

11 Robin Flower, *The Western Island*, (Clarendon Press, Oxford 1944/1974), p. 70.

12 Canon Sheehan's novel *My New Curate* (1900) gives a very unflattering picture of a secret, anti-clerical Fenian organisation. The curate unmasks the leader as an agent of Dublin Castle, and astonishes the villagers by further revealing that this is only part of a British, Freemason and Jewish conspiracy to subvert the faith and purity of the nation. (*My New Curate*, chapter 11). Canon Sheehan uses anti-

Semitism, just as the French Right was doing at the time in the Dreyfus affair, to blacken liberal or radical critics of conservative Catholic politics. In 1904, not long after the publication of *My New Curate*, a Redemptorist priest in Limerick reacted to the closing of his order's schools in France by the liberal government by setting his parishioners on the Jews of the city, a small community that had fled to Ireland in 1878 from a pogrom in Lithuania, and eked out a living by selling religious pictures and books to the poor. The priest, thirsting for action, and unable to imagine how opposition to the church's hold on education could arise other than through a sinister Jewish plot, organized a boycott of the Jews which pauperized the community and reduced it by half in two years. See Louis Hyman, *The Jews in Ireland* (Irish University Press, Dublin 1972, pp. 211–217). Arthur Griffith supported the Redemptorists in *The United Irishman*; Fred Ryan, Standish O'Grady, Michael Davitt and John Redmond denounced the campaign, as did James Joyce through his portrait of the Citizen in *Ulysses*, and through the choice of his main character.

13 James Connolly, Labour, Nationality and Religion', in *The Workers' Republic*, edited by Desmond Ryan (At the Sign of the Three Candles, Fleet St., Dublin, 1951), p. 194.

14 For the striking resemblance to Pearse's theory of the need for a blood sacrifice to shake the nation out of its political degradation see Canon Sheehan *The Graves of Kilmorna* (Longmans, Green and Co., 1915 rpt. Dublin, 1952, Phoenix), pp. 66–68.

15 Swift struggled to maintain the privileges of the Anglican church against the attacks of the dissenters and the liberals willing to grant them concessions. See J. C. Beckett, 'Swift: The Priest in Politics,' in *Confrontations* (Faber London 1972), p. 119.

16 W. B. Yeats, The Need for Audacity of Thought, p. 464.

17 Canon Sheehan, *Luke Delmege*, (Longmans, Green and Co. London 1902), pp. 351–2.

18 Douglas Hyde, *A Literary History of Ireland* (1899, rpt. Ernest Benn and Bernard Noble London/New York 1967), pp. 631. 634 and note p. 634 and *The Necessity for De-Anglicising Ireland* pp. 137–8 and note.

19 Daniel Corkery, *Synge and Anglo-Irish Literature*, p. 14.

20 *Ibid.*, p. 15.

21 See George Moore, *Parnell and His Island* (Sonnenschein & Co., London 1887, ed. of 1891), pp. 5–12, 35–8, 55–66 and 77–93 on the condition of the landlords and their views of the Irish.

22 See W. B. Yeats 'The Academic Class and the Agrarian Revolution' (1899) in *Uncollected Works* vol. 2, pp. 148–152.

23 Seán Ó Tuama, 'Daniel Corkery, Cultural Philosopher, Literary Critic: a Memoir', lecture delivered to the International Association for the Study of Anglo-Irish Literature in Uppsala/Sweden, August 1986.

24 Alice Stopford Green, *The Making of Ireland and its Undoing* (1908),

quoted in Daniel Corkery, *The Hidden Ireland: A Study of Gaelic Munster in the Eighteenth Century* (York University Press, 1924, rpt. Dublin/London 1967[2], p. 285.
25 R. R. Madden, quoted in Corkery, *The Hidden Ireland* p. 20.
26 Corkery, *Synge and Anglo-Irish Literature*, pp. 23 and 25.
27 Daniel Corkery, *The Fortunes of the Irish Language* (Talbot Press, 1954, rpt. Mercier Press, Cork 1968), p. 65.
28 Corkery, *Synge and Anglo-Irish Literature*, pp. 20–22.
29 According to Seán Ó Tuama, Gaelic literature did not become Catholic until the nineteenth century, see 'Daniel Corkery', his Uppsala lecture.
30 See D. P. Moran, *The Philosophy of Irish Ireland* pp. 19–20.
31 W. B. Yeats 'Compulsory Gaelic', *The Irish Statesman* 2 August 1924, in *Uncollected Works* vol. 2, p. 446.
32 Corkery, *The Fortunes of the Irish Language*, p. 21 and chapter 2.
33 Alice Stopford Green, *Irish National Tradition*, quoted by Corkery in *The Fortunes of the Irish Language* p. 25 with the comment: 'No truer word has ever been spoken about the history of Ireland.'
34 *Ibid.*, pp. 114–115.
35 George W. Russell — AE, *Selections from the Contributions to The Irish Homestead*, edited by Henry Summerfield (Colin Smythe, Gerrards Cross, 1978) vol. 1, p. 205.
36 Frantz Fanon, *Les Damnés de la Terre*, Paris 1961, p. 157.
37 Patrick Bolger, *The Irish Co-operative Movement* (Institute of Public Administration Dublin, 1977), pp. 107 and 259.
38 Ibid., pp. 239, 241–3, 262. See also Giovanni Costigan, *A History of Modern Ireland* (Pegasus, new York 1969), p. 266.
39 Erhard Rumpf, *Nationalismus und Sozialismus in Ireland: Historisch-Soziologischer Versuch über die Irische Revolution seit 1918*, Meisenheim am Glan 1959, pp. 40–82.
40 Marcus de Búrca, *The GAA: A History of the Gaelic Athletic Association*, (Cumann Lúthchleas Gael, Dublin, 1980), p. 2.
41 George Russell — AE, *Selections from Contributions to The Irish Homestead*, p. 2.

YEATS AND RELIGION

Mitsuko Ohno

All references to Yeats's plays are taken from *The Variorum Edition of the Plays of W. B. Yeats*, edited by R. K. Alspach (Macmillan, London, 1966), and to his poems from *The Collected Poems of W. B. Yeats*, (Macmillan, New York, 1966).

1 W. B. Yeats, *Autobiographies* (Macmillan, London, 1973), p. 12.
2 Graham Hough, *The Mystery Religion of W. B. Yeats* (Harvester Press, Sussex, 1984), p. 8.

3 W. B. Yeats, *Mythologies* (Collier Books, New York, 1969), p. 7.
4 *Autobiographies*, pp. 25–26.
5 *Autobiographies*, p. 89.
6 W. B. Yeats, *Essays and Introductions* (Macmillan, London, 1974), p. 28.
7 W. B. Yeats, *Memoirs* (Macmillan, London, 1972), pp. 100–101.
8 *Autobiographies*, pp. 378–379.
9 W. B. Yeats, *Explorations* (Collier Books, New York, 1973), pp. 31–32.
10 *Memoirs*, pp. 127–128.
11 Cyriel O. Sigstedt, *The Swedenborg Epic* (Swedenborg Society, London, 1981), p. 185. The first English translation of *The Spiritual Diary* (Vol. 1 out of the now available I–V: London, Swedenborg Society, 1977) was published in England in 1846. Yeats continued to read Swedenborg, as the markings in the pages of the books in his library show. *See* Edward O'Shea, *A Descriptive catalog of W. B. Yeats's Library* (Garland, New York, 1985) pp. 182, 296.
12 *Memoirs*, pp. 130–131.
13 'The People', *Collected Poems*, p. 149.
14 *Variorum Edition of the Plays*, p. 712.
15 Michael Meyer (editor), *The File on Strindberg* (Methuen, London, 1986), pp. 47, 57.
16 *Explorations*, p. 65.
17 *Ibid.*, p. 68.
18 Hough, op. cit., p. 72.
19 S. P. Swami, W. B. Yeats, (translators), *The Ten Principal Upanishads* (Faber, London, 1938 Second edition reprint), p. 10.
20 Sandra F. Siegel (editor), *Purgatory: Manuscript Materials Including the Author's Final Text* (Cornell Universiry Press, Ithaca, 1986), p. 26.
21 *Essays and Introductions*, p. 485.

JOYCE AND CATHOLICISM

Eamonn Hughes

1 James Joyce, *Ulysses*, The Corrected Text (Penguin, Harmondsworth, 1986) p. 17. All further references in the text as *U*.
2 James Joyce, *A Portrait of the Artist as a Young Man*, The definitive text (Jonathan Cape, London, 1968) p. 251. All further references in the text as *AP*.
3 Readers interested in the doctrinal aspects of Joyce's writings are directed to the works of such critics as J. Mitchell Morse, *The Sympathetic Alien: James Joyce and Catholicism* (Peter Owen Ltd/The Vision Press, London, 1959); William T. Noon, *Joyce and Aquinas* (Yale University Press, New Haven, Conn, 1957) and Robert Boyle, *James Joyce's Pauline Vision* (Southern Illinois University Press, Carbondale, Ill. 1978). Mention should also be made of Boyle's interesting

essay 'Miracle in Black Ink: A Glance at Joyce's Use of His Eucharistic Image', *James Joyce Quarterley*, 10 (Fall 1972) pp. 47–60.

4 Morse, *op cit*, p. ix.

5 The examples are taken from Edward J. Ahearn, 'Religious Values in Joyce's *Ulysses*', *Christian Scholar*, 44 (Summer 1961) pp. 139–45, and Beryl Schloessman, *Joyce's Catholic Comedy of Language* (The University of Winsconsin Press, London, 1985) respectively.

6 Terry Eagleton, *Literary Theory: An Introduction* (Basil Blackwell, Oxford, 1983) pp. 22–23. On the general issue of secularisation and culture see also: Chris Baldick, *The Social Mission of English Criticism 1842–1932* (Clarendon Press, Oxford, 1983); Edward Said 'Secular Criticism' in his *The World, The Text* and the *Critic* (Faber, London, 1984) pp. 1–30.

7 Matthew Arnold quoted in Edward Said, 'Secular Criticism', *op cit*, p. 10.

8 Richard Ellmann, *Ulysses on the Liffey*, corrected edition (Faber, London, 1974) p. 90.

9 F. S. L. Lyons, *Culture and Anarchy in Ireland, 1890–1939*, paperback edition (Oxford University Press, London, 1982) p. 13. Why Lyons should refer the issue to the judgement of 'most Englishmen' is perhaps explained by the allusion to Matthew Arnold in his title. If Lyons is right about this revulsion it explains something about the lack of awareness in critical response that this essay seeks to indicate.

10 Mention should be made, however, of the two histories of the Irish Catholic Church by David W. Miller, *Church, State and Nation in Ireland, 1898–1921* (Gill and Macmillan, Dublin, 1973) and J. H. Whyte, *Church and State in Modern Ireland 1923–1979* (1971) 2nd edition (Gill and Macmillan, Dublin, 1980) and also of Whyte's more analytically oriented *Catholics in Western Democracies: A Study in Political Behaviour* (Gill and Macmillan, Dublin, 1981). I am indebted to all three works in this chapter.

11 E. P. Thompson, *The Making of the English Working Class*, revised edition with new preface (Pelican Books, Harmondsworth, Middlesex, 1980) p. 412.

12 *Ibid*, pp. 412–419.

13 Miller, *op cit*, pp. 2–3.

14 W. J. McCormack, *Ascendancy and Tradition in Anglo-Irish Literary History from 1798 to 1939* (Clarendon Press, Oxford, 1985) p. 266. The pitfalls of taking an overly generalised approach to religion are well summarised in this brief quotation in which the Mohammedan (*hegira*), the Catholic (Joyce) and the Protestant (Weber) collide to no apparent purpose. This is odd from a critic usually fastidious about detail but it exemplifies the way in which Catholicism can be taken for granted rather than made the focus for analysis; so when McCormack calls for 'inquiry into the dominant political, social, and economic relationships in which and of which [Joyce] wrote' (pp. 253–4), religion is significantly absent.

15 It should be clear by this point that Louis Althusser's 'Ideology and Ideological State Apparatuses (Notes Towards an Investigation)' in his *Essays on Ideology*, paperback edition (Verso, London, 1984) pp. 1–60 has prompted much of my thinking on ideology *vis a vis* religion, not least because the essay's promised analysis of religion as an ideological state apparatus is replaced by Althusser's argument with God (see pp. 51–7). E. P. Thompson, indeed, refers to Althusserian Marxism as 'having many of the attributes of a theology'; E. P. Thompson, *The Poverty of Theory and Other Essays* (Merlin Press, London, 1978) pp. 4, 33. Thompson and Althusser are now the theoretical equivalent of Shem and Shaun.

16 I am grateful to Robert Welch for alerting me to the ambiguity of this phrase and for other comments.

17 Thomas McGreevy, 'The Catholic Element in *Work in Progress*', in Samuel Beckett *et al*, *Our Exagmination Round His Factification for Incamination of Work in Progress* (1929) (Faber and Faber, London, 1972) pp. 117–127, p. 121.

18 Richard Ellmann, *James Joyce* (Oxford University Press, Oxford, 1959) p. 626. Ellmann here quotes from two letters Joyce wrote to Harriet Shaw Weaver and Valery Larbaud on how he was directing criticism of his work; see Richard Ellmann (editor), *The Selected Letters of James Joyce* (The Viking Press, New York, 1975) pp. 341–2, 343–6.

19 Throughout this episode Haines' sole function is to be unable to understand the complexities of Stephen and the Irish. For further details see my ' "It seems history is to blame", *Ulysses* and Cultural History', Ideas and Production, 6 (Spring 1987) pp. 100–115.

20 F. S. L. Lyons, *Culture and Anarchy in Ireland, op cit*, p. 74. Lyons is here summarising the views of Sir Horace Plunkett.

21 George Moore, *The Untilled Field* (1903) (William Heineman, London, 1914) p. 43.

22 All quotations in this section are from the Ninth Article of the Apostles' Creed as glossed in the 1889 *Catechism*. The Creed remains largely unchanged between this and more modern versions except that Christ now 'descends to the dead' rather than 'into hell' i.e. Limbo. The point is not made flippantly but to illustrate that even 'the chief things that God has revealed [as] contained in the Apostles' Creed' can be altered. Joyce's Catholic background was one in which no bones were made about Hell or Limbo; indeed *A Portrait* without the hell-fire sermon would be unthinkable.

23 See J. H. Whyte, *Catholics in Western Democracies, op cit*, Ch's 2 & 3; Peter Nichols, *The Politics of the Vatican* (The Pall Mall Press, London, 1968) Ch 3.

24 This list is necessarily incomplete, for further details and the encyclicals themselves see Anne Freemantle (editor), *The Social Teachings of the Church* (Mentor/Omega Books, New York, 1963) and *The Papal Encyclicals in their Historical Context* (Mentor/Omega Books, New York, 1963).

25 Miller, *op cit*, p. 28.
26 See F. S. L. Lyons, *Ireland Since the Famine*, revised edition (Fontana, London, 1973) pp. 20–1, and Terence Brown, *Ireland: A Social and Cultural History, 1922–79* (Fontana, London, 1981) pp. 27, 30.
27 Miller, *op cit*, p. 63.
28 See F. S. L. Lyons, *Culture and Anarchy in Ireland, op cit*, p. 81n; on the fate of Ryan see also Lyons, *Ireland Since the Famine, op cit*, p. 239n, and Miller, *op cit*, p. 222; for O'Donovan see Brown, *op cit*, pp. 30–2; and for MacDonald see Miller, *op cit*, pp. 239–41, which bears out Sean O'Casey's more rumbustious remarks which are worth quoting because they reflect the sense of waste: 'When Maynooth at last got a professor who was a theologian, they didn't know what to do with him. So they concentrated on thinking what they could do to him. If he was let go on, he'd be stirring up trouble always.' *Inishfallen Fare Thee Well, Autobiography Book 4* (1949) (Pan Books, London, 1972) pp. 232–67; MacDonald is the book's dedicatee.
29 David Howell, *A Lost Left: Three Studies in Socialism and Nationalism* (Manchester University Press, Manchester, 1986) pp. 88–92.
30 Bernard Ransom, *Connolly's Marxism* (Pluto Press, London, 1980) pp. 19–20.
31 Oliver MacDonagh, *States of Mind: A Study of Anglo-Irish Conflict, 1780–1980* (George Allen and Unwin, London, 1983) pp. 90–103.
32 Miller, *op cit*, pp. 145–6.
33 Brown, *op cit*, p. 30.
34 *Ibid*, p. 35.
35 Seamus Deane, 'Joyce and Stephen: The Provincial Intellectual', in his *Celtic Revivals* (Faber, London, 1985) pp. 75–91, p. 78.
36 Richard Kearney, 'Introduction', in Richard Kearney (editor), *The Irish Mind: Exploring Intellectual Traditions* (Wolfhound Press, Dublin, 1985) pp. 7–38, p. 9.
37 M. P. Hederman, 'The Mind of Joyce: from Paternalism to Paternity', *loc cit*, pp. 244–66, pp. 244, 246.
38 McCormack, *op cit*, p. 241.
39 *Ibid*, p. 263.
40 F. C. Coppleston, *Aquinas* (Penguin, Harmondsworth, Middlesex, 1955) pp. 246–7.
41 Anne Freemantle (editor), *The Social Teachings of the Church, op cit*, pp. 47, 32–3, 27.
42 On Aquinas and the history of the concept of autonomy see Steven Lukes, *Individualism* (Basil Blackwell, Oxford, 1973) Ch. 8. For Joyce and nineteenth century concepts of autonomy see Dominic Manganiello, *Joyce's Politics* (Routledge and Kegan Paul, London, 1980) Ch3 ii.
43 George Moore, *Hail and Farewell*, (editor) Richard Cave (Colin Smythe, Gerrards Cross, 1985) p. 362. All further references in the text as *H & F*. See also Albert J. Solomon, 'A Moore in *Ulysses*', *James Joyce Quarterly*, 10 (Winter 1973) pp. 215–27.

44 F. S. L. Lyons, *Charles Stewart Parnell* (Fontana/Collins, London, 1978). Chapters 15, 16 and 17 cover the period of the O'Shea divorce and its aftermath and make it clear that the Irish Church held back for as long as it could and decided to throw its full weight against Parnell only when it became clear that he would fight on despite pressure from English Liberal nonconformists.
45 I am grateful to W. F. T. Myers for this information and for much helpful conversation during the writing of this essay.
46 James Joyce, *Stephen Hero* (Jonathan Cape, London, 1969) p. 199.
47 Boyle, 'Miracle in Black Ink', *op cit*, p. 48. According to the *OED* the sense of inward knowledge is, appropriately in this this context, a secondary formation from the sense of knowledge shared privately with another.
48 Anne Freemantle (editor), *The Papal Encyclicals, op cit*, pp. 157–61.
49 James Joyce, *Finnegans Wake*, third edition (Faber and Faber, London, 1964) pp. 185–6. All further references in the text as *FW*. See also Boyle, 'Miracle in Black Ink', *op cit*.
50 Adaline Glasheen, *A Census of Finnegans Wake* (Faber and Faber, London, 1957) p. 58.
51 Raymond Williams, *The Country and the City* (The Hogarth Press, London, 1985) p. 245.
52 T. S. Eliot, '*Ulysses*, Myth and Order', *The Dial*, LXXV (Nov. 1923) pp. 480–3.
53 Edward Said, *op cit*, pp. 16–20.

FRANCIS STUART AND RELIGION: SHARING THE LEPER'S LAIR

Anne McCartney

1 Francis Stuart, 'The Love, The Loss, The Dream' published in *The Irish Times*, 13 February 1988.
2 Francis Stuart, *Black List, Section H* (Southern Illinois University Press, 1971).
3 Francis Stuart, *Pigeon Irish* (Victor Gollancz, London, 1932).
4 *Ibid.*, p. 39.
5 *Ibid.*, p. 274.
6 *Black List, Section H*, p. 311.
7 Francis Stuart, 'An Interview with J. H. Natterstad', published in *The Journal of Irish Literature*, January 1976, p. 17.
8 Francis Stuart, *The Pillar of Cloud* (Martin, Brian & O'Keefe, London, 1974).
9 Olivia Manning, 'On The Pillar of Cloud', in *A Festschrist for Francis Stuart*, edited by W. J. McCormack (Dolmen Press, Dublin, 1972), p. 27.
10 Francis Stuart, *Redemption* (Victor Gollancz, London, 1949).
11 In 1942 Stuart wrote a novel called *Winter Song* which was sub-

sequently rejected by the German Propaganda Ministry and never published, however portions of it were used in *Redemption*.

12 Francis Stuart, 'Selections from a Berlin Diary 1942', in *The Journal of Irish Literature*, January 1976, p. 95.
13 Francis Stuart, *The Abandoned Snail Shell* (Raven Arts Press, Dublin, 1987).
14 *Ibid.*, p. 64.
15 *Ibid.*, p. 30.
16 Paul Ricoeur, 'Dialogue with Paul Ricoeur', in Richard Kearney, *Dialogues with Contemporary Continental Thinkers* (Manchester University Press, 1984), p. 24.
17 *The Abandoned Snail Shell*, p. 11.
18 Francis Stuart, *The High Consistory* (Martin Brian & O'Keefe, London, 1981), p. 46.
19 Francis Stuart, 'Novelists on the Novel', *Crane Bag*, Vol. 3, No. 1, 1979.
20 *Ibid.*
21 *Ibid.*
22 *The Abandoned Snail Shell*, p. 33.
23 'Interview with J. H. Natterstad', p. 17.
24 *The Abandoned Snail Shell*, p. 33.
25 *Ibid.*, p. 61.
26 *Ibid.*, p. 27.
27 *Ibid.*, p. 62.
28 *Ibid.*
29 *Black List, Section H*. p. 167.
30 Daniel Murphy, *Religion and Imagination in Anglo-Irish Literature* (Irish Academic Press, Dublin, 1987), p. 18.
31 Martin Heidegger, *Poetry, Language, Thought* (Harper & Row, New York, 1971), explores the growing, becoming character of language as a lived speech whose meaning is not definitively enclosed in its textual forms but grows and develops with the attentions of successive readers.
32 *Black List, Section H*p. 172.
33 So each abandoned snail-shell strewn
Among those blotched dock-leaves might seem
In the pure ray shed by the loss
Of all man-measured value, like
Some priceless pearl-enamelled toy
Cushioned on green silk under glass.

David Gascoyne, 'The Gravel-Pit Field', *Collected Poems* (Oxford University Press, 1965), p. 92.
34 *Black List, Section H*, p. 384.
35 *Ibid.*
36 Francis Stuart, *Memorial* (Raven Arts Press, Dublin, 1984).
37 Francis Stuart, *Faillandia* (Raven Arts Press, Dublin, 1985).
38 *Ibid.*, p. 128.

39 *The High Consistory*, p. 57.
40 *Black List, Section H*, p. 146.
41 *Faillandia*, p. 17.
42 *An Abandoned Snail Shell*, p. 11.
43 *Ibid.*, p. 67.
44 *The High Consistory*, p. 77.
45 *Ibid.*
46 Francis Stuart, Letter to J. H. Natterstad, received 9th March 1970, quoted in J. H. Natterstad, 'Francis Stuart, The Artist as Outcast', edited by Heinz Kosok, *Studies in Anglo-Irish Literature* (Bouvier Verlag, Herbert Grundmann, Bonn, 1982).
47 *An Abandoned Snail Shell*, p. 34.
48 'Interview with J. H. Natterstad', p. 19.
49 Francis Stuart, 'Literature and Politics', *Crane Bag*, Vol. 1, No. 1, 1977.
50 *Ibid.*

RECEIVED RELIGION AND SECULAR VISION: MacNEICE AND KAVANAGH

Alan Peacock

1 G. S. Fraser, Introduction to D. B. Moore, *The Poetry of Louis MacNeice (Leicester University Press, Leicester 1972), p. 10.*
2 Terence Brown, *Louis MacNeice: Sceptical Vision* (Gill and MacMillan, Dublin 1975); William T. McKinnon, *Apollo's Blended Dream: A Study of the Poetry of Louis MacNeice* (Oxford University Press, London 1971).
3 See Walter Allen's comments, Introduction to Louis MacNeice, *Modern Poetry: A Personal Essay*, 2nd edn. (The Clarendon Press, Oxford 1968), pp. vi–viii.
4 *Ibid.*, p. 88.
5 *Ibid.*, p. 35.
6 Cf. 'The Strand' and 'The Kingdom' VII, *The Collected Poems of Louis MacNeice*, ed. E. R. Dodds (Faber and Faber, London 1966), pp. 226 and 253.
7 *Modern Poetry*, p. 1.
8 *Collected Poems*, p. 540. henceforth, citations from this volume are included in the text under *CP*.
9 The first two words of the poem ('Aere perennius?') signal that this is to be an Horatian meditation, with particular reference to *Odes* 3, 1. Some citations from this and 1, 11 appear in my text; but see also, e.g., the allusion to 3, 13 in the mention of the Bandusian Spring (p. 540), that to 1, 12 and 3, 5 in the mention of Regulus (p. 541), and in particular the echo in 'deliciously laughing' Lalage (p. 541) of the 'dulce ridentem' Lalage of *Odes* 1, 22. The 'old yarn/of the routed

wolf' (p. 541) refers to the same ode. Horace's famous Sabine farm figures on p. 543. 'Lusisti Satis' ('You have played enough') on the same page is from *Epistles* 2, 2. For some comments on MacNeice's formal debt to Horace, see Robyn Marsack, *The Cave of Making: The Poetry of Louis macNeice* (Clarendon Press, Oxford 1982), p. 142.

10 Brown, p. 47.

11 Terence Brown, 'Louis MacNeice and The Poetry of Exile', *Twentieth Century Studies*, 4, November 1970, p. 81.

12 Brown, p. 1; *Modern Poetry*, p. 49.

13 *Ibid.*, pp. 24–25.

14 *Ibid.*

15 For an account of Horace's well-known sense of a correlation between the seasons in the natural world and those of a man's life, see Steele Commager, *The Odes of Horace* (Yale University press, Yale 1962), pp. 235 *seq*.

16 See D. B. Moore, *The Poetry of Louis MacNeice* (Leicester University Press, Leicester 1972), pp. 60–61.

17 'Experiences with Images', *Selected Literary Criticism of Louis MacNeice*, ed. Alan Heuser (Clarendon Press, Oxford 1987), p. 162.

18 See Commager, pp. 270–273.

19 I quote from *Rilke: Selected Poems*, trans. J. B. Leishman (Penguin Books, Harmondsworth 1964), pp. 63–65.

20 *The Odes of Horace*, trans. James Michie (Penguin Books, Harmondsworth 1967), p. 119.

21 'The Longley Tapes': Interview in *The Honest Ulsterman*, No. 78, Summer 1985, p. 26.

22 Patrick Kavanagh, *Collected Poems* (McGibbon & McKee, London 1964).

23 In Patrick Kavanagh, *November Haggard* (The Peter Kavanagh Hand Press, New York 1971); reproduced now in *Patrick Kavanagh: Man and Poet*, ed. Peter Kavanagh (National Poetry Foundation, University of Maine at Orono 1986), p. 241.

24 Marsack, p. 21.

25 Patrick Kavanagh, *The Complete Poems* (The Peter Kavanagh Hand Press, New York 1972), p. 279. Subsequent quotations from kavanagh's poetry are taken from this edition, identified as *CP* in the text.

26 Francis Stuart, 'Earthy Visionary' in . . . *Man and Poet*, pp. 383–386. See p. 385 Stuart's article is reprinted from *Hibernia*, 25th July 1975.

27 Michael O'Loughlin, *After Kavanagh: Patrick kavanagh and The Discourse of Contemporary Irish Poetry* (Raven Arts Press, Dublin 1985), p. 25.

28 Darcy O'Brien, *Patrick Kavanagh* (Bucknell University Press, New Jersey, 1975), p. 13.

29 'From Monaghan to The Grand Canal', *Man and Poet*, p. 249. Reprinted from *studies*, Spring 1959.

30 *Ibid.*, p. 255.

31 I would agree with Anthony Cronin that achievements such as 'The Paddiad' are sometimes too easily dismissed in appreciations of Kavanagh: 'Joyce is allowed the possibility of universalism where Kavanagh is not.' See *Heritage Now* (Brandon, Dingle 1982), p. 192. In connection with present topic, it might be argued (space permitting) how the techniques of the Dublin satires are relevant to the development of the casual, comic element in the later sonnets rather than somehow eccentric to the main lines of Kavanagh's development as a poet.

32 'From Monaghan to The Grand Canal', p. 255.

33 *Ibid.*, p. 256.

A MYTHOLOGY WITH WHICH I AM PERFECTLY FAMILIAR: SAMUEL BECKETT AND THE ABSENCE OF GOD

Lance St John Butler

1 *Molloy* pp. 167–168 (In *Molloy, Malone Dies, The Unnamable*, Calder and Boyars, London, 1959 where, alas, the proofreader has allowed the amazing word 'antechrist' to slip in.)

2 *Ill Seen Ill Said* (John Calder, London, 1982), p. 52.

3 *Watt* (John Calder, London, 1963), pp. 25–26.

4 As Beckett puts it in the Addenda to *Watt* 'No symbols where none intended.' Cf Deirdre Bair, *Samuel Beckett: A Biography* (Picador, Pan Books, London, 1980). p. 13.

5 Bair, *op cit.*

6 *More Pricks Than Kicks*(republished, Calder and Boyars, London, 1970), pp. 171–186.

7 *Ibid.*, p. 184.

8 *Ibid.*, p. 18.

9 *Ibid.*, p. 61.

10 *Ibid.*, p. 125.

11 *Ibid.*, p. 65.

12 *Watt* pp. 26–27. (Lourdes, of course, is in the Hautes Pyrénées and the Basses Pyrénées are now the Pyrénées Atlantiques, for what it is worth.)

13 *Ibid.*, p. 153.

14 *Mercier and Camier* (Calder and Boyars, London, 1974), p. 26.

15 *Ibid.*, p. 72.

16 *Ibid.*, p. 79.

17 *Molloy* p. 39.

18 *Ibid.*, p. 79.

19 *Ibid.*, p. 97.

20 *Ibid.*, pp. 100–101.

21 Ibid. pp. 167–168. (The question mark missing from the penultimate question quoted is also absent in this edition.)

22 Beckett died in December 1989, while this essay was in press. We may now say, therefore, that 'Later Beckett' extended from 1960 to 1989.
23 *More Pricks Than Kicks*, p. 109.
24 *Ibid.*, p. 172.
25 *Watt*, p. 133.
26 *Ibid.*, pp. 32–36.
27 *Ibid.*, pp. 37–38.
28 *Ibid.*, p. 157.
29 *The Calmative* appears in *No's Knife: Collected Shorter Prose 1947–1966* (Calder and Boyars, London, 1967), pp. 25–42. This talk of boys, goats and bare feet must remind us of *Waiting for Godot* (Faber and Faber, London, 1956; ed. of 1965).

> Vladimir: You work for Mr Godot?
> Boy: Yes Sir.
> Vladimir: What do you do?
> Boy: I mind the goats, sir. (p. 51)
>
> Vladimir: But you can't go barefoot!
> Estragon: Christ did.
> Vladimir: Christ! What's Christ got to do with it?
> You're not going to compare yourself with Christ?
> Estragon: All my life I've compared myself to him. (p. 52)

In this essay I have avoided discussing the religious intertexts that are responsible for so much of the power of this great play, preferring to concentrate on a wider range of Beckett's work. An essay which pursued in detail the way *Godot* depends utterly on Beckett's familiar mythology would largely repeat work done elsewhere.
30 *No's Knife*, pp. 34–35.
31 *Ibid.*, pp. 40–41.
32 Ibid., p. 62.
33 *Molloy*, pp. 26–29.
34 Ibid., p. 59.
35 Ibid., p. 78.
36 Ibid., pp. 90–91.
37 *Krapp's last Tape* and *Embers* (Faber, London, 1959). For a full and penetrating discussion of *Embers*, as well as of *Waiting For Godot*, *Endgame* and *All That Fall* cf. Hersh Zeifman, 'Religious Imagery in the Plays of Samuel Beckett' in Cohn, Ruby (ed) *Samuel Beckett: A Collection of Criticism* (McGraw-Hill, New York, 1975).
38 *The Unnamable*, p. 359.
39 *The Lost Ones* (Calder and Boyars, London, 1972), pp. 17–18.
40 *Not I* in *Ends and Odds* (Faber and Faber, London, 1977), p. 20.
41 *Footballs*, in Ibid., p. 37.
42 *All Strange Away* (John Calder, London, 1979), p. 24.
43 *Ill Seen Ill Said*, pp. 56–57.
44 note to follow
45 Cf. note 37, above.

46 Zeifman, op. cit., p. 93.
47 *The Unnamable*, p. 389.
48 *The Lost Ones*, p. 61.
49 *Ill Seen Ill Said*, p. 52.
50 Philip H. Solomon, 'Purgatory unpurged: time, space and language in *Lessness*', *Journal of Beckett Studies*, No 6, Autumn, 1980.
51 *The Unnamable*, p. 349.
52 German letter of 1937 reproduced in Cohn, Ruby (ed.) *Disjecta: Miscellaneous Writings* (John Calder, London, 1983), pp. 51–54 (translation by Martin Esslin pp. 170–173). In this letter Beckett also quotes Goethe's 'It is better to write NOTHING than not write at all.'
53 *Watt*, p. 164. (Conventional order restored.)
54 *Ibid.*, p. 201.
55 *Molloy*, p. 168.
56 *Worstward Ho* (John Calder, London, 1983), pp. 42–44.
57 In particular cf. David H. Hesla *The Shape of Chaos: an Interpretation of the Art of Samuel Beckett* (University of Minnesota Press, Minneapolis: 1971), also Hesla's review of a poor book on *Godot* in *Journal of Beckett Studies* No 7, Spring 1982. I might also point the reader towards by own *Samuel Beckett and the Meaning of Being* (Macmillan, London, 1984).
58 *Disjecta*, p. 150.
59 Ibid., p. 146.
60 *Ill Seen Ill Said*, p. 58.

PILGRIMS' PROGRESS: ON THE POETRY OF DESMOND EGAN AND OTHERS

Patrick Rafroidi

1 Seamus Heaney: *Wintering Out*, (Faber & Faber, London, 1972), pp. 59 and 79.
2 Paul Murray: *Rites and Meditations*, (The Dolmen Press, Mountrath, Portlaoise, 1982), p. 33.
3 Padraig J. Daly: *A Celibate Affair*, p. 32.
4 All references (unless otherwise indicated) are to that edition: Desmond Egan: *Collected Poems*. The National Poetry Foundation, Orono, University of Main, 1983; The Goldsmith Press, Newbridge, 1984; p. 224.
5 Desmond Egan: *Poems for Peace*, with an introduction by Sean MacBride (AFRI, Dublin, 1986), p. 27.
6 *Ibid.*, pp. 23–4.

NOTES ON CONTRIBUTORS

Lance St John Butler is a Lecturer in English at the University of Stirling in Scotland. He has recently been professeur associe at the University of Pau in France. He has edited volumes of essays on Beckett and on Hardy and has published *Samuel Beckett and the Meaning of Being* (Macmillan, 1984).

Peter Denman is a Lecturer in the Department of English at St. Patrick's College, Maynooth, Ireland. He studies at University College, Cork, and at the University of Keele, and has published a number of articles on Anglo-Irish Literature and on nineteenth-century supernatural fiction, as well as *Samuel Ferguson: The Literary Achievement* (1990).

Nuala Ni Dhomhnaill was born in Nenagh, Co Tipperary and brought up in the Kerry Gaelteacht. She published her first volume of poems *An Dealg Droighin* in 1980, followed by *Féar Suaithinseach* (1984), and *Feis* (1991). She has lived in Turkey and has four children.

Desmond Egan, born Athlone, Ireland, 1936. Educated in the midlands and at University College, Dublin. Married with two children. His published collections include: *Midland* (1972), *Leaves* (1975), *Siege!* (1977), *Collected Poems* (1983 and 1984). He has read with Allen Ginsberg and Ezra Pound and has been poet-in-residence in Osaka University, Japan, and University College, Dublin.

Ruth Fleischmann was born in Cork, was educated in Scoil Íte and Scoil Mhiire, studied at University College, Cork, and at the University of Tübigen in the Federal Republic of Germany. She taught English and German for four years at the University of Constantine in Algeria, and is now on the staff of the English Department at the University of Bielefeld, Federal Republic of Germany.

A. M. Gibbs is Professor of English at Macquarie University, Sydney, Australia. His most recent book is *The Art and Mind of Shaw: Essays in Criticism*.

Barbara Hayley was Professor of English at St Patrick's College, Maynooth. At Cambridge she was a Gulbenkian research fellow and a Fellow of Lucy Cavendish College. Her books include *Carlton's Traits and Stories of the Irish Peasantry and the Irish Nineteenth Century Anglo-Irish Tradition: A*

Bibliography of William Carleton, and an edition of the *Traits and stories*. She was engaged on writing a *History of Irish Periodicals 1800–1870* when she died tragically in 1991.

Eamonn Hughes is a lecturer in English at Queen's University, Belfast. He has written on modern Irish writing in general, on Joyce, Heaney, Patrick Kavanagh, and Field Day, and on the impact of recent cultural theory on the study of Anglo-Irish writing. A member of the Executive Committee of the British Association for Irish Studies, he edits the Association's *Newsletter*. He is also joint British editor of the *Irish Literary Supplement*.

Séamus Mac Mathúna is Professor of Irish Studies at the University of Ulster, having previously lectured at University College, Galway and the University of Uppsala, Sweden. He was educated at Queen's University, belfast, the University of Zürich and the University of Iceland. he specialises in Early and Classical Irish language and literature and in Modern Irish grammar. He has published work on various aspects of the Irish cultural tradition, including *Immran Brian: Bran's Journey to the Land of the Women*.

Anne McCartney is a graduate of the University of Ulster where she is now conducting reasearch on the novelist Francis Stuart.

Joseph McMinn is a Lecturer in English at the University of Ulster at Jordanstown. He has taught in America and Germany, and has published *Jonathan Swift: A Literary Life* (1991), *JOhn Banville: A Critical Study* (1991), and has edited *Swift's Irish Pamphlets: An Introductory Selection* (1991). he is currently working on an illustrated documentary of Swift's travels around Ireland.

Daithí Ó hÓgain, M.A., Ph.D was born in Co. Limerick in 1949, and is Lecturer in irish Folklore at Univesity College, Dublin. Has published eight books on aspects of Irish literature and folk tradition, the best-known of which are *An File* (1982), *The Hero in Irish Folk History* (1985), and *Fionn mac Cumhaill: Images of the Gaelic Hero* (1988). Also a creative writer, he has written four volumes of poetry and short stories in Irish.

Mitsuko Ohno is a Professor of English Literature at Aichi Shukutou College in Nagoya, Japan, and a member of the Yeats Society of Japan and IASAIL-Japan. Having studied in Japan and in U.S.A., she has developed an interest in comparative studies of Irish and Japanese literature, and published articles mainly on Yeats's plays and poems both in English and Japanese.

Alan Peacock is a graduate of Birmingham University. he has taught at Magee University College, Derry, and was Lees Fellow at Manchester University. He is now Lecturer in English at the University of Ulster. He is the author of a number of articles, mainly of a comparative nature, on English literature from the seventeenth century to the present. He is currently working on twentieth century Northern Irish writers and is editing a book of essays on the work of Brian Friel.

Patrick Rafroidi was a pioneer in developing Irish Studies in France. His untimely death highlighted the extent of his accomplishments in promoting Irish literature and culture. He was the founder and editor in chief of *Etudes Irlandaises*, President of the International Association for the Study of Anglo-Irish Literature, and founder of La Societe Francais d'Etudes Irlandaises. He translated the works of Brian Moore and Brian Friel into French and was the author of, among other books, *Irish Literature in English: The Romantic Period*, 2 volumes, (1972), *Aspects of Irish Theatre (1972) and The Irish Novel in Our Time* (1976).

Robert Welch, Professor of English at the University of Ulster at Coleraine, has published *Irish Poetry from Moore to Yeats* (1980), *A History of Verse Translation from the Irish* (1988); edited, with S. B. Bushrui, *Literature and the Art of Creation* (1988), and a volume of essays on George Moore. He is editor of *The Oxford Companion to Irish Literature* and Chairman of IASAIL. His first volume of poems, *Muskerry*, is due to appear in 1991.

INDEX